People Power:
The Building of a New European Home

Michael Randle

Dedicated to the memory of **Hugh Brock**, pioneer of non-violent action in Britain and former editor of *Peace News*, who died in 1985.

HAWTHORN PRESS

People Power: The Building of a New European Home

© Michael Randle 1991

Published by Hawthorn Press
Bankfield House, 13 Wallbridge, Stroud GL5 3JA, United Kingdom

Copyright. All rights reserved. No part of this book may be used or reproduced in any form whatsoever without written permission except in the case of brief quotations in articles or reviews.

Typeset in Plantin by Bookman Ltd., Bristol.

Printed by Billings & Son Ltd., Hylton Road, Worcester.

Cover by Nicholas Jones, Sheepscombe, Stroud.

Grateful acknowledgements are due to the
Joseph Rowntree Charitable Trust
for their generous assistance in publishing *People Power*.

*Cover photo by courtesy of Reuter/Popperphoto.
Photo by Claude Salhani.*

CIP applied for

ISBN No 1 869 890 29 9.

Contents

Foreword by John Berger	vii
Biography	ix
Acknowledgements	xi
General Introduction	xiii

Part I: *People Power: the Building of a New European Home* 1

Introduction	3
Chapter 1: Preludes to 1989	9
Chapter 2: Reflections on the East European Revolution	21
Chapter 3: People Power and the Future of Europe	68

Part II: *The Interviews* 101

Introduction to the Interviews	103
Helmuth Frauendorfer, Romania	108
Thomas Hackman, Finland	123
Marco Hren, Slovenia, Yugoslavia	131
Jan Kavan, Czechoslovakia	149
Elbieta Rawicz-Oledzka, Poland	167
Jirina Siklova, Czechoslovakia	172
Peter Szasz, Hungary	181
Knud Wollenburger, East Germany	188
Appendix 1 – Selected Chronology, Eastern Europe	198
Appendix 2 – Selected Chronology, Soviet Union	218

Warsaw University. Student strike prior to June 1989 Election.

East European Reporter

Liberated Bucharest. *Radek Sikorsky*

Torchlit procession in Budapest, against repression in Romania, Summer 1988.

East European Reporter

Column of complaints – Leipzig residents gather to read posters criticising living conditions and government policies, November 1989.   *Associated Press*

Foreword

I find this essay outstanding because of where it is written from. And this where is already in its title. It is written from deep within popular experience, and it has the long time-perspective that can imagine the building of a home. Within this text there is a mind of urgent patience. It does not forget and it does not deny the future. This already separates it from the instant chatter with which the media smother most news from the world. Michael Randle's text is separate from such chatter and by this very token it is closer to all of us. Recent European events have tended to fill most commentators with a kind of dread – perhaps because they took all the experts by surprise! Randle speaks of these same events, not as an expert, but with the calm of a thinker who has faith, faith in the past and faith in the potential of people. He recognises the dangers, he sees through illusions, he is, thank God, no utopian. But he writes nothing off! I suspect that this is because he is, first, very honest with himself. As a consequence he can then conjure up for us the end of the century we are living – and he does this, despite everything, with a pride that is inspiring.

John Berger, March 1991

Biography

Michael Randle was born in England in 1933 but spent the war years with relatives in Dublin. He has been active in the peace movement since registering as a conscientious objector in 1951. He was a member of the march committee which organised the first Aldermaston March against British nuclear weapons at Easter 1958, Chairman of the Direct Action Committee Against Nuclear War, 1958-61, Secretary of the Committee of 100, 1960-61, and a Council and Executive member of War Resisters International from 1960-1987. In 1959-60 he spent a year in Ghana, participating in the Sahara Protest expedition against French atom-bomb tests in the Algerian Sahara and helping to organise a pan-African conference in Accra. In 1962 he was sentenced to 18 months imprisonment for his part in organising non-violent direct action at a USAF base at Wethersfield in Essex, and in October 1967 to 12 months for participating in an occupation of the Greek Embassy in London following the Colonel's coup of that year. While serving the first sentence he became friends with George Blake, the British MI6 agent condemned in 1961 to 42 years imprisonment for passing secrets to the Soviet Union. In 1966 he assisted in Blake's escape and flight to East Germany. He and his colleague Pat Pottle are due to stand trial for this in June 1991.

Michael Randle has taken a keen interest in developments in Eastern Europe. In 1956 he undertook a march from Vienna to Budapest with leaflets expressing support for Hungarian passive resistance to the Soviet invasion and calling on Soviet forces not to fire on unarmed protesters; however, he was prevented from entering Hungary by Austrian border guards. In 1968 he jointly co-ordinated for War Resisters International simultaneous international protests in Moscow, Budapest, Sofia and Warsaw against the Soviet-led invasion of Czechoslovakia. In the 1970s and 1980s he collaborated with Jan Kavan and Palach Press in London in smuggling literature and equipment to the democratic opposition in Czechoslovakia.

He has a degree in English from London University (1966) and an M.Phil in Peace Studies (1981). The topic of his M.Phil thesis was *Militarism and Repression*. From 1980 to 1987 he was co-ordinator of the Alternative Defence Commission, contributing to its two major publications, *Defence Without the Bomb* (1983), and *The Politics of Alternative Defence* (1987). Since 1988 he has been co-ordinator of the Social Defence Project. He married his wife Anne in 1962; they have two grown-up sons.

Acknowledgements

This book was commissioned by the *Hugh Brock Memorial Fund* to commemorate the life and work of Hugh Brock, the pacifist and former editor of *Peace News* who played a central role in developing a tradition of non-violent direct action in Britain.

As the author, I am ultimately responsible for its contents. It was nevertheless shaped and informed by many meetings of the Social Defence Steering Group, set up in the autumn of 1987 in association with the School of Peace Studies at the University of Bradford. The essay which occupies the first part of the book therefore represents approximately the consensus of that group. I wish to express my thanks to all its members, whose names are listed below, and to thank also the members of the International Consultative Group of the project for their comments on the early draft outlines and chapters, and War Resisters International whose conference in Bradford in April 1990 on Social Defence provided encouragement and contacts.

Funding for the project has come principally from two Charitable Trusts – the Barrow & Geraldine Cadbury Trust in Birmingham and the Joseph Rowntree Charitable Trust in York. I wish to express my thanks to them and to the Puckham Trust which also contributed financially to the project. Finally I wish to thank the joint sponsors of the project, the Lansbury House Trust Fund, the Hugh Brock Memorial Trust and the School of Peace Studies at the University of Bradford.

Members of the Social Defence Project Steering Group:
Christina Arber, Howard Clark, Owen Greene, Bob Overy, Michael Randle, Carol Rank, Andrew Rigby, Walter Stein, Tim Milne-Wallis.

Members of the International Consultative Group:
Lennart Bergfeldt, Sweden; April Carter, England; Hugues Colle, France; Adam Curle, England; Rt Rev Tony Dumper, England; Nicholas Gillett, England; Jorgan Johannsen, Sweden; Lynne Jones, England; Isobel Lindsay, Scotland; Brian Martin, Australia; Wilhelm Nolte, Federal Republic of Germany; Michael Schroeren, Federal Republic of Germany; Linneke Schakenbos, Netherlands; Hans Sinn, Canada; Antony Weaver, England.

General Introduction

This book is divided into two parts. Part I is an analysis of the significance of the 1989 revolutions in East-Central and Eastern Europe for the notion of civil resistance and social defence. Part II consists of interviews, mainly with people directly involved in the events of 1989 or in the opposition movements that preceded them.

The first draft of the essay on People Power was completed in April 1990, but for various reasons its publication was delayed. I have amended and updated it as necessary.

The focus of the essay is the overthrow of authoritarian communist regimes by popular non-violent movements – not the subsequent political developments in the countries concerned. However, the select chronology in the Appendix includes a record of some of the major political developments in each country since the 1989 events, including the outcome of general and presidential elections, and the steps leading to the unification of East and West Germany. The latter was the single event in Europe of greatest international moment during 1990 since it confirmed and institutionalised the end of the Cold War and the division of the continent.

I have not sought to modify the optimistic note struck in the essay, even though the outlook at the beginning of 1991 darkened. It is important when the world is confronted by certain ominous political developments in the Soviet Union, by the resurgence of anti-semitism and of long suppressed antagonisms in parts of Eastern Europe, and above all by the horrendous war in the Gulf, not to forget the hopes aroused by the events of 1989 and the realities on which they were founded. In the longer term those events and their implications for human struggles remain crucially relevant.

The interviews in the second part of the book with individuals from East-Central and Eastern Europe were recorded at various times between July 1990 and February 1991. One of those interviewed, Thomas Hackman, is not from Eastern Europe but from Finland.

Finland occupied a unique position between East and West during the Cold War and it seemed fruitful to explore the impact of the 1989 events on that country.

The interviews provide additional information about, and analysis of, the situation in various countries both before and since the 1989 revolutions. But, above all, they provide invaluable insights into the thoughts and feelings of people directly involved. Contributions of this kind from people who were for a time 'the subjects of history' – to quote the words of one of the respondents – are essential to the task of evaluating these struggles and their potential outcomes.

Whatever reassessments may be made in the future, there can be no doubting the historic importance of the 1989 revolutions, and what they reveal about the potential of non-violent resistance in a modern European context. To quote again the same respondent:

> 'Personally, I was always conscious ... that the non-violent resistance would be a paradigm relevant for many other situations ... My feeling is that, just as the 1968 revolutions in the West provided a paradigm for many things that occurred in Western Europe, including the whole change in the culture there since then, so the East European experience of non-violence will prove a crucial paradigm for Eastern Europe for many years to come – and maybe not for Eastern Europe alone.'[1]

I hope that my essay, and the interviews in Part II, will contribute to our understanding of the events of 1989 and their implications both for Europe and the future conduct of international relations.

Michael Randle, March 1991

---

[1] Knud Wollenberger in his contribution to this book.

April Fool's happening *Dementi*

Student supporter at Warsaw University writing publicity for NZS strike, May 1989.

Johnathon Sunley

PART I

People Power:
The Building of a New European Home

Introduction

On 9 November 1989 an earthquake shattered the edifice of post-war European politics. This was the day on which the new politburo of the East German communist party (SED) announced that there would be free elections in the country and that henceforth East German citizens would be free to travel to the West. For all practical purposes the Berlin Wall – the ugliest and most powerful symbol of a divided continent – was no more.

For days the city erupted in a frenzy of rejoicing as East Berliners in their hundreds of thousands streamed westwards – not in most cases to settle but simply to visit the half of their city that for more than quarter of a century they had been able to see only on television. By the following day the GDR authorities had sent in demolition teams to open up new crossing points in the wall. The mayors of East and West Berlin met to discuss and celebrate. There was talk of a re-united Germany, even of disbanding the two military alliances.

That the events in East Germany marked the collapse of authoritarian communism throughout Eastern Europe was quickly confirmed. The day after the Berlin Wall was re-opened, Bulgaria's hardline communist leader, Todor Zhivkov, fell from power. In the following weeks, Czechoslovakia was paralysed by mass demonstrations and a general strike and in early December a new coalition government took office. In late December, Alexander Dubcek, the Party leader deposed by the Soviet-led invasion of 1968, was elected Speaker of the Federal Parliament, and Vaclav Havel, in prison only a few months earlier, was elected President. By Christmas, the Ceausescu tyranny had been toppled in Romania; and in all the Warsaw Pact countries except Poland, free general elections were scheduled for 1990.

The 1989 revolutions in Eastern Europe provide a dramatic demonstration of the potential of 'people power' – or 'civil resistance'. With the notable exception of Romania, they were accomplished without violence. (And even in Romania itself it was people power that toppled the Ceausescu regime and only subsequently that the army was forced to take on the Securitate in bloody street battles to prevent a counter-revolution). While Gorbachev's decision to abandon the Brezhnev Doctrine – thereby removing the threat of Soviet military intervention – had a crucial impact on the situation, the revolutions came about in most countries essentially because enough people were prepared to withdraw their consent and cooperation from discredited governments and to defy them in waves of non-violent strikes and protests.

This essay is about people power in the European context. It traces briefly the development of civil resistance in Eastern Europe and considers some of the lessons that can be learned from it. Drawing on this analysis, it goes on to consider its future role in the political development of Europe, and also how far advance preparations for civil resistance at a national level could enhance the security of individual states and of the region as a whole. To avoid overloading, the process of change in the Soviet Union itself is only cursorily touched upon, though of course the impact of the changes upon Eastern Europe is considered.

A note at this stage on terminology may be helpful. I use the term 'social defence' to denote reliance on civil resistance for the defence of the country and/or its established institutions. The term is used in this sense by probably a majority of writers and researchers in Europe working in the field. (In the United States the term civilian based defence is more widely used).

There are thus three specialist terms used in the essay in relation to its subject matter: *people power*, *civil resistance* and *social defence*. *People Power* and *Civil Resistance* are used interchangeably to denote civilian non-cooperation, intervention and other forms of non-violent action to resist oppression or achieve social and political objectives. The rationale for using both terms is that since the overthrow of Marcos in the Philippines in 1986, the term 'people power' has come into general use and is now familiar to a wide non-specialist audience through press and media reports. Civil resistance, however, is a more precisely descriptive term and is also frequently used in earlier literature.

Social Defence is the use of civil resistance in a particular context, namely to defend a country and/or its institutions against external or internal aggression. Like the term 'defence' in traditional military usage, social defence covers both preparation for resistance – which hopefully will deter aggression – and the resistance itself should aggression occur.

In this essay I use the term mainly in connection with defence at a national level where the elected government and state bodies would assume at least a degree of responsibility for organising and co-ordinating plans for civil resistance. However, the free institutions of a democratic country – such as trades unions, civil rights and peace organisations, political parties, the churches – might independently use, or prepare to use, civil resistance to defend themselves against the country's own government – for instance if it was introducing repressive and authoritarian laws affecting their autonomy or right to independent existence. Civil resistance of this kind, in the context of a struggle by grassroots organisations against an elected government which is overreaching itself is very different from one in which the country as a whole is facing an exterior attack, or an attempted military coup to overturn the constitution. Thus we can sub-divide social defence into *social defence at the national level*, and *social defence at a societal level* while again recognising the considerable overlap between the two.

The distinction between civil resistance and social defence is neither absolute nor clear-cut – indeed the latter is referred to in some writings as 'defence by civil resistance'. The reason for using a separate term is that resistance, and preparation for resistance, at a national level raises very particular questions and problems. The civil resistance we have witnessed in Eastern Europe in 1989 provides many valuable lessons and insights for the construction of a national system of social defence, but it would be wrong to extrapolate directly from one to the other without taking account of the very different circumstances involved.

In an essay of this length, the treatment of such issues cannot be comprehensive. The main objective is to make a contribution to the discussion of urgent questions that have been thrust onto the European political agenda by the hectic pace of change in the Soviet Union and Eastern Europe.

There have of course been previous studies of civil resistance and social defence, some the product of detailed and scholarly research. Yet there are obvious reasons for making a renewed effort at this time to introduce these topics into the mainstream of political debate. In the late 1950s and 1960s, coinciding with the rise of the anti-nuclear weapons movement in Western Europe, several studies of an alternative, non-nuclear approach to security advocated social defence. However, these had little impact on public policy anywhere, and when interest in alternative defence revived in the 1980s, research focused mainly on the possibilities of 'non-offensive' defence.

In essence, non-offensive defence is a military system strongly geared to the defensive, and with at most only a very limited capacity, if any, to take the offensive. If both sides, it is argued, could feel secure about their ability to ward off any attack the other was capable of launching, mutual confidence would be strengthened and the way would be open for substantial force reductions and for a more relaxed discussion of outstanding political differences. This concept appears to have had little immediate impact on strategic thinking in the West, though there is evidence that it was taken more seriously within the Soviet bloc and contributed to a shift in the Warsaw Pact's military doctrine.

But today a re-examination of the whole problem of European security, and of alternative defence proposals, is urgently required. The collapse of authoritarian communist regimes in Eastern Europe means that the Warsaw Pact now hardly exists as a cohesive force, much less a threat to Western Europe.[1] This does not mean that there are no dangers to the security of European states – change itself has unveiled long-repressed tensions and grievances, and has created problems as well as opportunities. But the dangers are such that they could be exacerbated rather than alleviated by the continuation of the system of military blocs established at the outset of the Cold War. Moreover, events in Eastern Europe in 1989 provide us with a dramatic contemporary example of civil resistance in a European context. Its successes - but also its limitations and ambiguities – are indicative of the contribution that social defence could make to national and regional security.

Although this study focuses on Europe, the wider relevance of people power is underlined by the upsurge in its use in the 1980s in many parts of the world. The term was coined to describe the mass non-violent resistance in the Philippines that overthrew the

---

[1] The Warsaw Treaty Organisation is due to wind up as a military organisation on 1 April 1991.

Marcos dictatorship in February 1986, but the phenomenon dates back as far as recorded history, and in particular played a prominent role in the Labour and trade union struggles from the 19th century onwards, in the anti-colonial struggle in India and elsewhere, and in campaigns for women's rights and civil liberties.

During the 1980s mass protest and non-cooperation have challenged established power with varying degrees of success in Korea, Chile, Haiti, South Africa, the Israeli-occupied West Bank and Gaza Strip, Nepal, Mongolia and elsewhere. In China, the student and worker protests of May and June 1989 brought Beijing and other major cities to a standstill and confronted the Chinese authorities with their most serious challenge since the communists took power in 1950. The non-violent protests were halted by the terrible massacre in Tienanmen Square and elsewhere in Beijing and have been followed by a wave of repression. But, especially after the fall of Ceausescu in Romania, it would be foolhardy to assume that we have seen the end of the story.

In the Soviet Union, the dramatic changes of the Gorbachev era have been widely interpreted as an example of 'revolution from above'. Without detracting from Gorbachev's initiatives and achievements, it is important also to recognise that pressure from below, and from the periphery of Eastern Europe and some of the non-Russian republics, have helped to dictate the direction and pace of change. One question as the new decade begins is whether, or in what form, the Soviet Union will continue in being in the 1990s, and whether Gorbachev can find creative answers to the challenge of economic stagnation and nationalist revolt.

People power can be used in pursuit of a variety of social and political objectives, not all necessarily desirable. In post-Zhivkov Bulgaria, a demonstration against the lifting of restrictions on the Muslim population in January 1990 was particularly worrying, as indeed have been the racialist overtones in the dispute between Armenia and Azerbaijan within the Soviet Union. However, the potential of people power to effect change – whether for better or worse – is the principal reason for paying close attention to it and carefully analysing its workings.

The potentially negative consequences of people power are also an argument for not treating it simply as a technique, but questioning the ethical and political assumptions underlying any given campaign of civil resistance, or programme of social defence. In relation to social defence, it is therefore necessary to ask whether it implies a strictly pacifist approach, and if not what is the nature of the overall defence system of which it is a constituent part, and how central a role social defence is to play within it.

Despite the dangers of populism, an important attraction of people power is that ordinary people can participate actively and directly in social and political change and in defending their communities and institutions. The reason it blossomed into a major factor in international politics in the 1980s is partially explainable through modern communications, especially television. This has facilitated the spread of information about the techniques of people power, and at the same time contributed to its effectiveness by enabling third parties – whether states or non-governmental organisations – to exert pressure on the authorities concerned to avoid bloody repression and seek a just solution. At the same time the increasing economic interdependence of states means that there is genuine leverage available to the international community in bringing pressure to bear on maverick states.

Another significant factor behind the increasing resort to civil resistance could be the sheer destructiveness of modern weaponry and the appalling human cost of civil and international war. However, at the state level the possibilities of social defence have still been given no more than the most cursory consideration anywhere. This is particularly anomalous in the case of the industrialised states of Europe and North America where a major international conflict could bring the ultimate destruction of nuclear war.

The essay is divided into three chapters. Chapter 1 considers the political and economic background to the events of 1989 in Eastern Europe. Chapter 2 looks at the revolts themselves, analysing their more immediate causes and the reasons for their success. Chapter 3 considers how civil resistance and social defence could contribute to the future development of European politics and security.

The diffusion of knowledge about people power, the creation of more favourable circumstances for its successful implementation, and the crisis of war in the age of weapons of mass destruction, mean that it is an idea whose time has come. I hope the present volume will help stimulate discussion about it and about its role in meeting the challenges in Europe and the wider world in the 1990s.

Chapter 1

Preludes to 1989

Introduction

The political earthquake that struck Eastern Europe[2] in 1989 was at once astonishing and predictable. Astonishing because no-one had expected such an early and dramatic collapse of authoritarian communist rule and Soviet hegemony throughout the region; predictable because – like the Californian earthquake – sooner or later it had to happen.

Ever since the end of World War II the fault lines have advertised their existence by intermittent rumblings and occasional major tremors – East Berlin 1953, Hungary 1956, Czechoslovakia 1968, Poland in a succession of crises culminating in the emergence and subsequent banning of Solidarity in 1980-81. To understand how the dramatic changes of 1989 in Eastern Europe came about it is necessary briefly to consider these earlier crises and the effect they had on the regimes in question and on Soviet-East European relations.

Clearly the developments in the Soviet Union and Eastern Europe in 1989-90 represent only the beginning of a process of social and political transformation. Many questions remain unanswered, many problems unresolved. The changeover from a centralised command economy to one where market forces again play a major role has never previously been undertaken. There are also enormous

---

[2]Although East Germany, Poland, Czechoslovakia and Hungary are strictly speaking part of East-Central Europe – as people from these countries increasingly emphasise – for the sake of simplicity we follow the usual practice of using the term 'Eastern Europe' to cover the former Soviet-bloc states outside the Soviet Union itself.

difficulties, varying in intensity from one country to another, in achieving a peaceful transition from authoritarian one-party rule to a genuinely democratic system. In some countries, too, the lifting of restrictions on freedom of expression and assembly has led to the resurgence of old rivalries and hatreds. The Soviet Union in particular faces a challenge to its very existence as its constituent republics demand greater autonomy or total independence, and as ancient ethnic, religious and territorial disputes re-surface.

Nevertheless, whatever the future may bring, there can be no going back to the pre-1989 political systems in Eastern Europe as a whole or to the earlier pattern of Soviet-East European relations. Nor, given the grassroots momentum for change created by *glasnost* and *perestroika*, could the Soviet Union itself return to the political-economy of the Brezhnev – much less the Stalin – period. No matter how painful or even disillusioning the period of reconstruction that lies ahead may be, 1989 clearly marked the collapse of the old order in Eastern Europe and the climax of a period of remarkable change within the Soviet Union.

This essay focuses on the collapse of the authoritarian communist regimes in Eastern Europe and the significance and possible future role of the nonviolent resistance that brought it about. Its analysis is based on three propositions about the long-term viability of any government. First the rulers themselves must be convinced of the legitimacy and moral purpose of their government and be able to command the allegiance of a sizeable proportion of the population. Second the government must prove itself capable of keeping the economy and society functioning at a reasonable level of efficiency. Finally and crucially, the government must be able to secure the cooperation, or at least the compliance, of the bulk of the population and/or the loyalty of the institutions of state coercion – the army, police and other security services.

In this chapter we consider the erosion of conviction and morale within East European governments, and of public support for them, from the period when Soviet hegemony was established in the region from 1945-47 to the early 1980s. At the beginning of the new decade the rise of Solidarity in Poland, and the multiplication of independent human rights and peace groups across the region, posed a new challenge to the authority of the one-party Leninist system, and led eventually to its overthrow. We also outline the causes of the economic stagnation in the 1980s that added a further explosive ingredient to the situation. In chapter two we consider how widespread discontent in Eastern Europe was channelled into effective nonviolent action.

1945–1981: The collapse of an ideology

To understand the extent of the moral collapse of the authority of Soviet-style communism in the post-war decades, it is necessary to recall the degree of popular support it commanded at the end of the war. The Soviet Union had played the crucial role in the defeat of Hitler, and communists had been prominent in resistance movements throughout Occupied Europe. The abuses and evils it opposed – imperialism, racism, the exploitation of working people – were real. Thus 1945 – despite the Stalinist purges of the 1930s and the shock of the 1939 Molotov-Ribbentrop Pact – was a moment of hope and renewal for the international communist movement and for many socialists who hoped that some of the measures of liberalisation introduced in the Soviet Union during the war would be maintained and extended. In France, Italy and Belgium, communist parties enjoyed mass support and participated in the post-war coalition governments until forced out, mainly as a result of US pressure.

It is true that communist regimes in Eastern Europe, with the exception of Yugoslavia and Albania, were essentially imposed from above and from outside by Soviet power. Nevertheless there was generally a base on which the communist parties and governments could hope to build. This was strongest in Czechoslovakia where in 1946 the communists won 38% of the vote in free elections, the largest share of any of the contestants. In Hungary in 1945 they polled a not-insignificant 17% of the vote, and even in Poland where the Party lacked a mass base, it did have the support of much of the intelligentsia – a key political force in Polish society.³ In Poland too, the communist leader, Wladislaw Gomulka, sought to introduce a form of socialism adapted to Polish needs to avoid the extremes of Stalinist collectivisation.

With the onset of the Cold War, and especially after Tito's defiance of Stalin in 1948, the Soviet Union tightened its control over Eastern Europe. Coalition government in Hungary and Czechoslovakia was brought to an end, and purges reminiscent of those in the Soviet Union itself in the 1930s swept across the region, entailing executions and mass arrests. Not only were non-communist and anti-communist organisations suppressed but also, and crucially, those communist leaders, such as Gomulka in Poland, who were seeking to introduce a form of communism adapted to domestic social and political conditions were purged and in many instances imprisoned or executed. However, it is apparent that the communist cause could still command loyalty, since some of the disgraced leaders were prepared to sign false confessions that would send them to their deaths in the mistaken belief that they would thereby be performing a last service to the cause of the Communist Party and the struggle against imperialism.

Wider disillusionment came with the revolts in Eastern Europe and their brutal suppression, following the death of Stalin in March 1953 and the attempt by Khruschev to liberalise Soviet-East European relations. The unrest in East Berlin and other East German cities in June 1953 was a harbinger of what was to follow elsewhere. Bertold Brecht records in his poem *The Solution* the reaction of an outstanding radical intellectual who had fled Nazi prosecution in the 1930s and chosen to live and work in the GDR after the war:

> After the uprising of 17 June
> The Secretary of the Writers Union
> Had leaflets distributed in the Stalinallee
> Stating that the people
> Had forfeited the confidence of the government
> And could win it back only
> By redoubled efforts. Would it not be easier

---

³Neal Ascherson, *The Polish August*, Penguin 1981, pp.69-70.

In that case for the government
To dissolve the people
And elect another?[4]

Again Brecht's reaction was a foretaste of that alienation of the intellectuals that would ultimately undermine communist authority throughout Eastern Europe.

Two events in 1956 were to shatter that sense of an historic mission shared by the communist movement worldwide, including the communist leaderships in Eastern Europe. The first was Khruschev's revelations in February at the XX Party Congress of the Soviet Communist Party concerning the extent of Stalinist terror – an indictment so devastating that for many years it was not publicly available within the Soviet Union. The second was the Hungarian revolution of October–November, crushed by Soviet tanks with the loss of over 20,000 lives. Now the Soviet Union appeared to be taking on the role of an imperialist power, and a reactionary imperialist power at that. The invasions dealt a mortal blow to the prestige of Soviet communism and spelt the beginning of the end of Soviet domination of the communist movement worldwide. Communist parties in many countries suffered heavy membership losses, including in some cases the loss of prominent intellectuals and theoreticians.

The invasion of Hungary was a watershed in another respect. It undermined the myth that once the Stalinist brand of communism had been imposed on a country it could not be reversed – except perhaps by an international war. The theory was not simply that any resistance would be crushed but that a decade or more of political indoctrination would make it almost impossible for people to think outside the categories of the system. This notion was fairly widespread in the late 1940s and early 1950s, particularly among Cold War protagonists in the West, and was popularised by the nightmare vision of George Orwell's *1984*. But in Hungary in 1956 young people who had been educated in the Stalinist system played an active part in the revolution. Indeed Eastern Europe won a reputation not for conformity but for a black ironic humour at

---

[4]From the translation by John Willetts in *Bertold Brecht: Poems*, Methuen, 1976.

the expense of the authorities. Thus in a sense 1956 represented a rekindling of hope. Rebellion might be crushed, but it was still a possibility.

Twelve years later, in 1968, the Czechoslovak Party Secretary Dubcek and the other reformers of the Prague Spring sought to apply the lessons of the Hungarian experience to avoid suffering Hungary's fate. Assuming that Soviet intervention in 1956 had been prompted by the fear that Hungary would quit the Warsaw Pact, Dubcek insisted on his country's commitment to the alliance. In fact his political reforms, and especially the easing of censorship and the moves towards democracy, posed a no less serious threat to the stability of the Soviet bloc than the prospect of Czechoslovakia quitting the Warsaw Pact. Once again Soviet tanks moved in to crush reform, this time leading the armies of all the Warsaw Pact countries except Romania.

The invasion was met with an historically unique resort to social defence on a nationwide scale. The Central Committee of the Czechoslovak Communist Party met in emergency session to condemn the invasion and encourage the population to engage in passive resistance. Tens of thousands of people did so, pouring onto the streets and urging the young soldiers of the invading armies to return home. Czechoslovak radio and television, broadcasting from secret locations, remained in loyalist hands for several days, reporting the protests and encouraging further resistance.

In the short run the resistance was successful. The Party leader Alexander Dubcek, and Prime Minister, Oldrich Cernik, had been taken to Moscow as prisoners were released. They permitted to return to Prague and resume office, but only after signing an agreement which gave the initiative back to the Soviet leadership. In the months that followed Dubcek and his supporters were isolated and in April 1969 he was forced out of office, and the long, dour process of 'normalisation' was able to begin in earnest.

Dubcek, Cernik and the other leaders probably owed their lives to the popular resistance. Moreover, the spirit of defiance could not be completely broken, and there are direct links, in terms of some of the individuals involved and the goals sought, between the resistance of 1968-69 and that of 1989.[5] The very harshness and rigidity of the

---

[5]See, for instance, the contributions in this volume from Jirina Siklova and Jan Kavan.

Czechoslovak regime between 1968 and 1989 reflected in part a defensive response to the threat of a revived mass opposition.

The Soviet invasion of Czechoslovakia, and the peaceful dignified response of the population, dealt yet another blow to the ideological claims of the ruling parties in the Soviet bloc. The cynicism of the population deepened behind a mask of conformity. In the West, the events spurred the progress of Eurocommunism.

In both Hungary and Czechoslovakia the overthrow of reform was followed by a programme of 'normalisation'. But this was to develop in very different directions in the two countries. In Hungary after an initial period of repression, and a purge of the communist party, the new leader Janos Kadar sought to win over the population by progressively introducing economic reforms and a degree of liberalisation. The New Economic Model adopted in 1968 involved decentralisation and allowing the market to play a greater role. Politically, Kadar adopted the position summed up in his dictum 'those who are not against us are with us'. The result was a relatively liberal 'consumer communism', probably accepted by the majority of the population as the best deal available in the circumstances.

In Czechoslovakia, however, economic decentralisation was blocked precisely because it was what the reformers of the Prague Spring had attempted to introduce in 1967-68. Instead the economy remained centralised, though with greater emphasis on the production of consumer goods. Here too, as in Hungary, there was an extensive purge of the communist party to weed out real or suspected reformers, but also a return to a harsh political regime where dissent was not tolerated. Czechoslovakia thenceforth was to remain one of the most hard-line Stalinist states in Eastern Europe until the dramatic overthrow of communist power in November–December 1989.

Poland in the post-war decades shared to some degree the experiences of all the countries of East-Central Europe in this period, but there were also significant differences. First, even in the Stalinist period the repression was less acute and the economy and society less thoroughly Sovietised than elsewhere. The attempt to collectivise Polish agriculture was unsuccessful, and the Catholic Church continued to exert a powerful influence. Second, Poland avoided the tragedy experienced by Hungary and Czechoslovakia of direct Soviet invasion, though this was a real danger in both 1956 and 1980. Third, the industrial working class proved itself powerful and determined enough to challenge the authorities from time to time and to plunge the country into a succession of crises. Finally, even during periods of repression, such as during the aftermath of the military takeover in December 1981, 'pluralism from below' flourished in Poland as nowhere else in the bloc.

Historians have observed a cyclical pattern in post-war Polish history. Following a period of crisis, a new party leadership takes over, pledged to economic and political reform, but after a promising start, autocracy and economic stagnation return, provoking a further rebellion and another change of leadership. In 1956 the reformist Gomulka was brought back as First Secretary of the Polish United Workers Party (the communist party) following riots and demonstrations in the industrial city of Poznan. By 1968 Gomulka faced a revolt of intellectuals and students, and in 1970 he was forced to resign in face of another mass working-class revolt. Gierek, his successor, lifted many restrictions and succeeded for a time in raising living standards. By the mid-1970s the economic boom was over, mainly as a result of the global economic dislocation brought about by the oil crisis, and there were serious riots and demonstrations again in 1976, which importantly brought dissident intellectuals and sections of the working class into closer contact. In August 1980, Gierek too was swept aside in the wave of strikes and occupations which led to the formation of the independent trade union Solidarity.

This last event, and the phenomenal growth of the movement in the sixteen months of its existence, created an entirely novel situation in a Soviet bloc country – one in which a mass independent working class organisation was legally recognised and exercised an effective veto on government policy. Solidarity was seen – quite rightly – as posing a fundamental challenge to the single-party Leninist system. Its emergence marked a crucial stage in the process of transforming widespread alienation in Eastern Europe into effective rebellion.

To add to the difficulties facing the Soviet leadership, in the 1980s the economy of the Soviet Union itself experienced a serious decline, as the effects of mismanagement and structural defects made themselves felt. This malaise also affected, to a greater or lesser extent, the countries of Eastern Europe.

The Malaise of Soviet Bloc Economies

Within the Soviet Union, the political impact of the collapse of its brand of authoritarian communism as a dynamic moral and ideological force was cushioned, throughout the 1960s and 1970s, by a steady and impressive growth in the Soviet economy, and improvements in living standards. However, by the beginning of the 1980s the economy was slowing down and the outlook was bleak. The economy could non longer be revived through a continued strategy of *extensive growth* i.e. concentrating investment and labour resources into raising the gross volume of production. What was now needed was *intensive growth* – improving productivity and the quality and diversity of goods, and making use of opportunities afforded by computerisation and new technologies.

However, the Soviet management, pricing and incentive system was ill-suited for such intensive growth. Moreover, the reforms needed to make the economy more efficient, and more responsive to the changing needs of society, had political implications which the conservative Brezhnev leadership was reluctant to accept. It required a free flow of reliable information, at least on economic matters, so that production could be geared to meet demand; it implied devolution of economic decision-making and a more central role for the market – and thus the relinquishing by the Party of an important lever of power; it probably implied a considerable measure of political democratisation.

Economic stagnation was likely to have political repercussions, and the appearance of Solidarity in Poland at just this juncture posed a particularly serious threat to the entire system. Sewern Bialer, writing in *Foreign Affairs* in the summer of 1981, forecast a 'harsh decade' ahead in the Soviet Union.[6] Though at times unduly alarmist, the article successfully identifies the crucial choices facing the Soviet leadership in the 1980s – repression or radical reform.

Bialer argued that the post-Brezhnev generation of Soviet leaders – who must soon take over the reins of power – might be more

---

[6]Sewern Bialer, 'The Harsh Decade: Soviet Policies in the 1980s', *Foreign Affairs*, Vol 59 No 5, Summer 1981.

open-minded in some respects than their predecessors but they were likely also to be less cautious. Domestically, their response to economic difficulties and a volatile political situation would probably be 'to strengthen the authoritarian character of the Soviet party-state' and 'resort to coercion in a less restrained manner than their predecessors in the 1970s'. They could be expected to attempt to reform the antiquated economic system but certainly not to follow 'the sort of reformist tendencies advanced by Dubcek in Czechoslovakia'.

In Eastern Europe, Bialer argued, the Soviet Union would be forced – again because of domestic economic difficulties – 'to maintain its domination by intimidation and the threat of the use of force.' He noted the significance of Polish developments: 'Soviet leaders', he wrote, 'see in Poland, their own imperial backyard, the greatest challenge of their postwar history as a national Polish revolution threatens to undermine the centralist Leninist state.'

In the event, however, Gorbachev did decide to tread the Dubcek path. His reform programme represents an attempt to find a creative solution to the country's problems, and he was prepared ultimately to go much further than Khruschev had been to put Soviet/East European relations on a new footing.

Eastern Europe at the beginning of the 1980s faced even more severe problems. Politically the gulf between the Party/State and people was deeper because of the way the Stalinist system had been imposed on the area in the late 1940s and because of subsequent Soviet interference and military intervention. Economically the situation varied somewhat from country to country, but nowhere was the outlook promising.

In terms of economic policy Hungary was at one end of the spectrum in Eastern Europe, the GDR and Czechoslovakia at the other. Hungary's New Economic Model, introduced in 1968, and the import of capital equipment from the West in the 1970s, brought the country relative prosperity during this decade by comparison with most of its East European neighbours. However, by the early 1980s its overseas debt was rapidly mounting, and elements in the party were arguing the need for more radical measures, including democratising the political structure.

The GDR, by contrast, provided the most successful model of a disciplined centralised economy. Like Czechoslovakia, it had the advantage of an established 19th century industrial base which had been expanded under Stalinism. In addition, during the 1970s it developed a close trading relationship with the Federal Republic, becoming almost an unofficial member of the European Community.

Czechoslovakia, after the 1968 invasion, gave priority to consumption over investment as a means of winning public acceptance. But though this brought short-term relief, it was a policy which would have dire consequences for Czechoslovakia's modernisation programme. And during the 1980s, both countries – like some of the older industrialised countries of Western Europe – witnessed a decline in their large scale traditional industries.[7]

Another difficulty faced by all the countries of Eastern Europe in the late 1970s was the sharp deterioration in the terms of trade with the Soviet Union, particularly in relation to the crucial oil imports. Between 1970 and 1980 the terms of trade had shifted in the Soviet Union's favour by 30 per cent. Moreover, the rate of increase in the supply of energy and raw materials from the Soviet Union to Eastern Europe slowed down as the former sought to take advantage of the higher prices available on the world market. As a result of this, and of increased difficulties in obtaining credit from the West, East European planners were forced to accept lower growth rates of industrial production and investment.[8]

To compound all these problems, there was a growing environmental crisis, exacerbated by the burning of lignite coal in power stations and chemical plants, and the generally inefficient and highly polluting heavy industries given priority in the Stalinist model of development. Thus it is not surprising that environmental issues were to prove a major rallying point for popular resistance in the late 1980s.

Finally it is important to note how disillusionment and economic stagnation reinforced each other to produce a spiralling crisis. The official ideology still proclaimed the communist ideal of equality and human brotherhood. This contrasted with the reality of authoritarian rule and the existence of a privileged bureaucratic elite – the *nomenklatura* – nominated and rewarded by the Party hierarchy.

---

[7] Jacques Rupnik, *The Other Europe*, Weidenfeld Paperback 1989, p.172.

[8] Jan Vanous, 'East European Economic Slowdown', in *Problems of Communism*, Vol XXXI No 4, July–August 1982, pp.1-19.

Little wonder then if there was almost universal cynicism and alienation. Marx had dreamed of a society based on the principle 'to each according to his needs, from each according to his ability'. Such an ideal could not be achieved in a situation of autocracy and official privilege, so instead of people working unselfishly for the common good, the temptation was for them to seek the maximum reward for the least effort. As one observer commented, discussing the Polish situation: 'The workers pretend to work and the government pretends to pay them.'

Conclusion

The impetus for change in the Soviet bloc in the 1980s sprang from a deep-seated economic and political malaise. An over-centralised economy, based on inefficient and high-polluting heavy industry, was failing to meet the changing needs of society and the international market, and laying the foundations for an ecological catastrophe. At the same time the gap between communist ideals and 'real existing socialism' bred disillusion and cynicism in the population and division even within the ranks of the communist parties. In Eastern Europe, intermittent unrest, and recurrent major crises, demonstrated the essential lack of viability of Soviet hegemony. At the beginning of the new decade the rise of Solidarity in Poland presented a particularly grave threat since it could serve as a model for organised working class revolt throughout the bloc. Yet when martial law was introduced in Poland in December 1981, and Solidarity outlawed, few would have prophesied the collapse of Soviet-style government by the end of the decade.

Chapter 2

Reflections on the East European Revolutions

The Dynamics of Civil Resistance

> Resolve to serve no longer and you will free yourselves. I do not ask you to push or shake, but simply to withdraw your support from the tyrant. You will then see him fall to the ground like a colossus deprived of its base.
>
> Etienne La Boetie – Discourse on Voluntary Servitude

In the last chapter we suggested that three things were necessary for stable government: confidence on the part of the rulers of their right and capacity to rule; a modicum of efficiency in the running of society and the economy; and the co-operation, or at least the compliance, of the population. This last element is crucial, since unpopular and inefficient governments can hold on to power for prolonged periods if they can persuade or coerce their populations into compliance.

Clearly any government, however repressive or authoritarian, is vulnerable to sustained, widespread non-co-operation by the population, and particularly by those in key sectors such as the civil service, power, transport, telecommunications and other industries, the mass media, and the police and army. True it can seek through control of the media and rigid censorship to bludgeon people into accepting the official ideology and the inevitability if not the legitimacy of its rule. It can also bribe a section of society while simultaneously making life as uncomfortable as possible for those who speak out openly against it. In the last resort it can seek to terrorise the population into submission, using its armed forces to wage warfare against them, and imprisoning, torturing or expelling those who continue to resist.

But a sustained resistance is likely to open up divisions within the ruling elite itself, throwing up factions favouring reform, or even the overthrow of the existing system. Disaffection and division are all the more likely if the economy and administration has largely collapsed and the morale of rulers and administrators has been eroded. At a certain stage in a revolt, staff and management in the official press or on the state radio and television, may refuse any longer to toe the line and begin to publish or broadcast news and discussions that further undermine the position of the authorities. Finally the armed forces – who are after all also part of the population and may find themselves being ordered to fire on sisters and brothers – can become disaffected. If the non-co-operation begins to extend to any serious extent to the key institutions of state propaganda and state coercion, the regime's days are numbered.

Examples of authoritarian governments' dividing and falling as disaffection spreads to the state's own forces are not hard to find. Tsarist rule in Russia finally collapsed at the point when, in the February 1917 revolution, whole regiments in Petrograd refused to obey orders to open fire on demonstrators. In Iran in 1979, after several thousand unarmed demonstrators had been massacred, the army commanders ordered their forces to return to barracks, and the Shah was forced to flee the country. In Eastern Europe, police and security forces refused to go on attacking demonstrators at a certain stage in both East Germany and Czechoslovakia. The most dramatic instance of this process was in Romania when again the army refused orders and turned against Ceausescu. However, there the revolution ended in bloodshed because one section of the state's forces, the heavily armed secret police, the Securitate, remained loyal to Ceausescu and attempted to stage a counter coup. Elsewhere the revolutions were completed without violence on the part of those seeking change.

In Romania the initial massacres in Timisoara might have deterred further demonstrations in a less heady atmosphere than that of Eastern Europe in late 1989 when authoritarian governments in one country after another had collapsed or agreed to end one-party rule. It was the persistence of the demonstrators even in the face of massacre that turned the tide. Even in China there was a point at which the loyalty of the People's Army seemed in doubt: some soldiers for instance refused to fire on the crowds and others even handed over their weapons to the demonstrators. But clearly there were important differences in the situations in China and Romania, and it is possible that support for the Chinese communist authorities simply had not been eroded to the point where a decisive revolt by the army was likely.

When massacre and repression succeed in ending full scale defiance, opposition has to take other forms. Indeed, although civil resistance is frequently thought of in terms of dramatic public confrontations in the streets, it is rare that a population mobilises itself in this way. If mass civil resistance is aiming not at a particular limited reform, but at a change in the whole system, it cannot anticipate early success unless the government's morale is already largely undermined, except when there are divisions within its ranks, or if the loyalty of the armed forces is in question. And it is most frequently in such circumstance that large numbers of people are moved to put their lives on the line in a non-violent insurrection.

At other times civil resistance may take a variety of forms according to what seems feasible or prudent, but three main categories can be identified. First there is the high-risk opposition of individuals and groups committed to bringing about a fundamental change in the system who engage in generally small-scale acts of resistance – somewhat akin in military terms to guerrilla warfare. This may involve open defiance, such as public statements denouncing official lies and propaganda, and a variety of clandestine activities such as the publication of *samizdat* literature, the distribution of material smuggled in from abroad and so forth.

Second there is the 'semi-resistance' of the wider population as its alienation deepens. This may involve relatively low-risk acts of defiance or disobedience, including forms of economic disruption that are hard for the authorities to locate – go-slows, the deliberate misunderstanding of instructions, and 'sullen insubordination'. This may be paralleled by symbolic acts which reaffirm a people's culture, identity and sense of their own history – the commemoration of important dates, decorating the tombs of popular leaders, wearing black armbands to mourn the loss of independence and so forth. More generally it expresses itself in disaffection, low morale, hostility to official propaganda and exhortations. These various forms of semi-resistance can erode the regime's base of support in the country, leading to its isolation, loss of morale, and loss of effective power. It can also set the scene for periods of mass open defiance which put the regime to the test.

Third there is the type of civil resistance which may be on a large or small scale but whose distinctive feature is that its aims are limited. These aims may for instance relate to economic conditions or environmental issues, or to particular local injustices or abuses. The importance of such campaigns is that they involve ordinary citizens in periods when revolutionary change is not necessarily just round the corner, and give them experience in organising, and confidence in their ability to affect events.

Such instances of civil resistance can of course escalate to the point where the system itself is directly challenged. It was economic issues that sparked off some of the major crises in Poland's post-war history; similarly strikes by Romanian miners in the Jiu valley in August 1977 confronted the Ceausescu regime with one of its most serious political challenges prior to the 1989 revolution.[1] In Bulgaria, Eco-Glasnost, an environmental group, succeeded in mounting major demonstrations against some of the policies of the Zhivkov regime in 1989 shortly before his resignation, and subsequently kept up the pressure for the move to full democracy.

Escalation in the sense of widening the scope of initial limited demands is also a common experience. Again Poland provides an outstanding example of this with the birth of Solidarity in 1980. In the Soviet Union too, Siberian miners who struck over pay and conditions in July 1989 struck again in October and added political reform to their list of demands.

The Vulnerabilities of Dictatorships

The more hard-line and totalitarian a regime, the greater is the inherent tendency for such escalation to occur. Where strikes, demonstrations and almost all organised dissent is forbidden, any protest takes on a political significance, however limited the original demands. In effect these regimes, by their very inflexibility, turn

---

[1] *Labour Focus on Eastern Europe*, Vol 1, No 5, November–December 1977, pp.8-12.

the simplest protest into an act of civil disobedience and therefore a direct challenge to their authority and legitimacy. Of course the ban on protests makes it more difficult to get them started in the first place, but when they do occur, and especially when tens or hundreds of thousands of people become involved, they threaten the regime to a degree that would not be true of comparable demonstrations in Western democracies.

Public expressions of dissent challenge totalitarian regimes at another level – they shatter the illusion of unanimity. This illusion is crucial to the self-image of regimes which do not allow rival political parties to compete for office in democratic elections. Despite the fact that a degree of pluralism had forced its way from below into the political systems of most East European countries by the 1980s, so they no longer represented the classic Stalinist model of totalitarianism, these remarks on the significance of mass demonstrations still applied in 1989 to a greater or lesser extent depending on the country concerned. They applied most fully in the case of the hard-line regimes of East-Germany, Czechoslovakia, Bulgaria and Romania. This factor goes a long way to explain the rapidity with which the regimes collapsed when faced with people power when governments operating under a more flexible system could have absorbed it or responded with reforms.

The power equation in Eastern Europe was of course complicated by the role of the Soviet Union. Without the threat of Soviet intervention, civil resistance would undoubtedly have removed authoritarian communist regimes at a much earlier date, or transformed them into something radically different – perhaps into the kind of democratic socialist government 'with a human face' that was Dubcek's goal in 1968.

In the post-Stalin era, the East European regimes were not straightforward Soviet puppets and enjoyed a considerable measure of autonomy. This is obvious from the marked differences by the 1980s in the situations in Hungary, for example, compared to East Germany and Czechoslovakia. However, the Soviet Union set rigid limits which any East European government overstepped at its peril, as Hungary discovered in 1956 and Czechoslovakia in 1968.

Nevertheless, for the Soviet Union invasion was a last resort, entailing costs and risks it much preferred to avoid. Indeed in the case of Poland in both 1956 and 1980-81, the Soviet Union teetered on the brink of invasion but thought better of it, no doubt because the Soviet leadership recognised that this would be a far bloodier and more hazardous business than in the case of small countries like Hungary and Czechoslovakia. Whether, despite this, Brezhnev would ultimately have intervened if Jaruzelski had not done so, in effect, on his behalf, must remain an open question.

Ideally what the Soviet Union wanted were regimes in Eastern Europe which both commanded popular support and remained its faithful allies. The only hope of achieving this was by allowing the regimes considerable leeway in domestic policy and even a degree of latitude in international affairs. But, prior to Gorbachev, Soviet tolerance did not extend to the introduction of political pluralism domestically, or defection from the Warsaw Pact in terms of foreign policy. What made the advent of Solidarity in Poland in 1980-81 so threatening to the whole Soviet system was that it was a major step in the direction of pluralism and challenged fundamentally the hegemony of the communist party.

Gorbachev's rise to power introduced a new element into the situation. However, at first it was unclear just how much freedom of manoeuvre the countries of Eastern Europe were to be permitted. Hungary and Poland in their different ways put Gorbachev's intentions towards Eastern Europe to the test in the course of 1988-89. Once it was established that the Brezhnev doctrine really was dead and buried, the way was clear for a straight confrontation between the regimes in East Germany, Bulgaria and Czechoslovakia and their alienated populations. In Romania, the situation was different because for many years the maverick Ceausescu dictatorship was beyond Moscow's control. Indeed, the inability of the Soviet Union to influence Ceausescu, and to get him to make concessions, was an important contributory factor to the violence which marked the end of his regime.

Revolt and Accommodation: the process of transformation in Eastern Europe

Civil resistance does not necessarily achieve success through the sudden and dramatic overthrow of an unyielding dictatorship as happened in Romania. Change indeed is more likely to be achieved without violence if the regime has earlier been pushed into introducing some reforms and a measure of liberalisation. This can happen in response to pressure from below, to the economic and other needs of the situation, and to criticism from within the ruling group.

In Eastern Europe, as in most situations of this kind, there was an interplay between revolt from below and accommodation and reform – sometimes accompanied by blatant attempts at manipulation – from above. In the Soviet Union the major impetus for change came from above with Gorbachev's programme of economic and political reform; but even there, the economic stagnation meant something had to be done soon and the lonely voices of dissent probably had more impact on the ruling Party than they were willing to acknowledge publicly at the time. Moreover, once a measure of democracy had been introduced, the upsurge of popular enthusiasm and revolt forced the pace of change and made it difficult for conservative forces to put the clock back.

The degree of interaction between the regimes and their opponents has varied across Eastern Europe. Even in the revolutionary upheavals of 1989, some continuity was maintained between the new caretaker governments and the former communist ones. Communists at the beginning of 1990 were represented in the coalition governments in Poland, East Germany and Czechoslovakia; in Bulgaria reform communists remained in power pending the elections after the opposition refused to join in a coalition; and in Hungary the new Socialist Party – created out of the now defunct Hungarian Socialist Workers Party – also formed the interim administration pending national elections. The changes should nonetheless be counted as revolutionary because they encompassed a *systemic* political change – from a centralised, single party system to a pluralist multi-party one.

Hungary

It is instructive to consider the process by which change occurred in different countries. In Hungary, post 1956, Kadar's reform communism and comparative liberalism created space both for independent groups and radical critics within the party. The former were regarded with suspicion, and attempts were made intermittently to suppress or co-opt them, as seen in the tactic adopted by the regime in relation to the independent Peace Group for Dialogue in 1982-83.[2]

But pressure for change mounted, both inside and outside the Party; commencing in 1980, the government-sponsored demonstration to celebrate Hungary's 1948 revolution had to contend with a rival alternative demonstration of radicals and reformers. From small beginnings, by 1987 the alternative demonstration attracted an estimated 1,500 people; although this was not a large demonstration in comparison with those that were to take place across Eastern Europe in 1989, it nonetheless indicated a significant trend.

In September 1987, 100 prominent Hungarian intellectuals signed an open letter to the Parliament calling for economic and political reform, including the establishment of a free press, and guarantees of individual freedom.[3] In January 1988, 600 people attended the inaugural meeting of the Hungarian Democratic Forum. Initially this was a talking-shop rather than a political organisation, and was led by the reform communist, Imre Pozsgay. Later in the year it was to become a centre-right political party and went on to win the largest share of the vote in the election of March 1990.

The demonstration on 15 March 1988 attracted over 5,000 people, and in the following May Caroly Grosz replaced Janos Kadar as head of the HSWP. He promised to speed-up reforms and to introduce a limited degree of pluralism, but rejected demands for a multi-party democracy. Within the Party, the pro-democracy faction was led by Pozsgay; outside it, pressure came from a growing number of grassroots organisations, including notably FIDESZ (the Association of Young Democrats) formed in March 1988, and several environmentalist groups.

The Spring of 1988 also saw the formation of the first independent trade union, the Democratic Union of Scientific Workers, and the

---

[2] See for instance *From Below: Independent Peace and Environmental Movements in Eastern Europe and the USSR*, Helsinki Watch Report, New York & Washington, 1987, especially pp.50-54.

[3] See *East European Reporter*, Vol 3, No 2, March 1988, pp.49-51.

establishment by the opposition of a new political organisation, the Network of Free Initiatives. Later that year, after the government had promised legislation to introduce a multi-party system, the Network formed itself into a political party, the Association of Free Democrats. (The Free Democrats took second place, behind the Hungarian Democratic Forum, in the elections of March-April 1990).

The pressure had its effect. Reflecting the national mood, the Hungarian Parliament began to assert its independence, and in December 1988 rejected all three variants of the budget proposed by the government, voting instead to cut the defence budget by 17 per cent and to reduce drastically the subsidy to the HSWP. In January 1989 the government took the first steps towards legalising a multi-party system, and in the succeeding months the old order began to break down in earnest. 80,000 people from thirty-one independent groups participated in the 15 March demonstration, and eight of the main groups formed an Opposition Round Table in preparation for talks with the governing party on a new democratic constitution for Hungary.

In May, the border fence with Austria was dismantled, and the government cancelled the joint Czechoslovak/Hungarian Nagymaros dam project on the Danube, a project that ecology and other opposition groups had campaigned against with increasing effectiveness since 1985. An estimated 250,000 people attended the official reburial of Imre Nagy in June 1989. In sanctioning the reburial, the reform communists were making a bid to identify their position with that of the 1956 revolutionaries. But the size of the turnout was a stark warning that the Party would be swept aside by the power in the streets if the pace of reform slackened.

In October, the HSWP changed its name and declared itself to be a social democratic party; in the same month Parliament banned the functioning of the Party in the workplace, and ordered the disbanding of the People's Militia. On 23 October, Hungary ceased officially to be a 'People's Republic', and in the following month Parliament passed a series of bills to establish a 'state of law', covering the establishment of political parties, electoral law, the setting up of a constitutional court, and reform of the penal code. The Free Democrats won a remarkable political victory when they pressurised the government to hold a national referendum on the date of the Presidential election and obtained a majority in favour of postponing it from 25 November (the date the government had proposed) until after the general election.

The process of ending one-party communist rule and creating a multi-party democracy was introduced in Hungary without the threat of an imminent revolution in the streets. In this sense the revolution came 'from above'. Nevertheless such a description of the process of change in Hungary is partial and unsatisfactory. It fails to do justice to the wider effects of the 1956 revolution which served notice on the government that the people would not be pushed too far. And it overlooks the contribution in the 1980s towards the opening up of a society of independent groups and individuals, and the mounting pressure from demonstrations.

Poland

In Poland the element of confrontation was more pronounced. General Jaruzelski never succeeded in imposing his authority on the country after the military takeover of December 1981 and the banning of Solidarity. Not only did Solidarity itself continue to function clandestinely but *samizdat* newspapers and journals were published on a scale unparalleled in Eastern Europe. Conscientious objection also became an important focus of opposition in the late 1980s. It had a political as well as a moral dimension: Solidarity had been nonplussed in 1981 by the willingness of young conscripts to cooperate in imposing martial law, and one intention of the Freedom and Peace (WiP) campaign on conscientious objection was to challenge the traditional attitudes towards conscription and military obedience.[4]

The general population remained sullen and uncooperative in response to government appeals. In November 1987 when Jaruzelski sought a mandate in a nationwide plebiscite for a package of economic reforms involving substantial price rises, the voters rejected it. In the following year a government-sponsored poll, whose results were leaked to the opposition, showed that four out of five Poles

---

[4]See the interview with Elbieta Rawicz-Oledzka in the present volume.

had 'an entirely negative view' of the government, and nearly two out of three thought there could be 'open political conflict' within the following twelve months.[5]

This prediction was borne out when a new wave of strikes hit the country in August, paralysing the coal mining industry, Poland's principal source of hard currency. Troops were ordered to take over major industrial plants, and curfews were imposed in the provinces of Szczecin, Kotowice and Gdansk. The strike ended inconclusively, but now at last the government began to make serious moves towards accommodating Solidarity. Ironically, the latter was far weaker at this point than it had been in 1980-81, or in the early years after the imposition of martial law: in the later 1980s smaller and more radical groups, notably Freedom and Peace, set the pace and style of opposition. However, the regime itself was at this point demoralised and vulnerable.

Round-Table talks between the government and Solidarity began in February 1989 and three months later the union was again legalised. Jaruzelski's strategy was to try to enlist the support of Solidarity in restructuring the economy, while retaining ultimate power in the hands of the Party. Thus in the elections set for June, the communists and their smaller allied parties were guaranteed 60 per cent of the seats in the key lower house, the Sejm.

In the event even this failed to ensure for them the retention of power. Solidarity won a sweeping victory at the polls, taking ninety-nine out of 100 seats in the elections to the Upper House, and all the seats it was permitted to contest for the Sejm. Further demoralised after such a massive defeat, the Party floundered, and the two smaller allied parties – the Peasant Party and the Democratic Party – deserted it. On 24 August, the Sejm appointed Tadeusz Mazowiecki, a Catholic intellectual and editor of *Solidarity Weekly*, the new Prime Minister, and on 12 September it approved his choice of a Solidarity-dominated cabinet. The new government introduced stringent economic measures and began the process of dismantling the communist state apparatus. The Party was stripped

---

[5]See the interview with Elbieta Rawicz-Oledzka in the present volume.

of its privileges and formally deprived of its leading role. A general election is scheduled for 1993.

Nonetheless, the Polish developments represented something short of the immediate overthrow of the former regime. A compromise formula gave Jaruzelski the presidency pending a future election, and gave communist party members four key ministries – Defence, Interior, Transport and Foreign Trade.

East Germany

In East Germany what occurred was closer to outright revolution – albeit non-violent. In August and September 1989 thousands of East Germans travelled to Hungary via Czechoslovakia hoping to make their way from there to Austria and then on to West Germany. Initially the Hungarian authorities tightened security along the Austrian border, but as the would-be emigrants continued to arrive, they were forced to set up refugee camps in Budapest and on the shores of Lake Balaton. Finally, on 11 September, to the consternation of the East German authorities, Hungary opened its borders. Hundreds more East Germans continued to arrive each day, while others, fearing that Czechoslovakia would close its border with Hungary, sought refuge in the grounds of the West Germany Embassy in Prague. (Those sheltering in the Embassy were eventually permitted to travel to the West in sealed trains). In total an estimated 225,000 people left East Germany from the beginning of 1989 until the opening of the Berlin Wall.[6] Many of those leaving the country were young, highly qualified people whose departure in such numbers threatened the economy and society with collapse.

At the same time the authority of the government and the communist Socialist Unity Party (SED) was being challenged by increasingly massive demonstrations organised by New Forum in Berlin, Leipzig, Dresden and other cities. New Forum itself was

---

[6]*Tearing Down the Curtain: The people's revolution in Eastern Europe*, an *Observer* team, Hodder & Stoughton 1990, p.72.

in part an attempt to save the country from collapse by encouraging young people to stay in the GDR and force the government to change its policies. When Gorbachev arrived in East Berlin on 7 October to join in the celebrations for the fortieth anniversary of the founding of the GDR, he found a country in turmoil. Both privately and in public he warned the East German authorities of the need for change, clearly signalling that Soviet tanks were not about to intervene as they had in 1953.

Further major demonstrations occurred throughout the country within hours of Gorbachev's departure. On 9 October, despite a daunting police and militia presence, 70,000 people took to the streets of Leipzig. When the security forces refrained from interfering or attacking the demonstrators – in contrast to their response on many previous occasions in various cities, including Berlin the previous night – the credibility of the Honecker regime was virtually at an end. The decision not to intervene was an acknowledgement that a 'Tiananmen Square' solution was not an option that the authorities were prepared to risk – or perhaps not one that the Soviet Union would permit them to risk. On 16 October, 100,000 people demonstrated in Leipzig while the Politburo met in an emergency session. Two days later, Honecker resigned as party leader and head of state, to be replaced by Egon Krenz.

It was not enough to resolve the crisis. The exodus and the mass demonstrations continued. On 7 November, after a million-strong demonstration in Berlin, the government headed by the veteran communist leader Willi Stoph resigned. At midnight on 8-9 November the wall was opened. Just over a week later, a coalition government was formed, headed by a reform communist, Hans Modrow, the party boss in Dresden who had led the demonstrations there only a few days previously; nearly half the members of the new cabinet were non-communists. Still the crisis continued. On 3 December two million people joined hands in a human chain across East Germany; on the same day the entire Politburo resigned. Over the next few days crowds stormed the offices of the state security police – the Stasi – in Leipzig and other towns. On 1 December the East German Parliament, the *Volkskammer*, abolished the constitutionally guaranteed role of the communist party, and on 6 December, Krenz resigned as party leader and head of state. The following day Round Table Talks began with opposition groups, which resulted in setting a provisional date for a general election.[7]

Allegations have subsequently been made that the popular revolution in East Germany was not all that it seemed, and that elements within the communist party and security services (Stasi), acting in concert with Moscow, plotted Honecker's removal in the autumn of 1989 and the installation of a Gorbachev-style reformist regime. In an interview for the Channel 4 television series *And the Walls came tumbling down*, the former Party Chief in East Berlin, Gunther Schabowski, gave details of the alleged plot, and claimed that Hans Modrow, not Krenz, had been the preferred candidate to replace Honecker as party secretary and head of state. There was, he says, insufficient support within the Politburo for this move, and the appointment of Krenz as a compromise candidate failed to stem the tide of revolt.

But even if everything Schabowski says is correct, it doesn't alter the larger picture. One would expect that elements within the ruling elite should have sought to change the leadership and modify policies in face of a nationwide revolt. Indeed it is self-evident that Honecker could not have been forced to resign without some prior planning within the politburo, and nor would it be surprising, given the nature of the regime and its relationship with the Soviet Union, if those involved sought the prior acquiescence of Moscow and of the GDR's own security services. None of this changes the fact that what occurred in East Germany was a revolution from below and that whatever attempts there may have been to manipulate or divert it failed completely.

---

[7]In the election held on 18 March the Christian Democrats (CDU) and their allies won a landslide victory. The CDU won 40.91 per cent votes cast, giving them 164 seats in parliament, while their nearest rivals, the Social Democratic Party (SPD) gained 21.84 per cent of votes and 87 seats. The former communist party, renamed the Party of Democratic Socialism, under their new leader Gregor Gysi, won a respectable 16.33 per cent, giving them 21 seats. But Alliance 90, made up of New Forum and Initiative for Peace and Human Rights, gained only 2.90 per cent, giving them 12 seats.

Bulgaria

It was again a mass exodus – this time of ethnic Turks – that played a major role in undermining the position of the Bulgarian Party leader, Todor Zhivkov. Since 1985 tough discriminatory measures had been taken against the ethnic Turkish community, forcing them to give up Turkish names and abandon many cultural and religious (Moslem) practices. In May 1989, Turks in various parts of Bulgaria staged demonstrations and hunger strikes to coincide with the human rights meeting in Paris of the Conference on Security and Cooperation in Europe. The demonstrations were organised by the Committee to Support Vienna '89, and the Democratic League for Human Rights; and their main demands were the right to speak Turkish, the right to practise the Moslem religion, and the restoration of Turkish names to those who had been forced to abandon them.

15,000 people took part in the demonstrations which were assaulted by troops and militia using dogs, smoke bombs, tanks, helicopters and guns. A number of people were killed (seven according to official figures, sixty according to participants and other witnesses), many more injured, and thousands arrested. Subsequently 5,000 were deported to Turkey, including the organisers and many community leaders.[8] These outrages were condemned at the Paris meeting, and the European Community cancelled negotiations for a new trade treaty. Over the next several months, 350,000 ethnic Turks fled the country, causing immense dislocation to social, political and economic life. Gorbachev, who visited Bulgaria in June, refused to endorse Zhivkov's anti-Turkish policy, and was reportedly embarrassed and angered because he had been seeking closer relations with the Turkish government. Within the Bulgarian Party and government some senior members, including the Foreign Minister, Petar Mladenov, decided it was time for a change.

Throughout the summer and autumn of 1989 opposition to the regime grew and became more vocal. Despite arrests and persecution, the Independent Society for Human Rights continued to press the case of the ethnic Turks. The Independent Discussion

---

[8]*Tearing down the Curtain*, p.90.

Club for Support of Perestroika and Glasnost, half of whose 250 members were in the Communist Party, presented a petition to the National Assembly on behalf of the Turks. Still more significantly, the environmental movement, Eco-glasnost, showed itself capable of bringing large numbers of people onto the streets to challenge government policies.

A CSCE environmental conference in Sofia from 16 October to 3 November provided Eco-glasnost with the opportunity they had been looking for. They demanded the right to participate in the conference as a non-governmental organisation, produced well-documented papers, and proposed that their secretary, Petar Beron, an outstanding zoologist, should be the conference's Executive Secretary.[9] In an effort to regain the initiative, the authorities released on bail six human rights activists held illegally for the previous three months. This only emboldened the opposition, and during the course of the conference they openly held meetings, demonstrations and press conferences, collecting signatures daily opposing a river-diversion scheme. Other independent groups, including the Independent Society for Human Rights, and the Committee for Religious Rights, also staged actions during this period.

On 26 October, the Security Forces lost patience with the Eco-glasnost demonstrators and brutally attacked 40 of them in the presence of foreign diplomats, conference delegates and journalists. Western and non-aligned delegates at the conference threatened a walk-out, and this produced an unprecedented apology from the Bulgarian authorities, acknowledging that the security forces had overstepped the mark. On 3 November, the final day of the conference, 5,000 Eco-glasnost supporters demonstrated in the centre of Sofia, marching on the national assembly and presenting a petition containing 11,500 signatures. On 24 October, Petar Mladenov, who had been Foreign Minister for eighteen years, tended his resignation. This provoked a political crisis that culminated in Zhivkov's removal on 10 November. However, street protests, and demands for full democracy continued. On 18 November 50,000 people

---

[9]Predictably the proposal was refused, although the government did include Beron as an advisor to the Bulgarian delegation. See *Tearing down the Curtain*, pp.93-94.

demonstrated in Sofia. The same number took part in a further demonstration there on 10 December where the demand was for talks between the government and a new opposition grouping, the Union of Democratic Forces. A few days later thousands of chanting demonstrators outside the television station won an apology from the chairman of Bulgarian television for what they claimed was a bias in news reports; two of the protesters were also invited to examine and comment on news scripts. On 11 December, the Communist Party proposed an end to its monopoly of power and the creation of a multi-party system. A general election was promised for May or June 1990.[10]

Czechoslovakia

Reform and concessions from above played scarcely any part in the process of change in Czechoslovakia if one discounts the desperate improvisations in late November and early December as power finally slipped from the hands of the Party. It seemed at first that the position of the Party and its leader, Milos Jakes, was unassailable.

In January 1989, hundreds of police with dogs and truncheons broke up a demonstration of 1,000 people attempting to lay a wreath in Wenceslas Square to commemorate the twentieth anniversary of the death of Jan Palach. On August 22 a protest in Wenceslas Square on the 21st anniversary of the Soviet led invasion of 1968, attracted 8,000-10,000 people, the majority of them young people. This time the police were, in the words of one participant, 'relatively restrained'. However, a further demonstration of 10,000 on 28 October, the 71st anniversary of Czech independence, was again viciously attacked by riot police, and 355 people were arrested. 10,000 was a respectable number, given the risks involved, but it would not be enough to topple one of the most hard-line governments in

---

[10]In the subsequent elections held on 10 June 1990, the former Bulgarian Communist Party, now renamed the Bulgarian Socialist Party, won a total of 211 seats as against the 144 seats won by their nearest rivals, the Union of Democratic Forces led by Petar Baron. Thus, uniquely in Eastern Europe, the former Communist Party was returned to power.

the Eastern Bloc. Some Western commentators concluded that the population was still cowed by the memory of 1968.

Then came the student-organised demonstration of 17 November. A crowd of 30,000 – representing the largest protest since August 1969 – was attacked and dispersed by security forces. The rumour spread that one student had been killed, and the population, far from being cowed by the massive show of force, was galvanised into revolt.

What followed was a week without precedent in Czechoslovak history. Every night for the next seven days, hundreds of thousands of people took to the streets of Prague, Bratislava, Brno and other cities. On 20 November, 200,000 filled Wenceslas Square; on 24 November there were an estimated 250,000-300,000, as many as the square could hold. Millions, inside and outside Czechoslovakia, were able to watch the unfolding drama on television.

There were poignant and funny moments: the demonstrators jangling their keys like bells and chanting 'Give the bells to the clowns!', and 'The dinosaurs must go!'; Alexander Dubcek, the Party Secretary deposed after the 1968 invasion, stepping onto the balcony overlooking Wenceslas Square on 24 November and extending his arms in a gesture of embrace to the people below; two days prior to that, Marta Kubisova, banned for many years from public appearance, singing from the same balcony the hymn of Comenius:

> May disputes and envy fade
> May the governing of your affairs
> Come back at last to you,
> My nation.[11]

On 21 November the Prime Minister, Ladislav Adamec, opened talks with Civic Forum, the coalition of opposition groups formed two days previously. Despite this conciliatory gesture, on 23 November the authorities ordered the People's Militia, under the control of the Communist Party, to 'restore order' in Prague. The Militia

---

[11]This incident is graphically described in John Simpson, *Dispatches from the Barricades*, Hutchinson 1990, p.175.

refused. It was a critical moment in the erosion of the Party's authority.

The climax swiftly followed. The BBC correspondent, John Simpson, describes the moment:

> That night, at the Magic Lantern, Alexander Dubcek was giving a slow fragile press conference where the questions were as restrained as the answers, when Vaclav Havel, who had been protecting him as carefully as a son, bounded up and announced in the most Shakespearean fashion of all the news that Miklos Jakes, the Communist Party leader, had resigned, together with other leading Party officials. One could only sit and marvel at the timing, as Havel in his shirt sleeves embraced the older man and people in the audience stood and applauded.[12]

But it was not quite all over yet. President Husak remained in office and it was not clear if the party was willing to accept full democracy. On 26 November Adamec joined Havel and Dubcek to address a crowd estimated at half a million at the Letna Field on the edge of Prague; Wenceslas Square could no longer accommodate the numbers wishing to protest.

Next day a two-hour general strike in support of democracy showed just how far support for the party had been eroded within its traditional power base in the factories. On 3 December the announcement of a new communist-dominated cabinet provoked further mass protests. An estimated 200,000 people again demonstrated in Wenceslas Square on 4 December, demanding a new government and the resignation of President Husak.

On 7 December, Adamec resigned, followed the next day by President Husak. On 10 December, with the prior agreement of Civic Forum and its Slovak counterpart, People Against Violence, a new Federal coalition government was formed. It was led by a reform communist, Marian Calfa,[13] but with a majority of non-communist ministers. Jan Canogursky, released from prison only ten days previously, was appointed Deputy Prime Minister. At the end of the

---

[12]*Ibid*, p.180.

[13]On 19 January 1990, Calfa resigned from the communist party. Calfa went on to head the new coalition government, dominated by Civic Forum and People Against Violence, after the June 1990 elections.

month Dubcek was appointed Speaker of the Federal Parliament, and Havel President.

As in the case of East Germany, there have been subsequent reports of a plot – involving reformers within the Party, the Czechoslovak security forces (StB) and the KGB – to manipulate the unrest in order to bring to power a stable, Gorbachev-style regime. The gist of the allegation is that the StB infiltrated *agents provocateurs* into the student demonstration of 17 November, took the head of the march and deliberately led it into the police lines where they knew it would be attacked. It is further alleged that the 'student' whose reported death provoked such an angry response from the population was in fact a police agent acting out an agreed charade. It is suggested that the conspirators calculated that the police violence and the reported death of a student would provoke a political crisis in which Jakes would be removed to make way for a reformist government. Parallel with this operation, there was to have been a determined effort to infiltrate and split the opposition forces so that the new government could strengthen its hold on power.[14]

These reports have been taken sufficiently seriously by the Federal Parliament for it to have established two successive commissions to investigate them. The first published its report in May 1990, concluding that there was suspicion, but no proof, that the attack on the student demonstration of 17 November had been pre-planned by the StB, possibly in collusion with the KGB. The second commission has yet to report its findings.

The significance of such a conspiracy, if if it did exist, has to be questioned. The self-evident fact is that it did not succeed. Far from pre-empting or diverting the revolutionary challenge to authoritarian communist power, the plot, if there was one, precipitated that challenge, and set in motion forces that the conspirators were quite unable to control. Moreover, to suggest that the Czechoslovak revolution would never have occurred but for a manipulated assault on demonstrators on 17 November is unconvincing, given the momentum for change sweeping East-Central Europe, and indeed the propensity of the security forces to attack those challenging the authority of the state.

---

[14] See John Simpson, *Dispatches from the Barricades*, Hutchinson 1990, pp.170-172.

In order to understand how ten days of mass non-violent protest were able to overturn a tough and repressive system, we need to remind ourselves that the fact the demonstrations could be held at all represented the virtual collapse of the authority of State and Party. This loss of authority was underlined by the support of the industrial proletariat for the general strike on 27 November, by a vote of television workers on 23 November to cover the protests, and by the refusal on the same day of the People's Militia and the specially trained riot police to continue using force against the protesters.

Romania

In Romania, there were no significant concessions by the Ceausescu dictatorship until he was ousted from power by a popular uprising and the disaffection of the army. Initially the revolution was achieved without violence on the part of the people. The massacre on 17 December of ethnic Hungarians and others in Timosoara when demonstrating in support of a local Hungarian pastor, Lazlo Tokes, provoked only anger and the spread of protest, despite a ban on all demonstrations.

On 20 December, after returning from a visit to Iran, Ceausescu declared a state of emergency in Timisoara and blamed the disturbances on 'terrorists, fascists, imperialists, hooligans and foreign espionage services'.

Next day, addressing a huge rally from the balcony of the Presidential Palace in the city centre of Bucharest, he was visibly shaken when his words were greeted with boos and catcalls. Security men hastily ushered him back inside the Palace. Part of the crowd broke into groups and conducted anti-government demonstrations. There were reports that some troops refused orders to intervene, but later in the day the protesters faced the guns and tanks of the army, the Securitate, and the police and many were killed and injured. There were clashes also in Timisoara and other provincial cities.

On 22 December, Ceausescu declared a national state of emergency, and the radio announced the 'suicide' of the Defence Minister, General Vasile Milea, describing him as a 'traitor'. In fact he had been shot by a member of the Presidential Guard after refusing to order troops to open fire on the crowds. Incredibly, despite the massacre of the previous day, a huge angry crowd again assembled before the Presidential Palace. This time soldiers refused to open fire and some ostentatiously unloaded their rifles in view of the crowd. The cry went up 'The army are with us'. People began storming the Palace. Ceausescu and his wife, Elena, narrowly escaped capture by fleeing from the roof of the building by helicopter. Only five days after the Timisoara massacre, Ceausescu's reign of terror was at an end. On Christmas day he and his wife were summarily executed.

It is important to stress that up to the point that the Ceausescu's took flight, the revolution had been entirely non-violent on the part of the protestors, though some soldiers in Timisoara took the part of the people and returned fire on the Securitate prior to 22 December. Ceausescu lost the ability to rule because a people driven to desperation refused any longer to co-operate or to be intimidated. Tragically, however, many more civilians were to be shot down by the Securitate, and there were to be several days of pitched street battles between the latter and army, before the revolution would be secure.

Could the Romanian revolution have been accomplished without resort to violence in self-defence on the part of the population, or on the part of elements within the army acting on their behalf? Probably not – or at least not at that time. If the Securitate had not been resisted by force it is likely that their counter-revolution would have succeeded and they would have instituted a new period of even harsher repression. It would have been the post-Tiananmen pattern in China over again. How stable any new repressive regime would have been, and how long it could have clung to power are, however, much more open questions.

In Romania – as in East Germany and Czechoslovakia – there have been subsequent allegations and rumours that what occurred was not a successful popular uprising but a carefully planned coup. The notion is categorically rejected by the now ruling National Salvation Front in Romania, but of itself this carries little weight since, if there was a coup, they are its beneficiaries.

No-one, as far as we are aware, is suggesting that the initial protests in Timisoara, or the subsequent demonstrations in Bucharest which brought about Ceausescu's flight from the capital, were other than spontaneous. The suggestion, however, is that a group of anti-Ceausescu communists who had been plotting his overthrow for some time used the opportunity to seize power for themselves.

The most concrete evidence of a coup comes from the testimony of two prominent members of the immediate post-revolutionary government, Silviu Brucan and General Nicolae Militaru. In March 1989 Brucan had been one of the signatories of a letter, published in the West, by six former Party leaders indicting the Ceausescu regime. Militaru was a former Defence Minister. Both claim to have played a leading role in an anti-Ceausescu plot which, they say, had enlisted support from within the army, the Securitate and (less extensively) the Party.[15] Although their testimony has to be taken seriously, one must also bear in mind that by the time they gave their testimonies they had become estranged from the National Salvation Front and President Ion Iliescu whose reputation and prestige would be gravely damaged if their allegations were accepted.

Circumstantial evidence for the coup theory is provided by the fact that the National Salvation Front emerged from the blue in the immediate aftermath of the revolution and that it has been led from the start mainly by communist veterans and apparatchiks. It also appears to be the case that the old *nomenklatura* retain their predominance in Romania's political and economic life, that human rights are again being violated and freedom of expression curtailed, and that the notorious Securitate forces have, for the most part, simply been incorporated into the new security police.[16]

Reports of plots and coups – not only in Romania but throughout Eastern Europe – need to be put into perspective. Under any dictatorial system, there are bound to be dissident factions within the ruling elite or party, and intermittent attempts to remove the current leadership by some form of coup. It is also predictable – one is tempted to say inevitable – that at moments of crisis and popular unrest the plots and conspiracies will multiply.

This is not necessarily an obstacle to the success of a popular movement for radical change. On the contrary, in some situations

---

[15]The fullest exposition of their claims was published in an interview with the Romanian newspaper *Adevarul* (Truth) on 23 August 1990. For the full text of the interview, see *East European Reporter*, Vol 4, No 3, Autumn/Winter 1990, pp.74-77.

[16]See the interview with Helmuth Frauendorfer in this volume.

it may be the *sine qua non* for success. It is crucial that popular movements for democracy should take advantage of any division and uncertainty among the rulers in a dictatorial regime. So if Brucan and Militaru and their co-conspirators did indeed succeed in enlisting sections of the Army and Securitate against Ceausescu, thereby making it more likely that at the critical moment they would take the side of the crowd against him, so much the better. It is still a victory for people power, not for the conspirators **unless the latter succeed in taking over the revolution and halting it in its tracks.** That is the crucial issue in the debates about plots and coups and manipulation in the course of the 1989 revolutions. It is no surprise at all that conspiracies should have occurred. The question is – did they succeed in thwarting the goals of the democracy movement, or did they chiefly weaken and divide the ruling establishment?

In East Germany and Czechoslovakia, it is evident that whatever conspiracies occurred to maintain the essentials of authoritarian communism in place did not succeed. In Romania the situation is less clear. This is one reason why the political situation there is so unsettled – although this seems largely due to the absence of a developed civil society and a mature opposition.

The potential, then, of civil resistance to change – or secure the overthrow of – even the most dictatorial regimes has been confirmed by events both in Eastern Europe and in other parts of the world in the 1980s. However, two central questions requre answers: What motivates populations, cowed by years of repression, to resist? And what provides the organisational base for their mobilisation.

Civil Society – the Base of Nonviolent Resistance

Although it is convenient to refer to authoritarian and totalitarian governments, in reality no government exercises, or can hope to exercise, absolute control. In practice governments are forced to seek a degree of accommodation with the bulk of the population. This raises two issues which are important to the understanding of civil resistance and the opportunities open to it. One concerns the spaces within any society where independent thought and community can exist and expand. The second concerns the interaction between the apex and the base – between regime and population – as the former seeks to retain control but finds it necessary to surrender some of its power in its efforts to do so.

Clearly any government, even the most authoritarian, would prefer to have a population willingly co-operating with it rather than one forced into sullen compliance by threats and terror. Stalin and neo-Stalinist regimes sought to achieve this by establishing as nearly as possible total control of the means of communication and education and by rigid censorship. Paradoxically, this tended to isolate them from reality and thus to render them more vulnerable in moments of crisis. Ceausescu in Romania seems to have been genuinely incredulous at the manifestations of his own massive unpopularity and to have gone to his death believing that he had been overthrown in a counter-revolutionary coup.

The power of the outspoken dissident in authoritarian states of left or right derives from the fact that they expose the gap between the official propaganda and reality as the people experience it. As Vaclav Havel observed, the majority of people are coerced into living a lie, to paying lip service to the official reality while confining the expression of their real thoughts and feelings to private occasions.[17] In a country like Czechoslovakia, what made individual critics like Havel, or relatively small groups such as Charter 77, so threatening to the state was that they gave open expression to the thoughts and feelings of millions of ordinary people. They were prepared to say aloud that the emperor had no clothes.

Until the mass revolts of late 1989, the independent and dissident movements in Eastern Europe and the Soviet Union were – with the exception of Solidarity – relatively small and often apparently isolated. In fact on the contrary it was the governments that increasingly lost touch with the people, most markedly in the case of the hard-line governments. Yet even in a country like Poland there was a genuine tragedy about the way the system isolated well-intentioned and initially popular reformers like Gomulka and Gierek.

When the regimes dealt harshly with their intellectual critics and small dissident movements, they did not do so simply out of spite

---

[17]Vaclav Havel in *The Power of the Powerless*, Hutchinson, 1985, pp.23-96.

but from a quite accurate appreciation of the threat they represented. Moreover after 1980-81, the phenomenal rise of Solidarity in Poland served as a reminder of how quickly the situation could change once people found a cause to rally behind and became alerted to the possibilities of concerted action.

Independent thinkers in Eastern Europe have developed the concept of 'civil society' to identify such groups, organisations and institutions which operate outside the control of the state and which, to a greater or lesser extent, offer a different perspective on the world from that of the ruling authorities. Some of the groups concerned may be formally proscribed, or face official harassment, so that even maintaining them in being represents an act of civil resistance. This was generally the case until recently in the Soviet bloc with respect to groups with political or quasi-political goals such as independent human rights, peace and environmentalist organisations, unofficial trades unions, and some religious groups.

The major Churches, after an initial period of persecution or harassment, were in the main tolerated in the post-Stalin period and their role in society grudgingly recognised. The Catholic Church in Poland provided a major institutional base for dissent and also played at times a mediating role between State and opposition. The election of the Archbishop of Kracow, Cardinal Wojtyla, as Pope in 1978, and his triumphal visit to Poland the following year, were developments of major significance. And at the parish level church buildings provided both a refuge and rallying point, especially in the period after the banning of Solidarity in 1981. In Hungary, the Catholic hierarchy was unsympathetic to some of the opposition's goals and bitterly opposed recognition of the right of conscientious objection. However, at a parish level it often provided significant support for the opposition. In East Germany, human rights and peace groups were mainly church-based, though here it was the Protestant Evangelical Church that was central. The necessary caveat to be added is that in the history of Eastern Europe the Churches have tended to be a conservative force, and sometimes an outright reactionary one. In pre-war Poland, for instance, there was a strongly anti-semitic current within the Catholic Church.

There are also formally a-political institutions and bodies which may nevertheless become a catalyst for change because they provide opportunities for the presentation of new ideas and for free discussion. The 1968 crisis in Poland was sparked off by the banning of a play in Warsaw with a strongly nationalist message written by a nineteenth century playwright. In Czechoslovakia from the late 1970s onwards, the authorities sought to suppress jazz and rock music, and the jazz section of the Musicians Union became a focal point for dissent and the counter-culture.[18]

The theatres in both East Germany and Czechoslovakia also played a major role in 1989 in rallying opposition. In East Berlin there was a tradition of political theatre which had flourished in the 1920s and early 1930s and was closely associated with Bertold Brecht. One theatre manager in East Berlin speaking on a British television programme confirmed that the theatres became highly politicised during the 1989 crisis, and told how theatrical performances would be followed by a political discussion involving the whole audience. In Prague, the basement of the Lantern Theatre became the headquarters of Civic Forum in the days leading up to the overthrow of communist rule.

Universities too were central in the 1989 revolutions – as they have been in almost every major political upheaval in recent decades, whether in the East, the West or the Third World. The dilemma for authoritarian governments in technological societies is that a more highly educated workforce is crucial to economic competitiveness and success, but the spirit of rational enquiry which must to some degree at least inform the work of institutions of higher learning is inimical to dogmatism. And while students, academics and the professional classes may not be able on their own to bring about a revolution or fundamental change, they can articulate discontents felt more widely in society and become a catalyst for effective mass resistance. Thus in Czechoslovakia, Vaclav Havel and other intellectuals grouped around Charter 77 provided a kind of think-tank for non-violent change; in addition, students initiated the demonstrations which subsequently gained the support of almost every section of the community. In East Germany and Romania too students were in the forefront of the civil resistance that led to the end of authoritarian rule.

---

[18]See Andrew Czepel, 'Official Bunk about Punk', *Labour Focus on Eastern Europe*, Vol 7, No 1, Winter 1984, pp.11-14, and 'Jazz Section Suppressed', *END Journal*, December 86-January 87, pp.3-4.

Significantly, the movements cut across class boundaries and class issues. Even in Poland where a specifically working class organisation, Solidarity, provided the motor for revolution, it was the alliance of workers and intellectuals behind a set of demands that transcended narrow class interests that was crucial. The 1956 crisis in Poland was the result of a working class revolt that began in the industrial city of Poznan. In 1968 when the intellectuals and students revolted they did so on their own, failing to enlist the support of workers. Two years later, in the crisis that toppled Gomulka, the workers appealed in vain for support from the universities.

Only from 1976 onwards did intellectuals and workers begin to work together more closely following the formation of KOR – the Committee for the Defence of the Workers. This group soon added to its title that of Committee for Social Defence (KSS), and KSS-KOR was to play a key role in the emergence of Solidarity. However, by the late 1980s, the Freedom and Peace group (WiP) were making much of the running in the opposition to the Jaruzelski government. This body, drawing its support principally (though not uniquely) from students and intellectuals, campaigned on the issues of conscientious objection, civil liberty, ecology and disarmament.

Elsewhere in Eastern Europe broadly based campaigns were central in the growing opposition. Human rights bodies formed the main base of opposition in the 1970s. From the early 1980s onwards, independent peace groups emerged as a significant force in response to the Euromissile crisis, to the resurgence of mass protest in the West, and to new Soviet nuclear deployments in Czechoslovakia and East Germany in 1983. The 'Berlin Appeal' of the Swords into Ploughshares movement in East Germany, issued in January 1982, attracted over 2,000 signatures. This called for a Europe free of nuclear weapons, the conclusion of a German Peace Treaty followed by the withdrawal of all foreign troops from both German states, and an end to the balance of terror.[19] In Hungary, the Dialogue group, formed in September 1982, attracted thousands of young people in a brief period of independent existence, and organised marches and public meetings. Human rights groups too, like Charter 77 in Czechoslovakia, increasingly emphasised security

---

[19]*From Below, op cit.*, pp.213-215.

and foreign policy issues in their statements, and became engaged in a discussion with the Western peace movements. Finally, from the early 1980s onwards, environmental and ecology issues, and groups campaigning around them, became more prominent.

The groups and organisations that constitute civil society have a significance beyond their potential as a base for future revolution. They can enhance the quality of the intellectual, cultural and spiritual life of those involved in them even under conditions of repression. When Vaclav Havel insisted on the importance of 'living within the truth', it was not in the expectation of the early downfall of the Husak regime. However, when people were ready to take on the regime in open non-violent rebellion, the work of Havel and the small band of independent thinkers associated with Charter 77 and other similar groups, affected the whole tenor of the revolution and facilitated a non-violent transfer of power.

Havel's influence extended far beyond the relatively few people who had read his statements or plays and he quickly became the acknowledged leader of Civic Forum. It was fitting that he should become the president of the republic when democracy returned to Czechoslovakia. But more important still is the fact that the debates about future political and security arrangements in Europe – including nuclear disarmament, the removal of all foreign troops and bases, and the right of the German people to come together in a single state if that is their wish – were subsequently reflected in Czechoslovakia's foreign policy. Indeed if the outlook in Czechoslovakia today is relatively hopeful, it is in no small measure due to the groundwork of Charter 77 and other civic organisations. By contrast, one of the many difficulties facing Romania comes from the fact that independent organisations and open debate were so thoroughly crushed during the Ceausescu years.

Finally, however, we should not overlook another set of organisations which, though they hardly constitute part of civil society, may at critical moments become agents of change – the Party itself and its various affiliated and satellite bodies such as client political parties, and the trades unions. Like all human institutions, no communist party is ever completely monolithic, there are always various factions and tendencies within it, including people committed to the ideal of building 'socialism with a human face'. The fact that ruling parites in authoritarian states are not entirely monolithic is a crucial lever for non-violent change. In moments of crisis especially, the radical wing may be able to take over the leadership of the Party – indeed such a move may even be supported by the Party conservatives because they see it as representing a chance to retain power. This occurred when Gomulka was made General Secretary of the Polish United Workers Party in 1956. In moments of national crisis, too, the satellite groups and parties of the communists have in several instances asserted their independence and thrown in their lot with opposition forces. This happened in Poland in 1981 and again in 1989, and in the East German Parliament in November 1989.

Opportunity and rising expectations: the spurs to action

But how are people moved *en masse* to risk life and liberty in open rebellion? One classic situation in which this is likely to occur is when rising expectations are frustrated, and when people judge that there is a genuine chance of achieving change. This broadly speaking was the situation in Eastern Europe of the late 1980s.

The frustration of rising expectations was related in part – but only in part – to the slowing down of the Eastern bloc economies in the 1980s discussed in the previous chapter. This, as we saw, hit some countries harder than others – Poland and Romania, for example, more than East Germany and Czechoslovakia. Indeed the relative prosperity of the latter two countries, and the fact that they do not have the burden of a crippling foreign debt, belie the purely economistic accounts of the radical changes that swept the region. This is not to suggest that the economic factor was unimportant. It is to recognise that it was one of a number of factors, and that, in so far as economic considerations were central, the increasing awareness of the gap between living standards in East and West was probably as important as the actual slowing down of the economy.

There were also particular frustrations in individual countries which cannot be analysed in detail in a general survey of this kind. In Poland, for instance, there had been a large expansion in higher education in the 1970s, reaching out into the working class. By 1975 about half of all students in higher education were workers or of working class origin. However, the prospects for social advance were largely blocked. There were few openings at managerial level because management had been saturated by an earlier generation of educated workers; and the Party – the other traditional means of advance – had become a largely self-perpetuating and quasi-hereditary institution.[20] It was these educated young workers, confined to the factory-floor, who provided much of the workplace leadership of Solidarity.

Awareness both of the economic gap between East and West and of the relative openness of Western societies sprang in part from access to the Western radio and television stations, including those with a specifically political purpose such as Radio Free Europe and Voice of America. (Illusions about Western life, it should be added, were also promulgated). In the GDR, in particular, West German television was regularly viewed by a large segment of the population. Not only were the East Germans presented with an often glamourised picture of life in the West, they were also able to observe the relative freedom with which opposition movements operated. Indeed in the early 1980s, East Germans could see pictures even on their own state-controlled television of hundreds of thousands of people in Western Europe taking to the streets in demonstrations demanding nuclear disarmament. Mass non-violent protests in other parts of the world from South Africa to South Korea to the Philippines would also have been reported. But if such mass protest was possible in the capitalist West and the 'Third World', why not also in socialist states?

Increased travel, and person-to-person contacts across the East-West divide, had a disruptive effect too. Travel restrictions for Poles were eased in the 1970s, and in the boom years of the early part of the decade large numbers of them availed themselves of the opportunity to take holidays in the West. In the GDR the restrictions on foreign travel were severe, but in the 1980s East Germans annually received around 40,000 visits from relatives in the West,[21] and pensioners were able to visit their relatives in the Federal Republic. Even in the hard-line states, such as Husak's Czechoslovakia, where foreign travel was a luxury reserved for the few, tourists from outside entering these countries helped to disseminate information

---

[20]Neal Ascherson, *The Polish August*, pp.136-137.
[21]*From Below, op cit.*, note 4, p.28.

and ideas. Moreover among the privileged few able to travel abroad were scholars and academics who might be influenced by what they saw and heard to influence others on their return.

In short, in a world made smaller by both communications and travel, populations living in the heartland of modern Europe could not be kept unaware of conditions elsewhere or isolated from wider intellectual currents. Stalin had attempted to achieve this in Eastern Europe in the post-war period, though even then with only limited success; in the age of the transistor radio, of video cameras and machines, of satellite broadcasting, of computers and of jet travel, it simply was not an option.

The crucial question of how, given the favourable atmosphere of popular discontent coupled with expectancy, the opposition went about the business of mobilising mass support requires detailed investigation in the various countries concerned. Clearly leaflets and posters were widely used to spread information about planned meetings and demonstrations. Presumably these were often produced on existing *samizdat* presses; however, some of the pictures on Western television indicate that the Czechoslovak students in particular were able to obtain access to up-to-date technology within the universities. The fact that tightly-knit institutions such as churches and universities frequently provided the base for organising would have facilitated communication among key activists. In Leipzig, New Forum adopted the strategy of holding regular demonstrations at the same time every Monday evening so that soon people knew when and how they could make their protest.

Considerable effort was devoted to ensuring that state controlled television gave adequate coverage to the demonstrations and to the demands of the protesters. The concern here, of course, was not simply to provide information but to force the Party/State to acknowledge the degree to which its authority was being challenged. In East Berlin, and much of East Germany, viewers could tune in to West German television and this itself presumably made it more difficult for the official media in the East to ignore altogether what was going on. In Czechoslovakia adequate television coverage of the demonstrations was a key demand of the opposition.

The process by which this demand was eventually met in Czechoslovakia is instructive. First the student protesters themselves took the initiative of making an amateur video of the 30,000 strong demonstration on 17 November where there were brutal attacks by the police. They arranged to have this shown on televisions in shopfront windows in Prague where large crowds soon gathered to watch. On 23 November, as street protests mounted, television staff passed a motion expressing dissatisfaction with the way the demonstrations were being portrayed, and demanding live coverage from Wenceslas Square and the broadcasting of the students' video. Voting was 4,900 in favour of the motion to 300 against.[22] In Romania too, the switch of loyalty by the television station was hardly less important than the decision of the army to side with the protesters.

International Influences on the 1989 Events

International factors can be no less significant than internal ones in setting the stage for a successful non-violent struggle. In the case of 1989 events, developments in East-West relations, as well as Soviet-East European relations, had a crucial impact.

The 'Gorbachev Factor'

Gorbachev's initiatives re-defined both sets of relations. By late 1987, when the INF Treaty was signed in Washington, he had largely mended his fences with the West. At the same time his reforms were providing a fillip to the radical opposition and reform communists alike in Eastern Europe. Thus when Gorbachev visited East Germany and Czechoslovakia in the spring of 1987 he was seen by the disaffected populations as an ally in the struggle against the tyranny of the local regimes, and greeted in the streets as a popular hero.

This effect may not have been intended. The evidence suggests

---

[22]*Observer*, 10 December 1989, p.11, based on a diary of events by 18 reporters from *Mlady Svet* (*Young World*).

that initially Gorbachev wanted a quiet life in Eastern Europe so that he could pursue his reforms at home without too many distractions; to this end he was prepared to live with the old authoritarian regimes. However, when it became clear that their continued presence was a source of instability, he was prepared to ditch them.

At first many of the radicals and reformers in Eastern Europe remained cautious, sceptical even. Khruschev too in the mid-fifties had been an advocate of reform and a critic of previous Soviet relations with Eastern Europe. But when reform in Hungary had brought it to the verge of multi-party democracy in 1956, and threatened its defection from the Warsaw Pact, Khruschev had sent in the tanks.

In 1987 – and even as late as 1989 – Gorbachev was still insisting on the need for a one-party system, at least within the Soviet Union. Moreover some of his early statements after taking office suggested that he was not yet willing to renounce categorically the Brezhnev Doctrine – the doctrine of 'socialist internationalism' invoked post-hoc by the Soviet leadership to justify its invasion of Czechoslovakia in 1968. Thus for a time it was an open question whether Gorbachev was sufficiently committed to the path of reform to risk the withering away of the Eastern alliance. It was an open question too whether his own hard-line critics within the Party would allow him to take such a risk.

Developments in Hungary and Poland in 1989 signalled his willingness and ability to recast Soviet East European relations and to rethink Soviet security needs. Visiting Warsaw in October, the Soviet Foreign Minister, Eduard Shevardnadze, quipped that the Brezhnev Doctrine had been ditched in favour of the 'Sinatra Doctrine': henceforth the countries of Eastern Europe were free to 'do it their way'.

The various elements of Gorbachev's programme were interdependent. He needed improved relations with the West to secure agreed cut-backs in the colossal military budget and to benefit from economic co-operation. But successful economic reform was inseparable from at least a measure of political reform. The latter quickly took on a momentum of its own within the Soviet Union itself and still more dramatically in Eastern Europe.

When the regimes came under direct threat from mass civil resistance, Gorbachev's nerve might have failed. Had it done so, and had he sent in Soviet troops like Khruschev and Brezhnev before him, the Cold War would have returned with a vengeance and the whole reform programme could have unravelled. The great merit of Gorbachev is that he has been prepared to follow the logic of his own policies, even where they led in unforseen directions. The crucial question today is whether he will show the same nerve and flexibility in dealing with the thorny problems of the non-Russian republics within the Soviet Union.

Once the revolts got under way in Eastern Europe, the Soviet Union used its influence to secure peaceful change. First hard-line leaders like Erich Honecker in the GDR were warned that they could not simply ignore the demands being made by the majority of the population. Secondly, a 'Tiananmen Square' solution was ruled out. There were press reports of Soviet warnings to leaders in the GDR and Czechoslovakia against attempting to use force. And although these cannot be confirmed, it is clear that the last thing Gorbachev wanted was a massacre of civilian demonstrators in Eastern Europe at a time when he was trying to build up Western confidence in the new Soviet policies. Moreover the close integration of Warsaw Pact forces meant that the Soviet Union could in effect exercise a ban on the use of the army against the population. Part of the tragedy in Romania, indeed, was that there was no outside power capable of restraining Ceausescu and the Securitate forces under his command.

Although it is important to acknowledge the impact of the Gorbachev factor in the transition to democracy in Eastern Europe, and to pay tribute to Gorbachev's own outstanding personal contribution to the process, it is also necessary to understand the pressures that brought him to power in the first place, and the dynamic that took over once he had embarked on the process of reform. Gorbachev has been the great facilitator in the shift towards democracy in Eastern Europe, but his rise to power, and his reform programme and policy initiatives were themselves the – highly creative – Soviet response to a political and economic malaise affecting the whole bloc, and to the recurrent crises caused by mass popular resistance.

Integration: the CSCE Process

The West exerted an influence on developments in the Soviet bloc in both a positive and negative sense. The CSCE process was the chief positive instrument, sanctions its negative corollary.

The Final Acts of the Helsinki Conference on Security and Co-operation in Europe (CSCE) were approved by the thirty-five participating nations in 1975. All European states of East and West (except Albania)[23] are members of the conference, plus the United States and Canada; they have also subsequently participated in a series of follow-up conferences. The Accords themselves set out the essential pre-requisites of future co-operation, and pledge the states concerned to respect each other's independence and territorial integrity. More importantly in the context of the present discussion, they commit the participants to respect the human rights and civil liberties of their own subjects. In this sense they represent a shift away from the absolute sovereignty claimed by nation states in the past.

The CSCE process provided the West with an important means of exerting pressure on Soviet bloc governments over human rights issues. There was of course a considerable degree of hypocrisy in the approach of some Western governments, including notably the United States, for when it suited their global strategy they were quite willing to support repressive regimes in other parts of the world, and even to undermine democratically elected governments. At worst, meetings could generate into Cold War slanging matches, with accusations and counter-accusations of human rights violations blocking fruitful discussion.

Nevertheless the CSCE process exerted a useful pressure down the years especially as the Soviet Union wanted to keep it alive for economic reasons and as a means of promoting arms control. The Helsinki Accords also provided the independent human rights and peace organisations with a legal instrument for pursuing their goals. Charter 77 in Czechoslovakia is the most obvious example of a body which deliberately set out to use the Helsinki Accords

---

[23]Albania subsequently announced its intention to join the Helsinki conferece.

to press the Czechoslovak government to honour its international commitments.

International Sanctions

The interdependence of national economies makes concerted international sanctions a potentially powerful coercive instrument – though one that can be used for illegitimate as well as legitimate goals. The problem, even when the ends are laudable, is how to secure agreement to apply sanctions and to enforce them effectively.

The US attempts to persuade Western governments to take concerted action against the Soviet Union after the invasion of Afghanistan met with little success. Its own grain embargo was immensely unpopular at home and its effects were largely nullified by increased Argentinian sales to the Soviet Union; in April 1981 President Reagan ended the embargo. The response to the proposed boycott of the 1980 Moscow Olympics was equally patchy, and US efforts to block the sending of equipment for the Siberian gas pipeline, and other projects in the field of oil and gas exploitation, were resisted in Western Europe.

After the imposition of martial law in Poland, the US again took the lead in initiating sanctions both against Poland and the Soviet Union. These included shelving negotiations with the Soviet Union on a new long term grain contract, suspending Aeroflot landing-rights in the US, and tightening restrictions on high technology exports. Poland itself was the target of a number of measures: its landing-rights in the US were suspended, and it lost fishing rights in US waters, and food aid. Other measures included a freeze on new credits on Export-Import Bank credit insurance, and the suspension of debt rescheduling negotiations and of Poland's most favoured nation status. Its membership of the International Monetary Fund was opposed.

Again the response to proposed sanctions in Europe was lukewarm. The European Community agreed to reduce imports of a few luxury Soviet goods – caviar, watches and furs – but this accounted for less than 2 per cent of Soviet trade with the EC. In general the EC refused to go further than promising not to undermine US sanctions. There was also a new and fierce controversy within the Western camp in 1982 when the US banned the export to the Soviet Union by American firms of oil- and gas-related equipment without US permission.

Despite these difficulties, the US measures against Poland seem to have had some influence on General Jaruzelski's domestic policies. He suspended martial law at the end of 1982 and granted a general amnesty for prisoners in July 1984. It was clear moreover from his own statements that these steps were aimed in part at persuading the US to ease its restrictions, and in fact the US did so in stages, including ending its opposition to Polish membership of the IMF in 1984.[24]

At a more general level the long-standing restrictions on high technology exports to the Soviet Union and Eastern Europe have probably acted as an incentive to reform. The Soviet Union needs Western technology and know-how for the success of its economic reforms, and it is now pressing for these restrictions to be lifted.

The use of sanctions raises complex problems which cannot be considered in detail here. Morally their use is justified only under extreme circumstances. Nevertheless we should note the contribution of Western and international pressure to the ending of the state of emergency in Poland, and in general acting as a restraint against heavy-handed repression and an incentive to liberalisation. Prior international agreement to apply immediately a range of forceful sanctions could act as a powerful disincentive to aggression and complement preparations within individual countries for civil resistance.

Following Saddam Hussein's aggression against Kuwait in August 1990, the UN imposed tight economic sanctions, coupled with a naval blockade, against Iraq. The imposition of these sanctions, and the subsequent war, occurred too late to be analysed in detail in this essay. Clearly, however, if sanctions had succeeded in ending Iraq's occupation of Kuwait without war, it would have created a dramatic and very hopeful precedent. The fact that the US and Soviet Union were able to act in concert, particularly in the early months of the crisis, also appeared to augur well for the future of the UN as a peacekeeping body. The argument as to whether or not sanctions

---

[24]See Margaret P. Doxey, *International Sanctions in Contemporary Perspective*, Macmillan Press 1987, especially pp.74-83.

could have been sufficient will continue to be debated. They were having a major impact on the Iraqi economy, but they needed more time to be fully effective. Instead of giving sanctions that extra time, however, the decision was taken to wage war on Iraq and drive its forces out of Kuwait by force of arms.

Transnational Action at Non-Government Level

Transnational co-operation and action at non-governmental level was at least as important as the pressure exerted internationally by governments. At the non-governmental level we can distinguish between powerful institutions operating across national boundaries, notably the Catholic Church, and grassroots movements.

The Churches

We have noted how churches within Eastern Europe acted as both refuges and rallying points for the democratic opposition. At a transnational level too, the churches were able to engage in dialogue with their counterparts in Eastern Europe and often with official and semi-official bodies. The strength of religious belief in Eastern Europe was such that governments seeking to broaden the base of their support could not afford to ignore the churches. Thus, from outside, the latter were able to exert pressure to have illiberal legislation removed, to secure the release of individuals, and generally to press for the observance of human rights.

The Catholic Church was in a particularly powerful position in traditionally catholic countries like Poland and Hungary. The impact in Poland of the election of Archbishop Carol Wojtyla as Pope in 1978, and his visit there the following year, have been noted earlier: these two events helped to prepare the ground for the nationwide rebellion that led to the birth of Solidarity in 1980.

The Churches also provided an outlet for communication to the wider world. Church-based organisations campaigned for religious toleration in the Soviet bloc and drew attention to particular injustices. Some indeed went further and engaged in smuggling religious and other literature to the East.

People-to-people co-operation

Political organisations, human rights bodies, and peace movements were all involved in people-to-people co-operation at a transnational level. East-West co-operation was one aspect of this phenomenon; East-East collaboration was probably even more crucial.

Long established human rights organisations, most notably Amnesty International, kept up a steady pressure on Soviet and East European governments. So too did some of the Socialist and Trotskyist groups in the West. In Britain during the 1970s and 1980s, the journal *Labour Force On Eastern Europe* provided information and analysis not readily available elsewhere.

From the early 1970s the London based Palach Press also performed an invaluable function in smuggling materials and equipment into opposition groups in Czechoslovakia and informing the Western media about developments inside the country.[25] Palach Press was also closely involved in the establishment in the 1980s of the East European Cultural Foundation to disseminate information from within Poland, Hungary and Czechoslovakia. In the Spring of 1985 the Foundation began publishing a regular new journal, the *East European Reporter*, which provides extensive coverage of human rights and peace activities in these and other East European countries.

Conservative or right-wing organisations and associated trusts have also been active. Some of the emigre groups operating in Western Europe, such as the Russian emigre organisation NTS, were on the right or extreme right of European politics, and although it is improbable that conservative groups in general had a major influence on developments inside the Soviet bloc prior to

---

[25] See interviews with Jan Kavan and Jirina Siklova in the present volume.

the 1989 revolutions, there is evidence that some are now operating as channels to transfer large sums to centrist and right wing political parties in the East.

In terms of the East-West dimension, co-operation between the sections of the Western movements and independent groups in Eastern Europe was probably the most important. The mass demonstrations in Western Europe at the beginning of the 1980s against Pershing II and Cruise deployments were widely publicised in Eastern Europe and ironically helped to stimulate the growth of independent peace movements there. They almost certainly also influenced the forms that non-violent protest took in Eastern Europe and the Soviet Baltic republics in the late 1980s – for instance forming human chains to enclose a site of symbolic significance or to link one location with another.

An important dialogue developed between leading intellectuals in the Western peace movement and people engaged in human rights and peace activities in Eastern Europe. Its origins were a series of exchanges between several independent thinkers in Czechoslovakia and Edward Thompson, a leading figure in the European Nuclear Disarmament campaign. These, and other statements from Czechoslovakia, were jointly published by END and Palach Press in 1983 under the title *Voices from Prague*.[26]

The annual END conventions which took place in various European cities from 1982 onwards were regularly attended by representatives of independent groups from Soviet-bloc countries, thus strengthening both East-West and East-East co-operation. At first most of the participants from the Soviet bloc were exiles living in the West but, in later years especially, some individuals still resident in Eastern Europe were able to attend. Moreover, letters and statements were regularly sent to the conventions from Eastern European individuals and groups. Notable amongst these was the *Prague Appeal*[27] of 1983, and Vaclav Havel's essay *The Anatomy of a Reticence*[28] addressed to the Amsterdam

---

[26] Jan Kavan and Zdena Tomin (eds), *Voices from Prague*, Palach Press/END, 1983.

[27] See 'Charter 77: The Prague Appeal', *East European Reporter*, Vol 1, No 1, Spring 1985, pp.27-28.

[28] The full text of Havel's statement was published in 1985 by the Swedish Charter 77 Foundation, Box 50041, S-10405 Stockholm.

END convention in 1985. At the Convention in Perugia the previous year a 'European Network for East-West Dialogue' was established which met regularly to work out a common position.

Perhaps the most significant contribution of the Network was a memorandum entitled *Giving Real Life to the Helsinki Accords*.[29] This was signed by several hundred individuals in East and West, including many Western peace activists, and presented at a meeting in Vienna in 1986 on the occasion of the resumed Conference on Security and Co-operation in Europe (CSCE). Like the earlier 'Prague Appeal' it gave equal weight to human rights and security, stressing the importance of detente from below, and the responsibility of people as well as governments for the future of the continent.

There was, however, a division within the Western peace movements over how much emphasis should be given to the issue of human rights in the Soviet bloc, and indeed how far co-operation with independent movements in the East should extend. Some felt the issue of human rights was at best marginal, at worst a serious distraction, hampering co-operation with governments and official Peace Committees in the East. The alternative view was that issues of peace and human rights could not be separated.

Grassroots co-operation between groups in different Warsaw Pact countries

Co-operation between independent groups in various East European countries developed from the late 1970s onwards, and was facilitated in fact by the END conventions during the 1980s. In 1978 the first of a series of meetings took place between KOR-KSS and Charter 77 on the Polish-Czechoslovak border. Increasingly too, independent groups from different Warsaw Pact countries developed

---

[29]The full text appears in *From Below*, Helsinki Watch Report, October 1987, pp.239-258.

joint campaigns and organised solidarity protests when individuals and groups in other states faced harassment and persecution.[30]

In May 1987, the Peace and Freedom group in Poland (WiP), created a precedent in Eastern Europe by successfully organising an international seminar in Warsaw, attended by peace and human rights groups from both East and West. Over 200 people attended, including 100 WiP activists, and participants from seventeen other countries. (Representatives from the independent Soviet peace group, the Group for the Establishment of Trust between East and West, were refused visas by their own government to attend). Although the organisers encountered harassment beforehand, and a number of Westerners were refused visas, the authorities did not attempt to disrupt the seminar once it had begun.[31] The following November, when a substantial contingent of Western peace activists came to Warsaw to attend a conference organised by the official Polish Peace Committee, they were able to meet and talk freely to WiP members.

International seminars were also held by independent groups in 1987 in Moscow and Budapest, the former organised by the Trust Group in May, just after the Warsaw seminar. In June 1988 Charter 77 and a new independent Czechoslovak group, the Independent Peace Association-Initiative for the Demilitarisation of Society attempted to hold a further international seminar in Prague. Almost forty people from seventeen countries of East and West attended, but the police made a succession of raids on the flats where workshops were taking place, and finally arrested and deported many of the participants. Despite this harassment, discussions did take place,

---

[30]For a report on the first joint meeting between Charter 77 and KSS-KOR, see *Labour Focus on Eastern Europe*, Vol 2, No 4, September-October 1978, p.7. For later developments in this East-East dialogue see for instance the Special Feature 'In Solidarity: Drawing Back the Iron Curtain between East and East', *East European Reporter*, Vol 3, No 1, November 1987, pp.23-26; and 'Torn Curtains: East-East Co-operation Flourishes', *East European Reporter*, Vol 3, No 2, March 1988; the issue is mainly devoted to this theme and includes an interview with Vaclav Havel entitled 'Why East and East must Meet'.

[31]For reports see Howard Clark, 'Warsaw – a dream come true', *War Resisters International Newsletter*, July-August 1987, p.7; also *East European Reporter*, Vol 2, No 3, 1987, pp. 56-59; and Richard Bloom, 'Provoking Peace in Poland', *END Journal*, Issue 28/29, Summer 1987, p.5.

usually in small groups, and a final report called for the setting up of a European Peace Parliament of non-governmental organisations.[32] The 'Helsinki Citizens Assembly' which took place in Prague in November 1990 represents the fruition of this idea and is discussed again in the next chapter. The potential long-term significance of the pan-European and North American grassroots dialogue and (partial) consensus is also evident from the fact that among the signatories of the memorandum were Vaclav Havel, now President of Czechoslovakia, and Jiri Dienstbier, its Foreign Minister.

The Role of Non-Violence

How was it that the overthrow of authoritarian power in Eastern Europe was achieved with little or no violence on the part of the population?

The non-violent discipline was maintained by the protestors for a mixture of pragmatic, ethical and humanitarian motives. In Poland in 1980, Solidarity accepted the argument of Jacek Kuron and KSS-KOR that the effect of resorting to violence would be to increase greatly the number of casualties without bringing the union any nearer to its goal. Widespread violence, moreover, was likely to provoke Soviet military intervention.[33] Thus the leadership chose the technique of occupying the workplace rather than engaging in mass street demonstrations, in part because the experience of earlier protests was that these would end in violent confrontation with the authorities. And although in 1989 mass street protests were the chief weapon of the civil resisters throughout Eastern Europe, there was general agreement on the need to avoid violence.

The pragmatic argument that violence would be counter-productive, possibly disastrous, presupposes the existence of an alternative

---

[32]See *East European Reporter*, Vol 3, No 3, Autumn 1988, pp.17-20.

[33]See Jan Zielonka, *Strengths and Weaknesses of Non-violent Action: the Polish Case*, Orbis, Spring 1986, especially the section headed 'Why Non-violence', pp.92-95

approach that could be more efficacious. It seems unlikely that the bulk of the population, or even of the leadership, adhered to a well-developed theory of civil resistance. Nevertheless the basic notion that state power rests on the compliance of the people is probably widely appreciated, if only at an instinctive level. Moreover the tradition of using strikes, pickets, demonstrations and hunger strikes for economic – and occasionally for political – goals is well established in every country that has undergone a degree of industrialisation. The 1980s also produced some dramatic examples of 'people power' in other parts of the world, and this no doubt helped to popularise the concept.

There is also evidence from Poland in 1980-81 of a conscious effort to disseminate ideas about non-violent resistance. Thus, the writings of some leading Western proponents of the concept and strategy were translated into Polish and published in *samizdat* form.[34] There is also evidence that the film *Gandhi* influenced the thinking of Czechoslovak students in 1989: according to one participant in the events, after the police had attacked the demonstration on 17 November, the students decided to follow the method adopted by the Gandhian resisters during the raid on salt compounds in 1930, when wave after wave of protesters went forward until beaten into unconsciousness by the police. Fortunately in Prague didn't come to that.

Many of those active in the protest movement, though not absolute pacifists, were influenced by ethical and humanitarian beliefs. Christian teaching played a part here, particularly in Poland and East Germany where the influence of Catholic and Evangelical Churches respectively was strong. A striking example of the conscientious efforts made to keep the demonstrations non-violent is the set of instructions included in the Church service in Nikolaikirche in Leipzig on 25 September 1989:

> To maintain self control and help others to do the same
> To seek dialogue – with neighbours and individuals
> To remain polite and correct
> No bad language

---

[34] The authors were Jean Marie Muller and Gene Sharp from France and the United States respectively. See Jan Zielonka, *op cit.*, p.93, footnote 7.

No whistling
Singing helps to overcome one's own anxiety and indicates non-violent intentions to the opposition
When arrest seems imminent, sit down and link arms
If arrested, call out your name to those remaining behind
When in a paddy wagon, call out the number of prisoners with you
During and after interrogation, do not sign anything
Do not give any information beyond that which is on your identity cards.[35]

In November 1989 as the number of demonstrators in East Germany swelled to hundreds of thousands, church-based activists in some instances formed human cordons to protect the lives of members of the Stasi, the secret police. And throughout Eastern Europe, for a variety of reasons, there was clearly a desire to avoid the tragedy of bloodshed and civil war.

There were, of course, resisters for whom the ideals of non-violence were central. As noted earlier, independent peace groups, some of them avowedly pacifist, played an important part in mobilising opposition to the regimes, or to particular aspects of their foreign and military policies. It is significant too that the cause of conscientious objection was taken up by almost all the human rights and peace organisations throughout the region. Thus on 18 March 1988, an appeal calling for the recognition of the right of conscientious objection was presented to the CSCE conference in Vienna signed by people active in virtually all the main peace and human rights groups in the Soviet Union and Eastern Europe.[36]

Whatever the motivation behind the adoption of a non-violent approach, its strategic significance was that it increased Gorbachev's room for manoeuvre. If it is true that the non-violent revolts of 1989 could not have succeeded without the changes in Soviet policy under Gorbachev, it is equally true that the Soviet Union could scarcely have retreated in good grace from the Soviet empire in Eastern Europe had it not been for the remarkable non-violent discipline of the protesters.

---

[35] Informant, Hans Sinn in a letter to Michael Randle dated 24 October 1989.

[36] The text of the appeal, and the list of signatures, was published in *East European Reporter*, Vol 3, No 2, March 1988, pp.68-71.

Conclusion

Revolutionary change in Eastern Europe was achieved in 1989 by determined but peaceful civil resistance. The economic and environmental crisis, the frustration of rising expectations, and the opportunity afforded by international developments, particularly including Gorbachev's reforms and initiatives, encouraged the populations to withdraw their co-operation and participate in mass demonstrations.

The insurrections succeeded where others before them had failed for several reasons. First, Moscow was setting the pace in economic and political reform. Second, Gorbachev ditched the Brezhnev Doctrine thus removing a vital prop from the unpopular regimes in Eastern Europe. Third, the non-violent nature of the revolutions prevented them from setting off a series of international crises and possibly from pushing Gorbachev, against his better judgement, into ordering military intervention.

Without the crisis in the Soviet system, and the pressure from below in Eastern Europe, the Soviet Union might never have embarked on the Gorbachev reforms. Equally, without Gorbachev the revolutions might never have been attempted or might have ended, as had previous revolts in Eastern Europe, in intervention and bloodshed.

Chapter 3

People Power and the Future of Europe

Introduction

People power is now a recognised force in modern history. It played a crucial role in dismantling the old order in Europe and it is hard to believe that it will not now play an equally central role in constructing and preserving the new. The purpose of this chapter is to sketch some of its possibilities.

We argue that people power – and civil society on which it must essentially rest – has a role in preserving and strengthening democratic control and respect for human and social rights in a Europe in transition. In the longer term, it can contribute, in the form of social defence, to the security needs of a new Europe.

The Evolution of a new Europe

The democratic revolutions in Eastern Europe and the Soviet Union are still in progress. They face many pitfalls and could be halted or reversed in a variety of ways. But an active citizenry aware of the potential of civil resistance and ready and willing to engage in it if circumstances so demand, could play a crucial role in shaping the new politics. We consider below some of the circumstances which could require the exercise of people power as Europe rebuilds.

Resisting the return of Dictatorship

There is first the possibility, at least in one or two countries, of a return to autocratic or totalitarian government in Eastern Europe. Given the reaction against forty or so years of communist rule, and latent anti-semitism, a new authoritarian government is more likely to be of the right than of the left. But even the latter could not be ruled out if there was a prolonged period of economic decline, mass unemployment and political instability. Such a situation could create a romantic nostalgia for the old order.

A coup backed by conservative elements in the army is one possible scenario. Another is a creeping dictatorship as government takes upon itself more extensive and arbitrary powers. Gorbachev's stampeding of the Soviet parliament in March 1990 into creating a presidency with sweeping executive power could set an ominous example in this respect.

The dangers of a coup or a slide into dictatorship are not equally great in all East-Central and East European countries, and it is important not to overstate the danger. In Czechoslovakia, because of its pre-war democratic tradition, the work during the 1970s and 1980s of Charter 77 and Civic Forum, and the maturity and popularity of its political leadership, the danger may be largely discounted. In the newly united Germany, political domination by the right or centre right within a continuing parliamentary system is a more likely prospect than a return to dictatorship of any colour. In Poland and Hungary too, we can take it that any attempt to reimpose one-party or arbitrary rule would be vigorously resisted by a large section of the population, mobilised by the various groups and organisations that now constitute a thriving civil society

But elsewhere the situation appears to be more volatile – in Yugoslavia, beset by nationalist and ethnic divisions; in Bulgaria; above all in Romania, where the old structures and ways of operating have never been entirely jettisoned; and in the Soviet Union itself.

The developments in post-revolutionary Romania raise pertinent issues.[1] In the presidential elections held on 20 May 1990, the acting

---

[1] See the interview with Helmut Frauendorfer in the present volume.

president and Salvation Front (NSF) candidate, Ion Iliescu, won an overwhelming 85.07 per cent of the vote; the NSF won 66.31 per cent of the votes in the elections to the National Assembly, and 67.02 per cent in the elections to the Senate.[2] Despite this massive victory, the legitimacy of the NSF government is strongly contested, notably by some of those in the forefront of the popular uprising against Ceausescu in December 1989.

Firstly, the opponents of the government point out, when the Front formed itself into a political party on 23 January 1990 and announced its intention to contest the forthcoming election, it was reneging on its initial undertaking to play a purely caretaker role, overseeing the transition from dictatorship to democracy. Its decision was seen by many as an attempt by members of the former communist party – strongly represented in the Front – to maintain their hold on power and to preserve the old authoritarian structures. It provoked the largest demonstrations – and counter-demonstrations – since the demise of Ceausescu, and led to the formation on February 1 of the Council of National Unity, a kind of mini-provisional parliament. But again its composition was such as to give the Front and its supporters effective control.[3]

On February 18, 250 protesters broke away from a larger demonstration in the centre of Bucharest and invaded the NSF Headquarters until expelled by soldiers. The following day between 5,000 and 8,000 miners from the Jiu valley were brought in to support the NSF, and a decree was passed banning spontaneous demonstrations. Officials of the National Liberal Party and the National Peasant Party denied any responsibility for the February 18 demonstration and complained of a campaign of systematic terrorism against them.

Secondly, although the election itself was reasonably fairly conducted (despite some abuses), the opposition parties were strongly disadvantaged in the run-up to the election. In particular the State-run television service was used to promote the NSF cause. Demands by the opposition parties that the elections be postponed to

---

[2] *Keesings Contemporary Archives*, 'News Digest for May 1990', p.37442.

[3] Each political party had three representatives on the Council, but 90 seats out of a total of 180 were reserved for workers, peasants, scientists, intellectuals, artists, students and ethnic minorities 'active in the revolution', all of them presumed to be supporters of the NSF. See *Keesings*, February 1990, p.37251.

give them more time to organise, were also rejected by the Front.

Thirdly, the Front is accused of exploiting chauvinist and racist sentiment in the country to consolidate its hold on power. It is accused, in particular, of giving encouragement to the extreme right-wing Romanian nationalist movement *Vatra Romaneasca* (Romanian Cradle) which has been at the forefront of attacks on ethnic Hungarians, most notoriously in the town of Tirgu Mures in March when a peaceful march by 5,000 ethnic Hungarians was attacked by a mob with scythes, axes and clubs, resulting in three people being killed and 269 injured according to official statistics. Romanian peasants were bused into the town during the disturbances and supplied with weapons and refreshment, and there is evidence that the organisers of the violence were able to make use of the facilities of the local state.[4] Moreover, whatever the degree of complicity of the government in the disturbances, it made use of them to revive the security forces, staffing them with many former Securitate personnel.[5]

International concern at the direction of events in Romania, however, did not reach serious proportions until June 1990 when again vigilante miners, armed with clubs and other weapons, were called upon by the government, this time to end a fifty-five day student occupation of one of the main squares in Bucharest. Reports indicate that violence was used not only against the students but against anyone who appeared cosmopolitan or likely to be sympathetic to the opposition. By the time the occupation was ended, there were many more anti-Front protesters in detention than former members of the Ceausescu regime.

At the heart of the problems besetting post-revolutionary Romania is the weakness of civil society due to the long years of repression under Ceausescu and the isolation of the country from outside influences. Neither the opposition groups thrown up by the December revolution, nor the reconstituted historic parties, were strong enough, or united enough, to provide an effective challenge to the NSF at the presidential and parliamentary elections; even allowing

---

[4]See, Julius Strauss, 'Ethnic clashes in Tirgu Mures', *East European Reporter*, Vol 4, No 2, Spring/Summer 1990, p.42, and Tom Gallagher, 'Romania, the Disputed Election of 1990', in *Parliamentary Affairs*, Vol 44, No 1, January 1990.

[5]Tom Gallagher, *op cit*.

for the disadvantages under which they were operating, they put up a very poor showing indeed.[6] Indeed the main hope for the development of a balanced democracy lies with the network of civic organisations co-ordinated since last November in the Civic Alliance.

However, one question of general importance raised by events in post-Ceausescu Romania is whether continued civil resistance following the overthrow of an autocratic regime, and the holding of elections, could itself threaten democracy. The answer must surely be that in some circumstances it could – for instance if it was aimed not at righting particular injustices or abuses of power but at bringing public administration to a standstill and thereby securing the overthrow of a genuinely legitimate government.[7] This points to the need for discipline and self-restraint on the part of civil resistance movements, a recognition that strategies and tactics may have to change in a changed situation.

Clearly there is no way of guaranteeing in advance that such self-restraint will be observed. It is more likely to be so, however, if the civil resistance movement from its foundation has been committed to the democratic process and if there has been mature reflection and debate within its ranks about what such a commitment entails.

The observance of a non-violent discipline provides a strong – though perhaps not an absolute – guarantee that civil resistance will not bring about the destruction of democracy. The state, with its enormous coercive powers, is normally *physically* capable of clearing streets and public buildings of non-violent protesters, or indeed of riding out strikes and other forms of non-cooperation except where these enjoy really massive support.

A government which uses undue force, however, will pay a political price for its excesses. By the same token so will the protesters if their actions come to be widely regarded as unreasonable and a threat to the democratic system; their civil resistance will tend at that point

---

[6]In the elections to the National Assembly, the recently formed Hungarian Democratic Union of Romania polled 7.23 per cent of the votes, the National Liberal party, 6.41 per cent and the Christian Democrat/Peasant Party 2.56 per cent. Compare these figures with the 66.31 per cent of the vote obtained by the NSF.

[7]This issue clearly arises in relation to the mass demonstrations in Bulgaria in November 1990 which finally brought down the elected Bulgarian Socialist Party government.

to be counter-productive and may result in public acquiescence in the use of force to suppress them. Thus in a democratic setting, the struggle between a government and a protest movement engaging in civil resistance is essentially a moral and psychological struggle rather than a simple trial of physical strength. Generally speaking, a government which collapses in the face of a non-violent campaign is likely to be one that has already forfeited public confidence. The corollary, unfortunately, is far from true. Given the balance of forces in the modern state, deserving movements may not succeed over a prolonged period in face of public indifference and state repression.

In Romania, in so far as the students and their supporters were endeavouring to prevent abuses of the democratic process, or discrimination against minorities, their campaign of civil disobedience was justified – for even in a mature democracy, civil disobedience is sometimes right and necessary. Whether their action was politically effective is a separate question. In the judgement of some commentators, the occupation of University Square in Bucharest – which began well before the May elections – was politically counter-productive and may have swung floating voters and those fearful of destabilisation behind the Salvation Front.[8]

Whatever the rights and wrongs of this particular case, it is clear that democracy still has only a precarious foothold in Romania and perhaps in some other former communist countries, and that non-violent initiatives of various kinds, including civil resistance where appropriate, could play an important role in maintaining it. Historically, civil resistance has been used on occasions to resist coups. In 1920, a general strike in Berlin thwarted an attempted right wing military coup – or 'putsch' – led by Dr Wolfgang Kapp.[9] In 1961, strikes and demonstrations in France played an important role in defeating the plans for a coup by extremist French generals in Algeria.[10] Clearly too, if civil resistance can topple dictatorships

---

[8]Tom Gallagher, *op cit.*

[9]The Kapp Putsch is analysed in Gene Sharp, *The Politics of Non-Violent Action*, Porter Sargent, 1973.

[10]For an analysis of the role of civil resistance in defeating the Algerian Generals' revolt, see Adam Roberts, 'Civilian Resistance in Defence: the Defeat of the General's Revolt' in Vereinigung Deutscher Wissenschaftler (ed) *Civilian Defence*, Bielefeld: Bertelsmann Universitatsverlag Reinhard Mohn, 1969.

already in power, it can be used to prevent their seizing power in the first place, or to prevent existing governments from assuming a dictatorial role.

The enshrinement of democratic rights and civil liberties in the constitution and laws of the state can of course provide an important safeguard against arbitrary government. Indeed one of the tasks of alert citizens committed to the democratic process is to monitor the evolution of the constitution and laws, and if necessary to mobilise the population against dangerous tendencies. Another is to try to ensure that, during a period of transition, the government does not adopt dictatorial practices that make the evolution of democracy more difficult.

In the Soviet Union civil resistance was used on occasions to put pressure not on the authorities but on conservative opponents of democratic change. Thus the pro-democracy demonstration by 200,000 people in Moscow in early February 1990 strengthened Gorbachev's hand within the Central Committee of the Communist Party where he was pressing for the abandonment of the guaranteed leading role of the party and the move to multi-party democracy. We can anticipate that in Eastern Europe too, civil resistance may sometimes be necessary not to oppose a government but to support it.

Extending Self-management and Democratic Participation

Clearly a healthy democracy requires also the active participation of citizens in representative political structures, including the political parties, and the organisations that go to make up civil society. This can be seen as the other side of people power, the constructive political programme that contrasts with, yet complements, campaigns of non-violent resistance to remove abuses and tyrannical structures.

Occasionally leaders of civil resistance movements may find themselves having to decide whether or not to accept government posts in a new political situation – a choice faced in 1989 by people like Vaclav Haval in Czechoslovakia, and some of the dissident activists in Poland.

Even where a new government is broadly representative of the forces involved in the non-violent campaign that removed an

autocratic system, or a puppet regime, it is vital that grassroots movements should maintain their autonomy and their willingness if necessary to engage in new resistance campaigns. They can thereby act as an essential counterbalance to bureaucratic state power.

It is possible that out of the struggles in Eastern Europe will emerge something new in terms of grassroots participation in the running of civic affairs and the economy, an enrichment of the democratic process. The desire that it should do so is certainly present among many of those who were active in the independent movements; this is clear, for instance, from the Appeal of the Helsinki Citizens Assembly cited later in this chapter. The British writer and journalist Neal Ascherson argues that the 1989 revolutions have in fact introduced something new, and of historic significance, into the European political scene. As he puts it:

> I think that 1989 caused a European mutation, introducing a new gene. It is carried by all these Forums, even though they will probably wither away in the next year or so. It is about self-managing societies, about the decline of state authority, about a new kind of power-sharing deal between the wealthy and the producers of wealth, about the rise of nationalities and the fall of nation-states.[11]

Dealing with Ethnic/Nationalist Clashes

The end of Stalinism in the Soviet Union and Eastern Europe has led to a revival of nationalist sentiment with all its ambiguities: on the positive side, a desire by peoples to take charge of their own affairs; on the negative side the stirring up of ancient feuds and hatreds.

Today, disputes and clashes between ethnic groups represent a potentially major problem in the Soviet Union and much of Eastern Europe. In the Soviet Union there is the obvious example of Armenians and Azeris; in Romania, of the Hungarian minority; in Bulgaria, of the Turks; in Yugoslavia, of the Albanians in the

---

[11]Neal Ascherson, 'Birds of an East European feather rise above the earthbound West', *The Independent on Sunday*, 15 April 1990, p.19.

province of Kosovo. Ethnic tensions are not infrequently linked to actual or potential territorial disputes with neighbouring states, making them a still more serious threat to stability. Armenians demand the return of Ngorno Karabach, the enclave ceded to Azerbaijan by Stalin in the 1920s. Transylvania, which was part of Hungary until the end of World War I, could become a contested territory between Hungary and Romania, especially if the Hungarians living there are subjected to discrimination or further mob violence.

Civil resistance alone is not capable of solving these ethnic and territorial disputes – indeed in certain forms it may even exacerbate them, providing a prelude to armed conflict rather than an alternative to it. Yet there is a role here for disciplined non-violent action. In Bulgaria in January 1990, following anti-Turkish demonstrations, thousands took to the streets to assert the right of everyone living in the country to civil liberty. Anti-Hungarian riots and pogroms in Transylvania in March 1990 are an ugly reminder of how destructive the old prejudices and hatreds can be. Yet the revolution that overthrew Ceausescu began with the efforts of the Hungarian community in Timisoara to protect their pastor, Laszlo Tokes, from deportation by the authorities, and Hungarian and Romanian communities made common cause in the bitter struggle against the dictatorship.

Joint action by members of the minority and majority community can sometimes jolt the conscience of a population and halt runaway chauvinist passions. Another possible option is non-violent intervention by third parties. This approach has been used on occasions in some of the intercommunal clashes in India. And in Cyprus in the early 1960s a small international team, acting in close collaboration with the UN peacekeeping forces, played a modest but constructive role in preventing clashes between Greeks and Turks.

Finally, the possibility of border conflict or even full scale military intervention over a disputed territory is a danger which several of the states in Eastern Europe have to guard against. Clashes between neighbouring states are indeed much easier to imagine at this point than a full scale war between the Soviet Union and the West. The existence of border disputes is, in fact, a reminder that questions of defence and security cannot simply be taken for granted in the new Europe. We return to this issue later in the chapter.

Civil Resistance in the transformation of the Soviet Empire

The nationality problem is encountered in its most acute and challenging form in the Soviet Union. If the 1989 revolutions in Eastern Europe marked the first phase in the breakdown of the Soviet Empire, the demands for autonomy or independence by non-Russian republics marks the second. For many nationalist movements in the Soviet republics, Eastern Europe showed what was now possible. Understandably, however, the Soviet leadership is far more worried about the possible disintegration of the Union than it was about the loss of hegemony in Eastern Europe. Thus Gorbachev, whilst not ruling out autonomy or even secession by the various republics, has shown in Tblisi, Baku, Vilnius and Riga that he is prepared to take military action to prevent unilateral secession.

Since 3 April 1990, seccession has theoretically been an option for the Soviet Union's constituent republics. But the procedure laid down is long and complex. There must first be a two-thirds majority for secession in a national referendum within the republic concerned, followed by a five year transition period. In the final year of this transition period, there might be a further referendum. Finally the decision to secede would be subject to ratification by the USSR Congress of People's Deputies.

The Baltic states of Estonia, Latvia and Lithuania argue that theirs is a special case because their incorporation into the Soviet Union occurred as a result of the secret protocols in the 1939 Molotov-Rippentrop Pact, protocols which the USSR People's Congress itself recognised in December 1989 as illegal. Despite this, in March 1990 Soviet forces were sent into Lithuania only two weeks after the overwhelming electoral victory of pro-independence forces there, and the subsequent declaration of independence by the Lithuanian parliament.

Perhaps the Lithuanians acted too hastily. They might have been wiser to follow the more cautious approach of their neighbour Latvia rather than throwing down a direct challenge to Gorbachev's authority which it was very difficult for him to ignore. But they avoided any use of violence either in the campaign for independence or in their response to the dispatch of troops from Moscow. In fact one deputy from the Lithuanian parliament told the BBC *Today* programme on 28 March 1990 that the authorities now planned 'a campaign of non-violent resistance and civil disobedience'; in other words they plan to rely on social defence rather than armed resistance to defend their newly declared independence.

Despite the dispatch of troops to Lithuania, the Soviet action during 1990 in the Baltic States was relatively restrained – compared, for instance, to the crack-down in the capital of Azerbaijan, Baku, in January 1990. The latter had been preceded by large-scale ethnic violence between Azeris and Armenians, giving the Soviet authorities a rationale for taking drastic action. (In fact the firepower was used not to save Armenians, who by that time had fled the city, but to attack the nationalist movement).

In the Baltic republics, no such pretext for the use of force existed. Moreover Gorbachev could hardly deny the authority and legitimacy of a Parliament and government in Lithuania chosen in free elections of his devising. There were, therefore, grounds for hoping in 1990 that restraint and diplomacy would resolve the problem of the Baltic states. However, in January 1991 Soviet forces returned in strength to the republics and there were violent clashes between them and the local populations, notably in the Lithuanian capital of Vilnius.

The genie of nationalism in the Soviet republics cannot now be put back into the bottle, and the violent disintegration of the Soviet Union is a real possibility. This would represent a tragedy for the Soviet Union and for the world which has placed such high hopes on Gorbachev's leadership. Perhaps, however, the Baltic Republics will still be able, by a combination of non-violent action with political tact and flexibility, to regain their independence and at the same time point the way for a peaceful transition of the Soviet Union from 'empire' to 'commonwealth'. The particular strength of mass non-violent action is that, like war, it can be a coercive instrument, but that, unlike war, it keeps open the door for mutual restraint and compromise.

The integration of states within larger pan-European structures, such as an expanded European Community or European Parliament, could also help ease the nationalist problems in the Soviet Union and Eastern Europe. In fact, the political trend in the late twentieth century is for sovereignty at the state level to be constrained by economic interdependence and by formal obligations under international treaties. The 1975 Helsinki Accords for instance – the outcome of the Conference on Security and Co-operation in

Europe (CSCE) – commits the countries concerned to respect not only each other's rights as states but also the freedom and civil liberty of their own citizens. To this extent the CSCE countries have in principle accepted a limitation of their sovereignty: they can no longer claim that the way they treat their own citizens is an exclusively domestic issue. Similarly the EC imposes regulations that affect economic activity within member states.

The tendency towards accepting a more limited definition of national sovereignty, and the fact of increasing economic interdependence, could permit the flourishing of local and regional nationalisms. On the one hand nationalist movements may more readily accept a degree of political and cultural autonomy that stops short of complete independence. On the other, even separation need no longer be seen as such a threat by the major partner involved. The independence of the Soviet Baltic States, for example, would almost certainly not mean an end to close economic co-operation with the Soviet Union. Moreover, if European integration proceeds, both the Soviet Union and the Baltic States could be part of the proposed European alliance favoured by Gorbachev, and perhaps eventually part of a European parliament.

Resisting economic exploitation and the destruction of the Environment

The elections in Eastern Europe in 1990 indicate a swing to the centre-right throughout most of the region. No doubt this is in part an understandable reaction against the abuses of communist rule. Right-wing think tanks, like the British Adam Smith Institute, have also been promoting versions of unfettered capitalism that no Western European country at this point would be prepared to contemplate.

Whether or not such extreme theories are accepted by the new governments, the changeover from a centralised to a more market-oriented economy will be fraught with problems. As many commentators have pointed out, this is a move without historical precedent; there are no models on which to base it. Unemployment is becoming a major problem. And with the price of basic foodstuffs, accommodation and public transport all set to rise steeply, and probably that of many other commodities, large numbers of people could face serious hardship.

In this situation a form of 'people power' which we don't normally regard as such is essential for the defence of many ordinary people – independent trade union activity, and agitation by bodies representing vulnerable sections of the community. This is an area in which co-operation at grassroots level across national boundaries, including the sharing of experience and of organisational skills, could be especially valuable.

Agitation need not be confined to the attempt to maintain or improve living standards – it can extend to questions of ownership and control in the new economy. Because of the long period of communist rule, these question may be – for the time being at least – more open than in countries where private ownership is firmly established. Thus there could be pressure, to give priority to worker-controlled co-operatives, or to schemes of joint ownership by the municipality and the workers.

Environmental problems will not of course disappear with the arrival of a market-oriented economy in Eastern Europe, they could even worsen. True, if there is a shift away from the Stalinist emphasis on heavy industry, and if more modern and efficient technology is introduced, this would ease the pressure on the environment to some degree. However, this amelioration could be more than offset if the absolute level of energy consumption increases dramatically, if there are very many more cars on the roads, and if in general Eastern Europe seeks to emulate Western consumerist lifestyles in the shortest possible time.

Environmental groups played an important role in the resistance that brought communist government in Eastern Europe to an end. In co-operation with colleagues in the West and in other parts of the world, their role in the future could be no less important.

Action for the Demilitarisation of Europe

We discussed in the previous chapter the role of peace movements in East and West. Clearly the situation has changed over the last three or four years. The intermediate range nuclear missiles whose planned deployment sparked off the mass demonstrations in Western

Europe in the early 1980s are being removed on both sides under the terms of the 1987 INF Treaty. Soviet forces in Eastern Europe were reduced unilaterally in 1988-89 and are now being withdrawn from Czechoslovakia and Hungary; in due course they will be withdrawn from the rest of Eastern Europe. At the CSCE summit meeting in Paris in November 1990, a Treaty on conventional forces in Europe (CFE) was signed, in which it was agreed to cut dramatically the number of troops and weapons deployed. If agreement can be reached at the resumed START talks in 1991, the size of US and Soviet strategic nuclear forces will also be significantly reduced.

In this situation, the danger is that the peace movements may feel that the initiative now lies with governments in general and with the two superpowers in particular. In fact, however, without pressure from below, a unique opportunity to restructure European security, and, in Gorbachev's phrase, 'to build a common European Home', could be lost. Thus even if the time of mass demonstrations is past for the time being, informed criticism and public action will be necessary if Europe is to be demilitarised and nuclear weapons finally removed from the continent.

In the concluding part of this essay we consider briefly these wider political and security issues, including the role of people power in a restructured security system.

People Power and European Security

The Alliance Context

The end of the Cold War has undermined the rationale for the system of rival military alliances. On the Eastern side, the Warsaw Pact had ceased by the beginning of 1990 to be a coherent military force, much less a threat to the security of Western Europe. On 25 February 1991, the Foreign and Defence Ministers of the six states concerned met in Budapest formally to disband the Pact as a military organisation. On the Western side, NATO remains in being and indeed has been enlarged, if not exactly strengthened, by the inclusion (with restrictions) of the newly united Germany in the alliance. But its fundamental purpose is no longer clear.

The dissolution of the Warsaw Pact poses security problems for its former member states. There have been suggestions that some of them might join NATO. But the NATO states themselves have shown no enthusiasm for this and it could hardly be welcome to the Soviet Union – unless, of course, NATO itself became a pan-European security system in which the Soviet Union itself was included. The hope that the CSCE would provide an alternative European security system may perhaps be realised in the long term but there is little prospect that it can do so in the near future. The determination of the NATO members to maintain their alliance represents the main obstacle to such a development. Thus a Czechoslovak proposal that the CSCE should have its own Security Council was not taken up and for the time being at least is not on the agenda. In August 1990, the Hungarian Prime Minister caused consternation when he floated the idea that Hungary, Czechoslovakia and Poland might form a military alliance, and the idea was quickly dropped.[12]

The West European states also face a dilemma. On the one hand they are unwilling to merge Western security structures – NATO and the Western European Union – into a pan-European security system; on the other hand some are now expressing anxiety at the prospect of a large neutral and perhaps demilitarised zone between NATO and the Soviet Union.[13]

Nevertheless, by force of circumstances, the former Warsaw Pact countries are for the time being likely to remain non-aligned if not formally neutral. Heavily armed neutrality along Swedish lines is one possible option. This, however, has serious drawbacks. It is expensive and thus represents a tragic dissipation of resources for states struggling to rebuild their shattered economies. More importantly, in a region fraught with historic tensions and disputes, it could prove dangerously destabilising. There are indeed few developments more likely to destroy the fragile peace of the new era than an uncontrolled arms race in the centre of Europe. An alternative option therefore for these countries is a combination of low-level military defence

---

[12]See Isobel Hilton, 'Warsaw Pact digs in its toes over forced cuts', *Independent*, 11 October 1990, p.13.
[13]*Ibid.*

with the kind of social defence discussed in this essay. Perhaps the recent experience of these countries of the power of civil resistance in overthrowing long-established and heavily-armed dictatorships will lead to public interest in this possibility.

If in due course a pan-European alliance takes shape, its role would be to provide reassurance and collective security for all the member states. Unlike NATO and the Warsaw Pact it would not be directed against a supposed external enemy but at ensuring that inter-state relations within the area are conducted according to agreed principles. Thus there would not be the same drive towards escalation in military expenditure and deployments that existed previously. The alliance could even become a vehicle for facilitating and monitoring the demilitarisation in Europe and providing security at ever lower levels of armament. It could also provide a more congenial framework than the previous system of rival alliances for the development of social defence and other non-military approaches to security.

Social Defence

The threat of a major war in Europe has diminished, but if it were to occur it would be an unmitigated disaster. There would be a strong likelihood of nuclear escalation, but even without that, the devastation would be immense. This is a prime motive for establishing non-violent procedures for resolving disputes and non-violent ways of engaging in conflict where it cannot be avoided. As we pointed out in the last chapter, one reason why the protesters in Eastern Europe avoided violence and armed insurrection was that they realised this would bring disaster rather than success. A major international war would be even more catastrophic for all the peoples of Europe; non-violent alternatives to the use of military force therefore cry out for serious consideration.

Social defence can be simply defined as people power – civil resistance – employed for the defence of a country and its institutions.[14] Like military defence it aims to deter attack as well as to

---

[14] See the definitions of civil resistance and social defence on pages 4-5 above.

provide a means of resistance should an attack occur. But whereas in the event of conflict the latter concentrates on destroying the opponent's military machine, social defence seeks firstly to deprive him of the political and economic objectives of the attack, secondly to undermine his power base at home and within the armed forces.

In the decades since the end of World War II, there have been a number of studies of the possibilities of social defence, some sponsored by governments. In Britain in 1958, the political commentator Commander Sir Stephen King-Hall called for a Royal Commission on the subject, though his call went unanswered. The British Defence White Paper in 1982 in a discussion of alternatives to the government's nuclear strategy, devoted several paragraphs to social defence, though only to conclude that it failed the crucial test of providing a deterrent against attack. However, governments in Sweden, Holland and France have funded studies of the topic, and a government commission in Sweden in 1984 concluded that social defence could complement the country's military security preparations.[15]

The East European revolutions of 1989 have given the debate a new topicality. First, they provide a demonstration of the potential of civil resistance in a European setting, and cannot be dismissed – as for instance Gandhi's resistance in India, or the 'people power' movement in the Philippines tend to be – as something alien to European culture or the Western psyche. Second, they have changed the political and strategic balance in Europe. This fact, and the dramatic changes in Soviet domestic and foreign policy under Gorbachev, have revived the whole European security debate.

Clearly an essay of this length cannot deal with all the issues thrown up by the concept of social defence: further in-depth studies are needed for this. Here we consider briefly three central issues: whether social defence can have a deterrent or dissuasive effect; whether some combination of military and social defence is feasible; and finally problems of transition, including the roles of government and civil society in constructing a social defence capability.

---

[15] See *Complementary Forms of Resistance: A Summary of the Report of the Swedish Commission on Resistance*, Swedish Official State Reports, SOU 1984:10.

a) Deterring attack

One of the prime tasks of a defence system in a democratic country is to preserve the freedom, human rights, and free institutions of the society. The developments in Eastern Europe since the imposition of Stalinist rule after World War II, have shown that the will to resist can persist even in face of the fiercest repression – the Ceausescu dictatorship, for instance, or Eastern Europe of the purges from 1948 to 1952. The revolutions of 1989 have further shown that under appropriate conditions mass civil resistance and non-cooperation can bring about a restoration of free institutions and democratic government. This experience, and the increasing evidence from other parts of the world of the power of civil resistance, indicate that the potential of social defence merits serious attention. No group, or institution or government seriously interested in ways of defending a free society can excuse neglecting it.

Clearly, however, it is far preferable to prevent the imposition of dictatorial government – whether from a foreign invasion or from within – than to have to struggle over a prolonged period for its overthrow and for the restoration of a free society. Can the sanctions that civil resistance is capable of imposing provide an adequate deterrent to a would-be aggressor?

Here we need to consider the deterrent element of traditional military defence. 'If you want peace, prepare for war' was the Roman adage that summed up the philosophy of deterrence; the ability to repel an attack and to visit retaliation on an aggressor was the surest guarantee that an aggression would not take place. If it did not always work, it was at least a rational calculation. We are after all dealing here with probabilities and relative risks, not certainties.

In the nuclear age the notion of deterrence has taken on a new dimension. The retaliation threatened is the devastation, even the total annihilation, of the opponent's society. But if the opponent too has a secure capability of striking back with nuclear weapons, the result would be the destruction of both societies – and in an all-out nuclear war, the devastation of the entire planet. In this sense the strategy of mutual nuclear deterrence is based on a threat which it would be irrational and disastrous ever to carry out.

The immorality of threatening the lives of millions of innocent people – much less putting the threat into effect – and the irrationality at the heart of nuclear deterrence, are the factors that have fuelled the anti-nuclear campaigns of the past several decades. And since we are dealing with relative risks, the disadvantages of relying on some form of conventional military defence, social resistance, or some combination of the two, have to be judged against the awesome alternative of the nuclear strategy still relied upon by the two superpowers.

A security policy resting chiefly on social defence has a dissuasive element. It has a 'defensive deterrent' element in so far as it threatens to deprive the aggressor of the intended objective of the attack – depending in part on what the objective is and the relative size and strength of the parties to the conflict. It has a 'retaliatory deterrent' element in so far as may undermine the aggressor regime – for instance by the spread of disaffection and mutiny among the armed forces. Thus if a potential aggressor calculates that the economic or strategic gains of occupying a territory may be largely nullified by non-cooperation, strikes and economic sabotage; that attempting to administer a country determined to resist could overstretch his country's military and administrative capability; that disaffection in the armed forces at home and abroad would give his opponents the opportunity to stage a coup or revolution – then clearly the deterrent element would be powerful.

In other circumstances, the deterrence element could be weak, even negligible. But this is sometimes true of the attempt to deter attack by military means – for instance where a small country on its own faces a large, well armed and hostile neighbour. Yet for much of the time, small relatively weak countries do manage to live side by side with powerful ones, and it is worth asking why this is so, for it may provide indications of how the deterrent element in social defence could be strengthened.

Here we may introduce the notion of a 'background deterrent' to aggression. Countries may intermittently attack one another but they do not do so continuously because of a whole range of constraints. Fear of military retaliation and defeat is one, but only one, of these. Others are the positive economic, political and diplomatic benefits of peaceful co-operation and the likely interruption or ending of these benefits if a country embarks on a war of aggression.

The advantages of peaceful co-operation may even be critical to the viability of a regime. To take a concrete example, certainly by the 1970s, and probably before that, the military occupation by Soviet Union and Warsaw Pact of Western Europe could have so disrupted the global economy that Eastern Europe and the Soviet Union itself could have faced economic crisis and internal unrest, even if the occupation had not been resisted militarily.

Other factors are a well-informed public at home, the opportunity for free expression, and a tradition of dissent. In other words a vigorous democracy and an active civil society can be an important, even a decisive, constraint on a government tempted to embark on foreign intervention. One reason why militarily powerful dictatorships are particularly feared is that this constraint is largely absent.

The background deterrent to aggression can be systematically enhanced. In a positive sense, this can be achieved by closer political and economic integration, for instance in a given region such as Europe. We consider this in more detail in later sections, and also argue that integration and co-operation should not be confined to governmental or commercial levels but should extend to civil society. In a 'negative' sense, deterrence could be enhanced if potential aggressors knew for certain in advance that concerted sanctions would be immediately applied. This could help to make good one of the weaknesses of civil resistance as a deterrent on its own, namely that its effects tend to be cumulative and slow acting.

If we think of specific scenarios, it is not difficult to imagine the smaller European states being deterred from, for instance, settling territorial disputes with a neighbour through aggression and occupation, by the prospect of mass civil resistance and concerted international sanctions. The tougher question is whether a superpower such as the United States or the Soviet Union could be deterred in the same way? And to raise what is perhaps the nightmare of the newly liberated states of Eastern Europe, and the unspoken fear that keeps West European states clinging to the idea of NATO, could such a security system deter the Soviet Union in some future, post-Gorbachev era, attempting to reassert its hegemony in Eastern Europe and perhaps extending it westwards?

To answer the question properly one would need to consider the process by which the Soviet Union had come to the point where it seemed to be in its interests to attempt such a move. But one can say firstly that integration into the 'common European home' – economically as well as politically – should reduce the likelihood of that situation ever arising. But if it did arise, the economic and political consequences for the Soviet Union of, in effect, re-starting the cold war, of overstretching its forces, of provoking rebellion at home and the unleashing of international sanctions, are factors no rational Soviet leadership could afford to ignore.

In the end there can of course be no absolute guarantee that any system of deterrence, including nuclear deterrence, will work. But if nuclear deterrence were to fail, the result would be unimaginable devastation. The failure of a system of non-military deterrence to restrain some future, more aggressive Soviet leadership would not rule out successful resistance, or even of a relatively rapid restoration of the status quo in some circumstances. For the moment, fortunately, the prospect of Soviet aggression against Europe seems remote. And overall the approach to security which would seem to offer the best prospect of maintaining the peace is one where the emphasis on military factors is reduced, and preparations for social defence systematically strengthened.

b) Combining military preparations and social defence

One solution proffered to the problem of deterrence and to other perceived weaknesses in social defence is to combine it with orthodox military preparations. Various approaches have been suggested. Preparations for civil resistance could be a 'fall-back' strategy in a system that relied primarily on conventional, non-nuclear defence. Studies of alternative non-nuclear strategies in the 1980s by academics and activists committed to nuclear disarmament, usually proposed this role for social defence. The fall-back strategy would come into operation if, for instance, the conventional forces were defeated in combat. It might also be used from the outset by a small country faced with hopeless odds militarily, or any country facing the threat of nuclear attack. Finally social defence might be considered as a suitable alternative to the use of military force in particular situations – for instance in disputes over fishing or mineral rights.[16]

---

[16]This approach is advocated for instance in the Alternative Defence Commission's *Defence Without the Bomb*, Taylor & Francis 1983. See especially the chapter entitled 'Defence by Civil Resistance'.

A mixed approach does not perforce imply a military strategy in which nuclear weapons play absolutely no role. NATO countries without nuclear weapons of their own could for instance continue to have a declared policy of relying on the US strategic deterrent, whilst simultaneously developing the option of social defence. Even countries like Britain or France with nuclear weapons of their own might wish to do so; indeed the French government has for some years funded research into non-violent alternatives to conflict. Generally, however, proponents of social defence have linked their advocacy of this method to a critique of war either from a totally pacifist perspective or from a 'just war' position which prohibits the use or threatened use of weapons of mass destruction. Moreover if social defence were to become an important element in the security system of a country, the moral as well as the pragmatic basis of the system would need to be clarified.

There are some obvious disadvantages to a mixed strategy of military and social defence. If war and non-violent resistance take place side by side, the moral and psychological impact of the latter could be largely nullified. Moreover, constraints on the use of force against unarmed demonstrators by invading or occupying forces could easily be swept aside in a war situation, even if the fighting was taking place in a different locality. The difficulty, however, if one argues for a total reliance on social defence, is to draw the line at which organised force will be used in any circumstances – for instance in dealing with armed criminal gangs internally.

Some researchers who advocate a mixed strategy have proposed steps to reduce the problems it clearly involves. They argue that the armed and unarmed resistance should be separated in time, place and in terms of organisation. Civil resistance would take place after the end of military hostilities (or possibly in some instances in place of them), but not while fighting was still going on. Organisationally the military and social defence structures would be separate though there would presumably be a system of liaison and coordination.

Clearly there are other possibilities. In Occupied Europe, and in many colonial struggles, civil resistance in towns and cities occurred side-by-side with guerrilla or conventional warfare. Moreover under conditions of military occupation, there would almost certainly be a section of the population committed to using military force whatever the previously agreed strategy of the government. But while reality is always more messy than theory, civil resistance would take on quite a different character if it became simply the civil component of a military strategy or operation. In such a situation not only would civilian resisters be more liable to face massacre, but their status as non-combatants would be questionable. Such points would need to be carefully considered in any national plan of resistance.

Whether ultimately a mixed strategy is viable, the reality is that there can be no overnight switch from reliance on military means to reliance on non-violent means of defence. In some form or other the two are bound to co-exist side by side, however uneasily, for a considerable period.

c) *Transition to Social Defence*

This brings us to the question of how the transition to social defence might come about. Here two principal models can be identified – the 'top-down' and the 'base-up' models. These are oversimplified descriptions, but serve to clarify the two approaches. In the 'top-down' model the government and its security advisors are persuaded of the merits of social defence and take responsibility for introducing it into the security system of the country. In the 'base-up' model, groups and organisations within civil society take the initiative in building up the community's capability for civil resistance.

Civil resistance is a form of struggle that has sprung from, and is particularly suited to, resistance at the grassroots of society. Historically it has been employed by oppositional movements working in voluntary association for common objectives. There are indeed those who question how far it can, or ought to be, incorporated into the bureaucratic and essentially coercive institutions of the state. Psychologically, it is difficult for any government to acknowledge publicly the possibility that its armed forces could face defeat. It may be reluctant too to embark on an educational and training programme for the population which could make the business of government more difficult in the event of civil resistance being employed against unpopular measures, or laws widely regarded as being unjust.

Thus one version of the base-up model of transition would be as follows. The state in the transitional phase would continue to deploy armed forces for the maintenance of internal order and defence against foreign attack. But their role, thanks to public debate and the pressure of informed groups, would be strictly defensive. The size and armament of the forces would also reflect the degree of confidence felt by the government in the capability of society to employ social defence, and in the effectiveness of the international system as a whole in dissuading any state from embarking on an attack.

Whether acknowledged or not, estimates of political intentions and of what we have called the 'background deterrent' do already enter into the calculations of all governments to some degree. Moreover one of the elements in the calculation is the immense difficulty an occupier would experience in attempting to govern a hostile and uncooperative population. Today, for essentially moral, political and economic reasons an all-out invasion by one West European state of another is virtually unthinkable, and they no longer arm against each other with this possibility in mind. Thus the transitional model discussed here is not as different as might first appear from the situation which currently exists in many countries.

In reality, the gap between the state and civil society is not absolute, and one would expect the impetus towards the adoption of social defence to come partly from above, partly from below. Centrally the state, for instance, could fund research projects and feasibility studies, and perhaps assume some responsibility for co-ordinating the development of social defence. At the municipal level, local authorities could have more direct charge for organising social defence within their area. The state and municipal authorities would presumably also have to play at least some agreed co-ordinating role in the event of an attempted coup or occupation. However, the essential base for resistance could remain in civil society.

Not all problems can be solved in advance, and if social defence ever does make a significant contribution to international security, arrangements and processes will vary from country to country. It is important that those committed to advancing the idea should not become paralysed in disputes which can only be solved by attempting to put ideas into effect. Even the vexed question of whether or not social defence implies a total rejection of military methods, or whether some residual role for the armed forces must be retained, can be resolved at a later point.

The Context of Transition in Europe

In an earlier section we reviewed briefly the alliance context in which social defence might be introduced in the coming years. The European political, economic and juridical context is no less significant. In general one can say that the more closely Europe is integrated the stronger will be the disincentive for states to go to war against each other, and the more effective will be the collective non-military sanctions that could be applied against an aggressor state.

The process of economic integration is likely to speed up in the period ahead. With German unification, the territory of what was previously the GDR has been incorporated into the Economic Community. Closer ties between the EC and several other East European states are also likely either on an individual basis or through agreements between the EC and the Soviet-based trading group Comecon – assuming that for the moment the latter remains in existence. Finally the European Free Trade Association (EFTA) – Western Europe's other economic grouping – is already involved in establishing closer links with the EC and is unlikely to stand aside from the integration process.

Economic integration could have a down side if it were to block the emergence in Eastern Europe of new co-operative forms of ownership and management, or lead through pressure from the IMF and World Bank to a particular model of development being imposed on the region. These unfortunately are real dangers which may require new campaigns of civil resistance to combat.

One can also anticipate integration at other levels. Hungary, Poland and Czechoslovakia, for instance, have applied for membership of the Council of Europe. Others could follow. One important benefit of this is that it would tend to strengthen the democratic development of the countries concerned since the observance of democracy internally is one of the conditions of membership. In due course one could expect to see the emergence of a pan-European Parliament.

The CSCE provides a key framework for furthering East-West co-operation and building a 'Common European Home'. It has the advantage of involving the other world superpower, the US, in the integration process. As noted earlier, the CSCE states are committed to respecting each other's independence and territorial integrity, and also the human rights and freedoms of their own citizens. Demilitarisation, co-operation for economic development and the protection of the environment, are among the other commitments set out in the Helsinki Final Acts (1975).

Moves to secure integration at the official, inter-state level need to be matched by the strengthening of civil society across national boundaries. This, as we have seen, was crucial in the struggles in Eastern Europe in the 1980s; it is likely to prove no less so in meeting the challenges of the new Europe beyond the Cold War, and providing the base for building social defence at a European level.

An important initiative in this respect is the 1990 Prague Appeal to establish a permanent Helsinki Citizens Assembly. The Assembly held its first meeting in Prague in October 1990 bringing together independent organisations from East and West committed to the Helsinki process. To quote from the Appeal:

> Overcoming the division of Europe is the job especially of civil society, of citizens acting together in self-organised associations, movements, institutions, initiatives and clubs across national boundaries. It means the creation of new social relationships, new forums of dialogue through which citizens can negotiate with governments and each other, put pressure on political institutions, and indeed, resolve many issues without the direct involvement of governments. It means the expansion of public i.e. non-state, non-private, spheres of activity and the creation of a European public opinion.[17]

The terms of the Appeal show clearly the desire to see something new emerge from the revolutions in Eastern Europe in terms of democratic participation – to introduce, in the words of Neal Ascherson cited above, 'a new gene' into European political life. It is an effort to continue the co-operation and dialogue between human rights, peace and environmentalist groups in various countries of East and West, including notably the Western peace movements. Originally planned before the historic changes in Eastern Europe, its direct antecedents were the Network for East-West Dialogue established at the 1984 European Nuclear Disarmament Convention, the appeal

---

[17]The text of the Appeal is available from Mient Jan Faber, c/o IKV, PO Box 18747, 2502 ES's-Gravenhage, Netherlands.

entitled Giving New Life to the Helsinki Accords presented in 1986 to the Vienna CSCE conference, and the international seminar in Prague in 1987 organised by Charter 77 where it was resolved to establish a permanent European Peace Assembly.

The Longer Term Perspective: Nuclear Abolition

The prospect of radical demilitarisation in Europe has been opened up by the East-West detente, by progress in arms control negotiations and by the dissolution of the Warsaw Pact. It makes little sense in this situation for NATO to be considering the deployment of a new generation of air-launched cruise missiles armed with nuclear weapons. Rather it is time to reconsider seriously the elimination of nuclear weapons.

Progress in arms control and demilitarisation, provides a crucial opportunity to tackle the nuclear issue. Moreover, once demilitarisation in Europe passes a certain point, the question of nuclear weapons can hardly be avoided. A continuing capacity by countries in East and West to destroy each other simply does not square with reducing conventional forces to minimal levels, or the adoption of a strategy of non-offensive defence.

Discussions between the two nuclear superpowers on strategic nuclear forces must also address ultimately the question of totally eliminating nuclear weapons and all weapons of mass destruction. Morally the actual use of such weapons is indefensible; in terms of human and environmental consequences their use would be an act of madness. In the end no security system can be stable which has such madness at its core.

When Gorbachev proposed at the 1986 Reykjavik summit the total elimination of nuclear weapons by the turn of the century, many Western leaders reacted with alarm and dismissed the suggestion as dangerously utopian. But circumstances have changed. We have now had the 1987 INF Treaty which for the first time got rid of a whole category of nuclear weapons. At the Paris summit of the CSCE in November 1990, a new Conventional Forces in Europe (CFE) Treaty was signed which will drastically reduce the size of non-nuclear forces in Europe and minimise the risk of surprise attack. Finally, despite certain difficulties, a treaty on strategic nuclear weapons

(START), again drastically reducing deployments, seems at least a reasonable possibility in 1991. Sooner or later abolition must be put back on the agenda.

But while there have been many volumes written on nuclear strategy, remarkably little consideration has been given to the possibilities and modalities of *global* nuclear disarmament. Advocates of nuclear deterrence have for the most part regarded the whole notion as utopian. Peace researchers and activists have tended to concentrate on moral issues or on nuclear disarmament in a more limited context – for instance in one country or region. The studies in Britain by the Alternative Defence Commission, for instance, considered the possibilities of a non-nuclear security policy by Britain and Western Europe – though much of the argument, and many of the proposed alternatives had a more universal application.[18]

One person who has put forward a considered proposal for global nuclear disarmament is the American author and political commentator, Jonathan Schell, in his book *The Abolition*.[19] Schell devotes the first part of his essay to 'defining the great predicament'.

> In sum, the underlying *human* question that the invention of nuclear weapons confronts us with is whether we will live or die as a species, but the underlying *political* question, which must be tackled before the human question can be favourably resolved, is how disputes among nations are to be handled in a world in which war has been spoiled as an instrument of state policy.[20]

Schell also graphically summaries the moral issue posed by reliance on nuclear weapons:

---

[18] See Alternative Defence Commission, *Defence Without the Bomb*, Taylor & Francis, 1983; and ADC, *The Politics of Alternative Defence*, Paladin, 1987.

[19] Jonathan Schell, *The Abolition*, Picador, 1984.

[20] Schell, *op. cit*, p.27. Schell clarifies his point by noting that war has been spoiled 'in those theatres of potential conflict in which the rivals are abundantly armed with nuclear weapons, as the United States and the Soviet Union are. In other theatres, in which one or both powers lack nuclear weapons, nations can and do go on fighting wars'. – p.26.

The bishops boldly ask us whether we are willing, under any circumstances, to kill countless millions of innocent people,[21] and to this their and our immediate impulse is to cry out 'No!' And, indeed, at one point the bishops state that we must say a clear 'no' to nuclear weapons. If I may use myself as an example, I know that if the nuclear button were on my desk and a nuclear attack were launched against the United States I would be unable to retaliate in kind. I would utterly lack the 'resolve' to do this. In fact, my whole resolve would be that it not be done. This 'retaliation' would seem to me to be a separate, new, unspeakable crime in its own right, which was in no way an appropriate response to the unspeakable crime that had just been committed against my country.

As I see it, it would in fact, not even *be* retaliation, since most of the people it would kill – innocent citizens, including children – would have had nothing to do with their government's criminally insane decision. Yet I know that this unwillingness of mine would, if it were generalised into a policy, be so far outside the pale politically as to have virtually no acceptance. In that sense, to truly say 'no' to nuclear weapons forces one into a position that is politically irrelevant – at least as far as present policy is concerned.[22]

The second part of Schell's essay can be seen as an attempt to bridge the gap between moral imperative and political realism. He confronts the argument that it is literally impossible to abolish nuclear weapons since the knowledge of how to make them will now always be with us. The argument, Schell points out, is a non-sequitur: it conflates two quite separate questions – whether the weapons can be 'uninvented', and whether they can be destroyed and their future manufacture and use prohibited. Schell advocates the total abolition of nuclear weapons under international inspection, and argues that the very fact that the weapons could not be uninvented would provide an 'existential (nuclear) deterrent' to aggression.

Schell, in short, is arguing for a system of nuclear deterrence without the nuclear weapons in place – 'weaponless deterrence' as he calls it. His proposed Abolition Treaty would actually authorise, and establish the guidelines for, the re-manufacture and, ultimately, the use, of nuclear weapons against an aggressor, including an aggressor who had secretly manufactured a limited number of

---

[21]A reference to a statement on nuclear war by US Catholic Bishops in 1984.
[22]*Ibid*, pp.76-7.

nuclear weapons,[23] or had openly defied the Treaty, and was attempting to hold the world to ransom. He envisages a lead time of six to eight weeks from the day manufacturing of the weapons recommenced to the point at which they would be ready for use, and argues that this would allow a breathing space for diplomacy and second thoughts, and greatly reduce, by comparison with the present situation, the danger of war by accident or miscalculation. Other elements of the proposal include the building up of anti-missile defences which would probably be concentrated on defending the means to re-start nuclear weapons production and delivery, and the retention of conventional forces geared as far as possible to defence.

The proposals are clearly unsatisfactory as they stand. They fail to resolve the moral issue – as indeed Schell himself freely acknowledges – since they involve not only a conditional intention to use nuclear weapons, but also a continued command and control system to ensure that nuclear rearmament could take place, and nuclear war actually be waged if necessary, at very short order. They probably fail equally the test of political realism, though that is something no so easily determined as truly radical proposals which challenge long-standing assumptions are bound to appear unrealistic at first presentation.

Nevertheless there are important insights in the essay. Because we cannot turn back the clock to a pre-nuclear age, the situation of our world of sovereign states has been subtly but radically altered. It is no longer in the 'state of anarchy' as defined by classical political theory, since war is not a rational option any more, at least between the major powers with a nuclear capability. 'Nuclear weapons,' as he puts it, 'have knocked the sword of war from our hands. Now it is up to us what we will pick up in its place.'

The central weakness of the essay is that Schell doesn't actually suggest anything that we might pick up in its place. His proposals cover various institutional moves to eliminate nuclear weapons and strengthen the peace, but he does not devote any attention to what happens if peace breaks down despite these arrangements. In particular the problem of wars between non-nuclear states, and

---

[23]A limited number, because it is assumed that a system of international inspection and control would prevent cheating on a substantail scale to go undetected.

how they could embroil the major powers, it never adequately considered.

Significantly, however, Schell does note that an important bar to world conquest – the nightmare that preparations for defensive war or collective armed security are designed to prevent – comes from the aroused national consciousness of local people and their increasingly successful resistance to foreign domination. He continues:

> The single great exception to this local takeover from great powers is in Eastern Europe, where the continued Soviet domination is ultimately maintained by occupying armies. But even there local resistance – especially in Poland – though it is not yet intense enough to expel the Soviets, makes one wonder how long this anachronistic form of control can last.[24]

We do not suggest that the people power which played such a central role in ending this anachronism provides a total answer to the dilemmas of the nuclear age. But we do see it as an essential and indeed crucial element in the process of abolishing nuclear weapons, and – in a way that Schell's plans fail to do – the threat of future nuclear conflict.

Critics of nuclear disarmament argue that the abolition of nuclear weapons would make the world not safer but infinitely more dangerous. This is not an issue which can be proved either way. However, the proposition that often accompanies that statement, namely that nuclear disarmament would return the world to the strategic situation that existed prior to World War II, is clearly incorrect. Schell's point about the inevitable continuance of an 'existential deterrent' applies even if nuclear weapons had been unequivocally prohibited under international law and safeguards were in place to prevent nuclear rearmament under any circumstances. Any potential aggressor would know that despite such safeguards, and despite whatever undertakings an opponent has given never to resort to nuclear weapons, any *global* war could quite quickly become nuclear.

This aspect of the debate hinges on a calculation about risks. Without the existence and actual deployment of nuclear weapons,

---

[24]Ibid, pp.145-6.

would the major powers become complacent about the immense destruction that even a conventional war would bring, and about the prospects of a race to nuclear Armageddon, and thus be tempted to go to war? Or does a world where the US and the Soviet Union, and several other states, are poised for the indefinite future to launch weapons of mass destruction, represent a greater threat to peace?

Those involved in producing this study take the second view. However, the strictly *strategic* debate is inevitably open ended; there is no way of settling the issue beyond dispute. Historical examples may throw some light on the argument, but cannot settle it if only because the situation itself is without precedent and because there can be no empirical test of the rival hypotheses.

But the fact that the strategic arguments *per se* cannot decisively settle the question does not make the wider debate about whether or not to retain nuclear weapons any the less urgent. On the contrary, it is clearly a debate of momentous importance on whose outcome the very future of human life on the planet could rest. The implication is that the debate belongs in the arena of the human, not the exact, sciences; here the goal can only be, in the telling phrase of the literary critic F.R.Leavis, 'the common pursuit of true judgement.' In that pursuit, past experience, rational calculation of probable outcomes but – crucially – moral intelligence – must take their place.

Conclusion

In this essay we have sketched the development of civil resistance in the Eastern Europe revolutions on 1989. Without resistance Eastern Europe would still be experiencing authoritarian communist rule; but without the non-violent discipline, the struggle would probably have ended in the tragedy of another Soviet intervention and the recrudescence of the Cold War. Because there was resistance, and because it was non-violent, the 1990s – despite recent setbacks – open in a more hopeful context than any decade since the end of World War II.

The successes of civil resistance in Eastern Europe should dispel any notion that it is something alien to the European tradition or irrelevant in the European context. In fact the political, economic and environmental challenges now facing Europe require an alert civil society and grassroots organisations ready to engage in civil resistance. As regards security, the situation in Europe created by the end of the Cold War and the withering away of the block system, means that defence by civil resistance – what we have called social defence – could play an increasingly important role. In the longer term, if nuclear weapons are to be abolished, social defence could become the cornerstone in a new security system.

Clearly many issues raised here require discussion at greater length. The principal aim of this essay is to draw attention to them in the hope of stimulating such discussion and thought. Civil resistance – people power – moved centre stage in struggles in many countries and continents in the 1980s. It is time it received the attention and creative reflection it deserves. Developed with due seriousness, it could yet be the key to ridding the world of the twin scourges of dictatorship and war and to building more genuinely democratic societies.

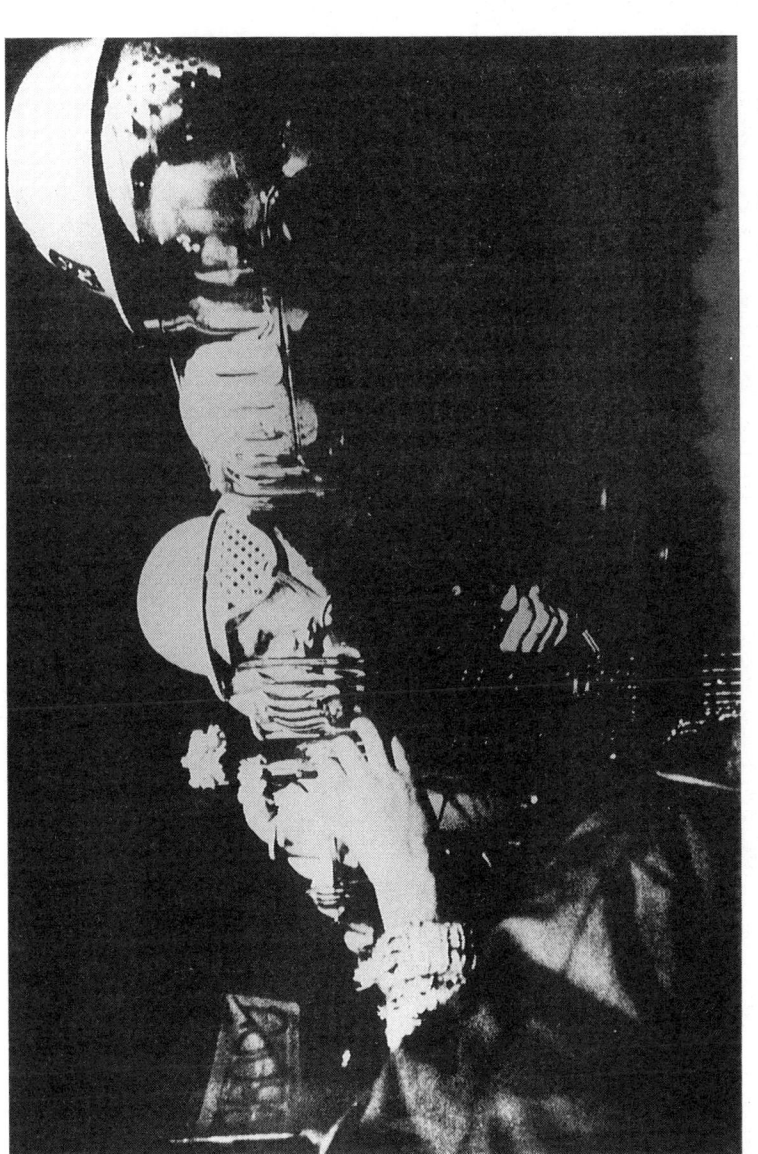

The gentle revolution, Prague, November 17, 1989.

East European Reporter

Celebrating the velvet revolution, Prague, November 1989.

East European Reporter

PART II

The Interviews

Introduction to Part II

The reasons for devoting the second half of this book to interviews with people involved directly – for the most part – in the revolutions of 1989, or the events leading up to them, have been touched upon in the General Introduction. The interviews provide first hand information about the situation as it existed in the various countries concerned at that time, and as it has developed since then; more importantly, they help us to understand how and why people were willing to take the enormous risk of opposing the authoritarian regimes they confronted. Such an understanding is as crucial to developing people power as the analysis of how it can unseat illegitimate authority.

I am struck by the often intensely personal reasons people give for their involvement in the opposition, an involvement that always entailed great risks and sometimes heavy costs for them and their families. 'I became involved', says Jirina Siklova, from Czechoslovakia 'because I wanted to be able to look my children in the face.' 'I had to ask myself', explains Helmuth Frauendorfer from Romania – 'What am I? Am I a writer, or am I man who can speak with others and then tell the Securitate what has been said?' 'Speaking for myself,' says Elzbieta Rawicz-Oledzka from Poland, 'I can say that there came a point when I felt that the situation in the country was quite unbearable and that I simply had to do something to try to change it.'

Of course there were broader political, social and economic factors underlying the 1989 revolutions and these are discussed both in my own essay and in the interviews. Nevertheless what the respondents say about their personal involvement and motivation tell us much about the character of the East European revolutions. One has a sense of quiet heroism, rather than of the grand heroic gesture; of a shared commitment to human dignity, free expression, and democratic politics rather than to either a narrow political programme or some grand ideological scheme; of a belief in ironic humour and moral challenge, rather than violence, as ways in which the pretensions of the old order could be punctured and its power undermined.

The absence of violence – except in the case of Romania – was a notable feature of the 1989 revolutions. Most respondents stress that this was the only practicable way forward, especially given the danger of provoking a Soviet military intervention. But Marco Hren, from Slovenia, draws attention to the difficulty of drawing a sharp distinction between pragmatism and principle because there was a meeting point between the two in a deep and widespread desire to avoid bloodshed. He also suggests that, in his country at least, the 'wave of energy' from the Western peace movements in the early 1980s had an important impact. Peter Szasz says that bloodshed was avoided in Hungary in part because reformers inside the communist party persuaded it that change was necessary; Knud Wollenberger too notes the unwillingness of most of the East German leadership to shoot down civilians peacefully protesting.

Revolutions, it is often said, devour their own children. In Eastern Europe the former dissidents have been – in many instances – not so much devoured as marginalised. True, Havel and Walesa are now the presidents of their respective countries, and there are former 'dissidents' in the governments and legislatures of several East European states. But both Civic Forum in Czechoslovakia, and Solidarity in Poland are deeply split, with many of the former activists taking a critical stance towards the new governments. Elsewhere the marginalisation process has gone further. In the former GDR, West German politics and political parties have effectively taken over. In Romania, many of those in Timisoara and elsewhere who were at the forefront of the opposition to Ceausescu, now bitterly oppose the government of the National Salvation Front, and complain of harassment and even persecution. Knud Wollenberger, of the former GDR, eloquently expresses the sense of loss. 'For a time we were the subjects of history ... now again we have become its objects.'

Jirina Siklova, however, had foreseen this outcome before the revolutions ever took place. In a paper written in 1988, she argued that if the opposition succeeded in overturning the old system 'they will lose their political unity, cohesion, special position and the goals for which they have fought'. The inheritors of the new situation would be the people of the 'grey zone' – the 'qualified but politically conforming people who support officially the regime while simultaneously favouring the opposition.'

Does this mean that the former 'dissidents' and opposition movements have no role now that something akin to normal democratic politics has replaced the authoritarian regimes of the post World War II period? This is far from the view of any of the respondents. On the contrary they are at one in believing that such groups and movements have a vital function to perform in promoting a non-violent political culture. Crucially this means nurturing – or, in the case of Romania virtually creating – civil society, i.e. the free association of individuals for social and political goals outside state structures. Helmuth Frauendorfer sees the civil movements, linked since last November in Civic Alliance, as the key to the gradual emergence of democracy in Romania. 'My hope,' he says, 'is that they can build up a political culture, because that is what is missing in Romania. There are so many quarrels and fights between the parties, such extreme accusations and counter-accusations – it's completely destructive.'

Knud Wollenberger makes a similar point in discussing the future role of non-violent action:

> I'm not only referring to resistance as such, but to a non-violent approach which includes learning how to build a democratic culture. It was not only the dramatic street protests that were significant in the East European revolutions, but also the fact that, at least within the framework of the peace movement, people learned to deal with each other despite holding different ideas. It was learning to accept that opposing views could be expressed in the same room without one side or the other being forced to back down. It took years for us to learn that. And I guess it will take years for the majority of the population, or of the politically interested population, to learn, even emotionally, how to live in a pluralist society.

Jan Kavan from Czechoslovakia sees the Helsinki Citizens Assembly – an international body with its headquarters in Prague – as a way of linking civil society across national boundaries.

I hope ... that the Assembly – along with other non-governmental organisations – will emerge as a strong and influential movement within the next two to three years. There is a shared determination to create a framework which would allow individuals and non-governmental groups – what we used to refer to as the informal structures of civil society – to determine their own future and their own quality of life. Above all there is a determination to find nonviolent means of solving outstanding problems, and a commitment to non-violent change towards a freer and more just European-wide society.

It is clear, unfortunately, from the interviews, that social defence – in so far as it concerns systematic preparations *by a government* for non-violent resistance – is not yet on the political agenda in Eastern Europe. There appear to be two main reasons for this. First, with the dissolution of the Warsaw Pact, the winding down of the Cold War and the gradual withdrawal of Soviet forces, there is no imminent sense of exterior threat and so defence questions have not been given a high priority. Second, the new governments are preoccupied with more immediate internal problems, notably keeping their economies afloat, and, in some cases, dealing with ethnic and nationalist tensions.

It is no coincidence that the exception here is Slovenia. Slovenia is part of the Yugoslav Federation but voted in December 1990 for complete independence. There the possibility of intervention by Federal forces is at the forefront of people's consciousness, and, as the interview with Marco Hren shows, the state government is paying serious attention to social defence as a means of consolidating and defending Slovenia's independence.

There is a parallel situation developing in the Baltic States whose parliaments have voted for independence from Moscow. I have not been able to interview anyone involved in the independence struggle in any of the Baltic States, but there have been several calls by prominent politicians in the three states for 'Gandhian resistance' and 'civil disobedience'. The interview with Thomas Hackman from Finland also confirms the keen interest, at least in Latvia and Estonia, in the potential of civil resistance.

In most of Eastern Europe it would seem that if civil resistance is to be developed it will have to be done initially by the groups and organisations of civil society. Nevertheless, Jan Kavan expresses

Introduction to Part II

the hope that in due course East-European governments will take an interest in the notion:

> ... I do believe that this notion of social defence will eventually enter into the consciousness of some of the political leaders. They are not necessarily unsympathetic to the idea of social defence, or opposed to it on ideological grounds; it is rather that developments in that part of the world have not placed the idea at the top of the political agenda. I think it will be put on the agenda relatively soon as governments and politicians have to discuss the role of their countries within the new Europe, and within the new European security system.

I hope that the testimony of the respondents will be read not only for the light they throw on the tasks so movingly accomplished in Eastern Europe in 1989, but for the potential they reveal for 'people power' in building the new European home and developing alternatives to war and violence between people and between nations.

Helmuth Frauendorfer

Interviewed 4 February 1991. Helmuth Frauendorfer, a poet and writer, was born in Romania in 1959 in the countryside near Timisoara. He is from the German minority in Romania which has now been all but dispersed. He studied German and English in Timisoara where he contributed a literary page in German to a students' review, and directed a theatre group. In both his writings and his theatre work he was often critical of the regime and in 1984 was interrogated and beaten up by the Securitate. In December 1987 he was forced to leave Romania.

Since then he has lived in Berlin, working with other Romanian exiles to publicise the situation in his country and Ceausescu's war against his own people. On November 15 1988, a year after the revolt in Brasov, he co-ordinated a Day of Action for Romania in which people from many countries participated. Subsequently he and friends founded the Human Rights Committee for Romania within the Heinrich Böll foundation, a committee for which he worked full time as co-ordinator until December 1990. The committee organised many international actions and conferences, documented the situation in Romania, and informed the Western media about it. In October 1990 the committee, in collaboration with opposition groups in Romania and the Helsinki Federation for Human Rights, organised the first international human rights conference in Romania, in the town of Timisoara.

Helmuth Frauendorfer is married. He has no children. He explains that he and his wife decided against having children as long as they lived in Romania. This was firstly because it was impossible to provide properly for children there; and secondly, because they did not want 'to give Ceausescu children' – to co-operate in the national campaign for every family to have at least four children.

MR: Perhaps we can start with the human rights conference you organised, in collaboration with others, in Timisoara last year. Was Timisoara chosen as the venue for symbolic reasons?

Helmuth Frauendorfer: Partly for symbolic reasons, this being the town in which the so-called revolution against Ceausescu began – and I emphasise so-called. But it was also because in Timisoara there is a different political atmosphere from the rest of the country. I made several journeys for research purposes to Romania and I could see that Timisoara was the only venue where such a conference could take place. In other towns and cities, for instance Bucharest, I am sure the authorities would have tried to organise a boycott of the conference.

There are historical reasons for this special atmosphere in Timisoara. The western part of Romania – the region of Banat in which Timisoara lies – has experienced a different cultural influence from the rest of the country. Until 1918 Banat was part of the Austro-Hungarian Empire.

MR: How does Banat relate to the region of Transylvania?

Helmuth Frauendorfer: Most people when they talk of Transylvania are including Banat. But Transylvania is in fact the more northern and central part; Banat is the south western part.

MR: What led you personally to oppose the Ceausescu regime, given the tremendous risks involved?

Helmuth Frauendorfer: I started as a child to write some verses – I can't call them poems! – and I read many books. I began to realise that my childhood wasn't so beautiful and so happy as the teachers and others would have me believe. As I grew up, I began to ask myself what was the reason for this, and to criticise some aspects of the society in my writing – including my journalistic writing for as long as I was allowed to publish.

The most important event for me occurred in 1978. I was the youngest member of a literary group at that time and was approached by the Securitate who tried to co-opt me as an agent. This was a turning point in my personal life. I had to ask myself – 'What am I? Am I a writer, or am I a man who can speak with others and then tell the Securitate what has been said?' I came to the conclusion that I couldn't do this. Instead I went to the people the Securitate had asked me to spy on and warned them about what was happening. Obviously the Securitate were extremely angry, and from then on they started to collect information about me. In 1984, when I was interrogated, they showed me what they had collected. It included my poems, other writings, my artistic work – and the conversations I had in the literary group. They knew everything.

MR: Presumably, then, they had succeeded in recruiting others in the group to act as spies.

Helmuth Frauendorfer: Exactly so. I then saw just how perverse was this whole system and the extent of the repression directed against the people of the country. During the 1980s the repression became harsher and harsher. I said to myself that if I was to be a writer in such a society, I must speak out against this repression and against the whole personality cult of Ceausescu. I could only do this through my writing – I am not a politician, or a soldier. Writing was my only weapon.

MR: How isolated were you in doing this? Were there other people in the literary group, or other groups, who joined you in this work? This question touches upon a larger one: how far was there an embryonic civil society in Romania during the Ceausescu years?

Helmuth Frauendorfer: Civil society didn't exist in Romania then, and nor does it today. We were a few writers, a minority in a double sense. We were a minority being Germans; and inside the German minority, we were again a minority because most of the German writers conformed with the system. Our group comprised a few people like Richard Wagner, Herta Müller, and William Totok. We tried to make contact with young Romanian writers, but it wasn't easy. Some contacts existed. But most of them as they became older and had a job they wanted to hold on to, were unwilling to risk trouble with the Securitate, and so preferred to remain silent. It was no joke to have trouble with the Securitate. People were beaten up. People died. So contacts were very limited.

MR: What about contact with the Hungarian minority? Was that any easier?

Helmuth Frauendorfer: The Hungarians who were politically active – as Geza Szocs for example – lived in Transylvania. You have to understand that communication is nearly impossible in Romania. We didn't have telephones, and the mail was strictly censored. You couldn't say anything controversial in a letter because you knew that it would land on the desk of the Securitate. For these reasons we had very little contact with the Hungarian minority; there were a few contacts, but only a few. Still I wonder now why we didn't make a greater effort to establish contacts. We didn't attempt to make contact with them, and they didn't attempt to make contact with us.

MR: Given that situation of total repression, how do you explain the events of 1989 when suddenly tens of thousands of people took to the streets?

Helmuth Frauendorfer: It was an expression of desperation. The revolt started in Timisoara in a small way as a Hungarian religious phenomenon. The people in Pastor Tokes' community expressed their solidarity with him by forming a cordon in front of his house to prevent his forcible removal. His bishops, in collaboration with the Securitate, had proposed expelling him to another part of the country. This Hungarian religious phenomenon turned into an anti-Ceausescu phenomenon between one day and the next. When more people joined the vigil outside Tokes' house they didn't only shout 'We want Tokes!', they also started to shout 'Down with Ceausescu!' The people were in despair. Despair and desperation drove them onto the streets. It was an entirely spontaneous revolt.

MR: Did Romanians at that point join the ethnic Hungarians?

Helmuth Frauendorfer: Yes they joined in solidarity with the Hungarians. You should know that Timisoara is a multi-cultural town. Hungarians, Romanians, Germans, Gypsies, Bulgarians, Jews – all live there, and people from every community came onto the streets.

MR: Did events in other parts of Eastern Europe, and developments in the Soviet Union under Gorbachev, help to trigger the revolt?

Helmuth Frauendorfer: Yes, of course. Without the overthrow of the regimes in other countries, the revolt in Romania would not have been possible. What happened in Czechoslovakia, in Poland, in Hungary, in Bulgaria, and last but not least the GDR had a tremendous impact. People saw that Romania was the last to retain its dictator.

Of course the situation in Romania was incomparably worse than that in other countries. Every evil was multiplied several times over. There was more cruelty, more brutality, more repression than anywhere else in Eastern Europe. Then the whole thing exploded.

At first it was an explosion – and now you can see that it was also an implosion.

After a few days, the trouble spread to Bucharest. Ceausescu fled, leaving a political vacuum. Iliescu and his friends who formed the National Salvation Front were at that time the only group organisationally competent to fill the vacuum. He stated at first that the Salvation Front government was purely transitional, a caretaker administration that would take charge until a properly elected government could be installed. The mistake they made was to reconstitute themselves as a party and to seek to retain power.

MR: Was it a mistake, or was it the plan all along?

Helmuth Frauendorfer: You know there exist today in Romania at least ten variants of conspiracy theories. I know that there were small-scale conspiracies, but there was no pre-planned *putsch* by Iliescu. He and his fellow conspirators only came on the scene when the vacuum was created by the downfall of Ceausescu. Having obtained power on 22 December, they then made the decision to retain it, and not to destroy the old structures.

The whole *nomenklatura* under Ceausescu is unchanged. Iliescu and his friends made a pact with the *nomenklatura* which allowed the latter to retain their position and privileges. The Salvation Front government didn't even disturb or destroy the Securitate. For example I know that the major who interrogated me in 1984, Major Adamescu, is now again an officer of the new security service, the 'Romanian Information Service'. It consists almost entirely of the same people as the Securitate, only a few have been changed. And it is functioning in much the same way.

I can give you an example from last Friday. My wife phoned to Timisoara to talk to her mother. They were able to talk, but the moment her mother started to tell her how cold it was in the house – how they had to keep all their outdoor clothes on, and stay in bed for warmth – they were cut off. My wife phoned again, and this time when her brother started to tell her how cold it was, they were interrupted and we could hear the distorted voices as the tape machine was wound back.

Still the security services cannot operate in quite the same brutal way as before; they are afraid to do that. So there is a change. Indeed in general, although the changes have not been as great as expected, and as were needed, still things are different from before. There can be no complete return to the situation that existed under Ceausescu.

MR: Does this mean there is an opportunity for a genuine democracy to develop?

Helmuth Frauendorfer: The development of democracy will be a difficult process because society is not prepared for it. There is also too much disinformation being circulated in Romania. During the elections for example, it wasn't the case that the election results were falsified. The problem started before the election when the television – which is under the direct control of Iliescu – was used to spread disinformation. Thus the authorities were able to manipulate the people. Furthermore, the opposition parties are weak, and some are simply not serious. A real political opposition simply doesn't exist.

The only hope I have for Romania resides in the small, step by step work of the Civic Alliance. The Alliance was set up last November and consists of civil movements from Timisoara, Bucharest, Cluj and other parts of the country. My hope is that they can build up a political culture, because this is what is missing in Romania. There are so many quarrels and fights between the parties, such extreme accusations and counter-accusations – it's completely destructive.

The greatest danger of all comes from nationalism. That hatred of everything which is not Romanian, that whole xenophobic and chauvinistic dimension which was one of the pillars of Ceausescu's power, is now manifesting itself.

MR: Is this happening spontaneously or is it being manipulated for political ends in the way Ceausescu had previously done?

Helmuth Frauendorfer: It's a combination of both. It is the old hatreds resurfacing – against Hungarians, for instance, against the gypsies, and against others. But the fears and prejudices are also being manipulated by *Vatra Romaneasca*[1] which has very good contacts with the Salvation Front. The Front and *Vatra Romaneasca* are collaborating. This is one of the greatest dangers I see threatening the development of democracy in Romania.

MR: Are there ways in which the Civic Alliance and its various constituent groups can combat this xenophobia and its exploitation for political ends? Have they been able to do anything about it?

---

[1] *Vatra Romaneasca* – literally 'Romanian Cradle' – is an extreme right-wing organisation with overtones of fascism which was set up in Transylvania in January 1990. It openly espouses anti-semitic and anti-Hungarian policies.

Helmuth Frauendorfer: They are trying. But, as I said, they will not be successful from one day to another, or from one year to another. It is a work of little steps over a long period.

MR: In the meantime do you see the National Salvation Front government retaining power?

Helmuth Frauendorfer: Yes. It is sad, but that's how it is. The problem is there is no alternative to it. The Civic Alliance isn't a political party – and, as I said to them, it's good that they are not a party. It is necessary to have a civil, non-parliamentary corrective to the government. But the opposition political parties are not working at all. You can forget them.

MR: Are there links between Civic Alliance and the Helsinki Citizens Assembly which held its first international gathering in Prague last October?

Helmuth Frauendorfer: In October, the Civic Alliance had not yet been founded. But someone from the Timisoara Society did attend the Prague meeting, and it is a member of the Alliance. I hope now the contacts between Civic Alliance and the Helsinki Citizens Assembly will continue and be strengthened. One of the aims of the conference I helped to organise in Timisoara last October was to put civic groups, students, and so on, in touch with groups in other countries and with international bodies. Amnesty International sent an observer to the meeting as did the Helsinki Federation of Human Rights and other human rights organisations from different countries. I had also observed that in every town in Romania there were small groups working for human rights but that they had little contact with one another. Thus another crucial function of the conference was to establish links between groups within Romania.

MR: Coming back to the revolution itself, do you think there was any way in which the violence and the street battles between the army and the Securitate could have been avoided?

Helmuth Frauendorfer: No. In November 1989 I wrote a commentary for a Berlin newspaper in which I said that it was too late now for peaceful change in Romania; any change would be a bloody one. No other way existed. The structures of the dictatorship were too brutal.

MR: But up to the point that the Ceausescus fled from the roof of the palace in the helicopter, hadn't the revolution been non-violent?

Helmuth Frauendorfer: No, it had been violent, very violent in Timisoara.

MR: Yes, but wasn't the violence at that stage entirely on the side of the authorities. My impression is that the pitched battles between the army and the Securitate came later after the Securitate tried to stage a counter-revolution.

Helmuth Frauendorfer: The violence began, certainly, on the part of the authorities. The people had no possibility of using violence as they had no weapons. The people demonstrated peacefully, but at the same time called out 'Down with Ceausescu!' in a very forceful and vehement way. The government answered with violence. The army, police and Securitate all took part in the shooting of people. Later on a few army officers refused to give the order to shoot, and finally the army went over to the side of the people. In Bucharest that happened on 22 December. In Timisoara it happened earlier.

MR: I hadn't realised that about Timisoara. However, the argument I make in my own essay is that what brought about the overthrow of Ceausescu in the first instance was the same people power that ended communist regimes in the rest of Eastern Europe. The demonstrators were very viciously attacked, and in that sense of course the revolution was more violent even at that stage than elsewhere. I take your word for it that some soldiers in Timisoara did go over to the side of the people and return the fire of the Securitate before Ceausescu fled from the Presidential Palace on 22 December. But surely the decisive factor in forcing Ceausescu's resignation was not that some soldiers fired back on the Securitate but that people took to the streets in their tens of thousands, and refused to be intimidated, despite brutality and massacre.

Helmuth Frauendorfer: Yes, of course. It wasn't the soldiers who brought about the revolution but the people.

MR: It is extraordinary, even puzzling, that people had the courage to keep coming back again and again to demonstrate, even after the massacres had begun.

Helmuth Frauendorfer: I can only repeat that it was despair that drove them to it. A new winter was on its way with freezing temperatures. Their lives were in ruins. They had nothing more to lose.

MR: At a certain point, after Ceausescu was executed, the fighting died down and the Securitate stopped shooting people. Now in view of what you say about most of the Securitate people being back in their old positions, do you think the Salvation Front struck a deal with them?

Helmuth Frauendorfer: If only I knew the answer to that! I would be very glad indeed to know it. However, the fact is that at that time, in the last days of December, the Securitate people were really terror stricken. I have been told how they abandoned their homes for fear of what the people might do to them. At that moment, Iliescu had the opportunity to destroy the whole structure of the Securitate. But he didn't do it. My belief is that at the end of December or the beginning of January, the Salvation Front started to make a pact with the Securitate. Iliescu's pretext was that now he needed the Securitate since these were the people with the expertise.

MR: On a somewhat related issue, I have read two explanations for the decision summarily to execute the Ceausescus. The first is that this was a desperate measure to try to prevent a successful counter-revolution by the Securitate. The second is that the Salvation Front wanted to avoid the embarrassment of a full-scale trial which would have revealed the complicity of many of their own members in the crimes of the previous regime.

Helmuth Frauendorfer: Both of these explanations are true. If they had not executed Ceausescu, there was a possibility that the Securitate would have continued their attacks and succeeded in their attempted counter-revolution. That danger certainly existed. But it is also true that in a proper trial Ceausescu could have revealed many embarrassing facts about most of the members of the Front. I have now seen the whole video of Ceausescu's trial. It was conducted in a completely Stalinist way. It was a mockery of a trial, a complete fiasco.

But there is other evidence in support of the second of your two explanations. Charges have been brought against a few – a very few – members of the former government, and high-ranking members of the Securitate. But nothing has been done about bringing them to trial. Furthermore all the charges relate to the period 16-22 December 1989; none of the other activities of the Securitate officers are mentioned. Now those accused are saying – 'I was in bed – I was at home!' Again, it's a perverse fiasco.

This is symptomatic too of one of the most dangerous trends in Romania. So many people are preoccupied only with the future and are not prepared to examine their own history. They do not ask the question, why was Ceausescu able to establish such a harsh dictatorship in Romania? People are not willing to analyse their own past responsibility. They are afraid to do so because most of them participated in one way or another. It is a question in everybody's consciousness – what have I done during this whole period of dictatorship?

MR: The question of how Ceausescu was able to establish the dictatorship is a very large one, raising many issues. But do you want to say a little about it, and about why it was so much more extreme than dictatorships elsewhere in Eastern Europe?

Helmuth Frauendorfer: This has to do in part with Romanian history. Romania has never had a truly democratic system. There is no democratic tradition there such as exists for example in Czechoslovakia. One must not forget that Romania existed as three countries which obtained their independence in 1878. Prior to that they were under Ottoman domination, and only in 1918 were they united in Greater Romania. After World War II they again lost some territories to the Soviet Union and Bulgaria. All these periods of foreign domination made it almost impossible for the people to develop a sense of their own identity. For the same reason nationalism and chauvinism are very strong; they are symptoms of this lack of a sense of identity. It also explains why a strong leader finds it so easy to be acclaimed. For the same reason the development of democracy is proving very difficult at the present time. The Western part of the country has had a different historical experience – for instance Banat with its Austro-Hungarian past – and this explains the gap in the level of development between the Western and Eastern parts of the country.

But there are other factors underlying Ceausescu's success. He took over the leadership of the communist party in 1965 with a liberal image. Then in 1968, he refused to participate in the invasion of Czechoslovakia and this enormously consolidated his position. He played on anti-Soviet sentiment in the country and its corollary nationalism; these were the twin pillars of his power. Whenever there was a development that threatened his regime, such as for instance the miners' strike in 1977, he would warn of the danger of a Soviet intervention. So everyone was quiet in order not to provoke the Soviet Union.

The Western countries also helped to consolidate the dictatorship.

MR: He was given a knighthood, of course, by the Queen.

Helmuth Frauendorfer: Yes, for example! And West Germany and the United States also cultivated him. He visited the United States in 1973, the only East European leader to do so. I have here some very beautiful pictures of Ceausescu, his wife and his son in Hollywood in a Donald Duck car! Nixon was one of his admirers and paid an official visit to Bucharest. Western countries closed their eyes to the internal politics of Ceausescu – as they did with Saddam Hussein until last year. They supported him because they saw him as someone who was independent of Moscow. But that wasn't the case. He was very dependent on Moscow, in both a political and economic sense. His gestures of independence were of a trivial nature; they were political pirouettes. The Western countries acclaimed him, and said how good he was, because for instance, he was the only East European leader who dared to send his sports teams to the Los Angeles Olympics!

MR: However, the decision not to join in the invasion of Czechoslovakia in 1968 was of a different order.

Helmuth Frauendorfer: Oh yes, certainly. And that was the most important thing as far as establishing his credentials is concerned.

However, in 1971, Ceausescu went to China, and on his return started his own mini cultural revolution within Romania, bringing to an end a period of relative liberalisation initiated by his predecessor, Gheorghiu-Dej. Ceausescu never promoted liberalisation; he inherited a situation where some liberalisation was under way that he could not immediately halt. Instead he exploited it for the purposes of his foreign policy.

All the apparent moves towards liberalisation in the Ceausescu period were bogus. Let me give you an example. In 1974, Ceausescu declared that censorship in Romania was abolished. What this meant, however, was simply that the office of censor was done away with while censorship itself was intensified. The chief editor of a newspaper had to act as a censor. In addition Ceausescu created a so-called Committee for Socialist Education whose role was to vet everything that was published. So now there was a double censorship. Yet in the Western countries, Ceausescu was acclaimed for having abolished censorship!

MR: Was the external support he received very important to Ceausescu in retaining his position?

Helmuth Frauendorfer: Yes, it was crucial. It enabled him to show his own people how important he was, and how highly he was regarded, at an international level.

MR: How far was the dearth of contact between Romanians and the outside world a factor in allowing Ceausescu to establish his dictatorship? In the GDR, for instance, most people could tune in to West German television and get a wider view of the world, but I presume there was nothing comparable available to people in Romania. It was also very difficult, I understand, to have personal contacts with people in the West or in other countries of Eastern Europe.

Helmuth Frauendorfer: It was forbidden but it was not altogether impossible to have contacts with people from other countries. Still you are right, it was difficult and dangerous. Ceausescu passed a law which stated that if you had any contact with a foreigner you must inform your chief or the Securitate about it. Of course, the law was often ignored, and we did have our contacts. A few days ago, Iliescu reactivated this law so that every foreigner now has to present himself at the police station. As from 18 February 1991, Romanian Television broadcasts in German and Hungarian were also cut by half. The youth programme on television, and the programme in which representatives of different political parties were given the opportunity to put forward their views, have also been cut.

As for obtaining information, Romania did not have a source in their own language comparable to that available to the GDR in the form of West German television. But those who lived in border areas did not watch Romanian television but tuned into, for instance, Yugoslavian, Hungarian or Bulgarian stations. Moreover people who were particularly interested could listen to Radio Free Europe, the BBC, German Radio, all of whom broadcast news bulletins in the Romanian language. They listened to foreign broadcasts and were very happy when they could hear the truth. But this was all. They didn't think of acting together to make the truth widely known in their own country. Some people thought of doing so but not a sufficient number to create new political thinking. Most people were too preoccupied with the day to day problems of getting enough to eat to spend time thinking about political issues.

MR: Nevertheless when the rest of Eastern Europe was in upheaval in 1989, word about that obviously got around – and presumably there wasn't much about it on Romanian television or in the official press.

Helmuth Frauendorfer: There was no mention of the 1989 events in the GDR or the rest of Eastern Europe. Indeed there were many such 'white spots' in the official press and media coverage down the years. Lech Walesa was never mentioned; he didn't exist as far as the official media was concerned. The Soviet Union never invaded Afghanistan! Here sources like Radio Free Europe, and Yugoslavian television were helpful in filling in the blank spaces.

MR: But wasn't there a language problem in the case of people tuning into Hungarian or Yugoslavian television?

Helmuth Frauendorfer: Well, you have to remember the mixed population in Romania. Also, people would begin to learn the language. I have a friend, for example, living in Timisoara, who has been listening to Yugoslavian television for ten years and now speaks perfect Serbo-Croat! In any case many of the foreign films shown on Yugoslavian television were not dubbed, and quite a few people could understand films in English or German or French.

MR: On a different issue, one thing I found puzzling was that it was miners from the Jiu valley whom the National Salvation Front government were able to call upon to break up the student demonstrations in Bucharest in June 1990. Yet it had been miners from that same area who had most seriously challenged Ceausescu's regime in the 1977 strikes. How do you account for this?

Helmuth Frauendorfer: It was miners from the same area, but not the same miners! The miners who struck and demonstrated in 1977 didn't remain there; Ceausescu brought in others to replace them.

Iliescu was also very astute. In January 1990 he spent a few days in the Jiu Valley holding discussions with the miners. He knew they were an important political force, despite the fact that the pits are not economically viable and don't pay their way. He gave them a guarantee that they would be able to remain there and keep their jobs, that they would have better equipment and provisions, higher salaries and so on.

MR: Has there been any subsequent attempt by the opposition groups, or by Civic Alliance, to improve relations with the miners' leadership, and bring them round to a different point of view?

Helmuth Frauendorfer: Since the troubles of last June, contacts have been established with some of the miners involved, and a few of them have expressed their regret about what happened. It hasn't been easy, but I understand that efforts to improve relations are continuing.

MR: On the other side, do you think it was a mistake for the students and other opposition groups to have engaged in demonstrations involving mass civil disobedience – blocking the city centre in Bucharest and so on? The Salvation Front had, after all, been elected by a massive majority, and, despite some manipulation and malpractice, could claim to be a representative government. It could be argued that it was undemocratic to try to force them from office by action in the streets.

Helmuth Frauendorfer: From a moral point of view, I do not feel competent to answer this question because the events ended so tragically. But one must not forget the extent to which people were manipulated before going to the polls. One cannot say it was undemocratic for protesters to try to force the Salvation Front out of office since the preparations for the election were undemocratic. A month ago a former Securitate officer acknowledged that the Securitate – now renamed the Romanian Information Service – were given orders to carry out a campaign of intimidation and disinformation in relation to the elections. The operation was code-named 'Rose' – because the rose is the symbol of the Front.

However, speaking more generally, it isn't enough to take to the streets and shout 'Down with Iliescu!' as long as you have no alternative. That's the core of the problem in Romania, and again it reflects a lack of political culture. I agree with the sentiment – 'Down with Iliescu!' He is not doing what people expected. But what is the alternative?

MR: Did the Salvation Front invite the opposition to join with them in a coalition government – as for instance the government in Bulgaria did before it was finally forced from office in November 1990?

Helmuth Frauendorfer: Yes, they did so last December when the demonstrators again tried to force the government to resign. Iliescu made a kind of pact with Campeanu from the Liberal Party, and offered three ministerial posts to the opposition. But it was no more than a symbolic gesture; it had no political significance.

MR: Would it be your judgement that the Salvation Front has such a hold on the levers of power, and the means of influencing people, that they will be victorious again in the next general election scheduled for 1992?

Helmuth Frauendorfer: We have to see how the National Salvation Front itself develops. You mustn't forget that it is a heterogeneous grouping. It hasn't yet even formally constituted itself as a political party, though it will have to do so this year. It is quite incredible – but that is the situation! The Front is a combination of the old communist *nomenklatura* and the technocrats centered around Petre Roman.

MR: Would some of the technocrats within the Front welcome a move towards a more democratic form of government?

Helmuth Frauendorfer: Some of them, yes. There clearly are political struggles going on within the Front. But the struggles are not sufficiently visible; they are happening behind closed doors. As a result you are not even sure who is in charge in Romania. Is Iliescu controlling the Securitate, or are they controlling him? What is the role of the army? Inside the latter too there are factions. There are older officers who are generally reactionary, but there are also younger officers who want to democratise the army. Recently, however, CADA – the Committee of Action to Democratise the Army – has been banned.

MR: On a related issue, how open is Romania now, in terms of freedom of expression and association, and so forth?

Helmuth Frauendorfer: Freedom of association is a reality. However, bureaucratic methods are used to handicap political groups unpopular with the authorities. They cannot ban the organisations of civil society, but they can make life extremely difficult for them. For example, in Spring 1990 many members of the opposition faced death threats by phone and letter. One cannot say for sure that these emanated from the Salvation Front. But the latter had launched tough campaigns against the opposition, and the threats had all the hallmarks of past Securitate operations.

In the case of opposition newspapers, the authorities don't allocate them adequate supplies of newsprint. *Romania Libera*, for instance, has had problems getting sufficient newsprint. However, there are as many illegal as legal ways of obtaining it! For the most part the opposition newspapers manage to get the newsprint they need, but they have to pay extra for it, and it's a daily struggle. One cannot continue indefinitely in this way.

Corruption is widespread. Under Ceausescu, a whole structure of corruption was built up, and continues to exist today. Corruption, indeed, represents one of the major threats to the future of Romania.

Thomas Hackman

Interview recorded in Berlin, 22 July 1990. Thomas Hackman was born in Helsinki in 1963 and is a Council Member of War Resisters International. Since 1984 he has been a member of the board of the Union of Conscientious Objectors, the Finnish section of WRI, serving as chairperson for the Union in 1988–89.

MR: The events in Eastern Europe have clearly had a major impact on East-West relations. But Finland as a neutral country was outside the direct confrontation of the Cold War period and was thus in a different position from member countries of either NATO or the Warsaw Pact. How do you judge the influence of the 1989 events on a) the peace movement and b) the wider political scene in Finland?

Thomas Hackman: Let me begin with the wider political scene. One has, first of all, to understand the thrust of Finnish foreign policy since the end of World War II. 'Finlandisation' is the concept generally employed throughout Western Europe to characterise Finland's foreign policy and implies a habit of not criticising the Soviet Union. In fact this approach, as I see it, is the product of a more fundamental decision to separate morality from foreign and security policy, and to pursue the national interest in a completely pragmatic way. Thus Finland refrained from criticising not only the Soviet Union but also unsavoury aspects of Western and US policies. Instead, Finland tried to keep a kind of neutral quietness and in some instances to take positive initiatives – for instance over the Helsinki CSCE conference.

I would say that the government has not yet taken on board the fact that there are no longer two superpowers dominating the world scene – that we have moved into a multi-polar system at the international level. This means that the position of a small country like Finland is completely different from before. The gradual falling apart of the Soviet Union in particular has major implications for Finnish foreign and security policy because in the past these were based on an appraisal of Finland's geo-political position in a situation of bi-polar confrontation.

As regards the impact on the peace movement, I would say first that in most Western countries that part of the peace movement that was closely aligned to the pro-Moscow World Peace Council has fallen apart, or is in the process of doing do. This is less true, however, in the case of Finland. That part of the peace movement has been through a crisis, but it has responded by making significant policy changes. Thus the Peace Committee has become more radical than before – radical in the sense of moving closer to pacifism.

There seems to be a greater divergence of views between the generations within the peace movement than between the organisations as such. However, I'm not sure how much this has to do with developments in Eastern Europe. The differences chiefly relate to working methods; on questions of policy there is a broader consensus.

One very positive result of the East European events is that there is a tendency for young people to become more radical, more willing to do quite daring actions, and actions which may last several days. This spring there was an occupation of the university administrative building which took three days and had a lot of active support from the students. We also had a civilian service strike which went on for one month. There are examples too of individual actions. Thus four total objectors (to conscription) went on hunger strike as the same time as the civilian service strike, and three of them continued their fast for thirty-nine days before being released.

It seems that many young people have come to appreciate the power of non-violent action as a result of the successful actions in Eastern Europe. Another important consequence is that whereas traditionally radical politics have been associated in people's minds exclusively with left or Green parties, the events of 1989 in Eastern

Europe have provided a new context for the idea. People realise that they can be radical without aligning themselves with traditional left or traditional Green movements. This has opened gates for people who have not been politically active before but have a desire to see certain changes.

MR: Now that the blocs are dissolving, has there been any rethinking at the political level of Finland's traditional policy of armed neutrality?

Thomas Hackman: The official policy remains unchanged, but military expenditure is rising. There are plans to buy new war planes and other weapons. In fact in percentage terms Finland's military expenditure is expanding more rapidly than that of any other European country. But the overall military budget is still comparatively low – 1.5 per cent of GNP – though could rise to 2 per cent within the next decade.

MR: Is this increased military expenditure due to the sense of an external threat, or to the desire for prestige – or how is it to be explained?

Thomas Hackman: You have to understand that whereas in Western Europe the military build-up has been closely tied to enemy images, this has not been the case in Finland. Of course there were always people who had some kind of enemy images, but relatively few people actually regarded either the Soviet Union or the United States as enemies. The situation in which they foresaw Finland's army playing a role was if a conflict broke out between the two superpowers. In the changed situation people can build up new scenarios – for instance some kind of crisis in the Baltic region, or an ecological catastrophe in the Leningrad region which could cause a large influx of refugees to Finland. What exactly the army would be expected to do in this last situation is not clear. To shoot down the refugees at the border, perhaps! However, the main point is that because our military policy has not been tied to enemy images, the withering away of the enemy image in other parts of Europe hasn't undermined it in the way it should have done.

Nevertheless there is a sense in which traditional military thinking is under threat. There are signs that the previous consensus support for Finland's military policy is breaking down. The socialists and the Greens have stepped up their demands for measures of disarmament. There are also signs of new thinking within the Social Democrats where some people are arguing that maybe Finland should disarm as other countries in Europe are doing.[1]

MR: In this situation where future security policy is being considered, is the idea of social defence an element in the debate?

Thomas Hackman: No, not to a significant extent. Occasionally the idea surfaces in some discussions, but since the 1970s there has been very little discussion of social defence as a national policy. Many movements, of course, especially the ecological movements, adopt non-violent methods in their struggle, but that's a rather different matter. The concept of social defence is mainly one that has been used by the peace movement when challenged to say what it proposes the country should do in certain situations. Part of the difficulty in a way is that most people in Finland feel reasonably secure from outside attack and don't see the need to consider new approaches to security.

MR: You mentioned in our informal discussion before the interview the impact of developments in the Soviet Baltic republics. Could you say something on this?

Thomas Hackman: Historically, Finland has had close ties with the Baltic Republics, and especially with Estonia where the language is very similar to Finnish. Moreover, the Estonians can watch Finnish television, and Finnish people Estonian television. There is also the fact that the Baltic states became independent from Russia at the same time as Finland. They did not, however, have such a strong independence movement, nor did they enjoy the same degree of autonomy as Finland had done prior to full independence. Also many Finns have something of a bad conscience about the Baltic States because Finland kept quiet about their situation after World War II.

Yet another bond is the fact that Estonia is using similar methods in its independence struggle to those used by Finland at the beginning of this century. You can understand this because Estonia now is in an analogous situation politically to Finland at the turn

---

[1] In a letter written in January 1991, Thomas Hackman adds: The social democrats now seem to have reached a consensus on military policy with the centre and the conservatives. This probably means they will support an expansion of the military budget.

of the century; it was taken over illegally but enjoys some degree of autonomy, and has its own governmental structures. It also has an official legal status which is better than the actual situation. For all these reasons the Estonians are using the same kind of arguments that the Finnish independence movement used.

The independence movements in both countries have been non-violent, though both lacked a non-violent ideology and adopted non-violent methods for pragmatic reasons. Perhaps in Estonia and the other Baltic republics, the commitment to non-violent action has somewhat deeper ideological roots than was the case in Finland; still it is quite obvious talking to people in Estonia that the main reason they are non-violent is that they see it as the only way forward for them.

There does not seem, however, to be the same resurgence of militarism in Estonia that occurred in Finland after it gained its independence. Of course Finland experienced a civil war at that time, so the situation was very different. The interesting question, given the strength of non-violent resistance movements in the Baltic republics, is how the state in each country will react to them when independence is achieved. In Finland, once it became clear that independence was coming, the politicians tried to dampen down the non-violent campaigns because they began to see them as a potential threat – raising the prospect of many people objecting to army service and so on. We will have to wait and see if there is a similar trend in the Baltic republics.

MR: Has there been much contact between the independence movement in Estonia and the peace and non-violent action movements in Finland?

Thomas Hackman: There were quite a lot of contacts. They began some while back, but became increasingly important over the last two years. However, the Estonian movements have a different political basis from the peace movements of Western Europe. For instance, although many conscientious objectors are pacifists, they are not organised on the basis of pacifism but on the basis of resistance to the Soviet army as an occupying force. The contacts have therefore mainly come about as a result of particular projects, such as the 1990 END Convention in Helsinki and Tallinn, where there is a common interest. The Churches too have a lot of contacts, as have the political parties. It's amazing to see that almost all political parties – from Right to Left – were very satisfied with the policy of the People's Front in Estonia. They all saw their own objectives reflected in these movements. Something of major significance was happening in Estonia and each political party wanted to claim that the movement represented all the things it had always stood for.

MR: Is there a feeling that the Baltic republics are part of the Scandinavian group of countries and that after independence there might be close trading, defence and other links between them and other Nordic countries?

Thomas Hackman: The situation is different in relation to the three Baltic republics. Estonia and Latvia are definitely seen as forming part of the Nordic region. The attitude to Lithuania is different. It is seen as being more like Poland – not least in being rather chaotic! Finnish people also tend to think that the Lithuanians have not been as clever as the Estonians in their independence struggle. Despite this, there is talk of including all three countries in the system of Nordic co-operation.

MR: What do most Finns, in your view, perceive as the main external threats they have to guard against?

Thomas Hackman: People are mainly worried about the ecological threat, especially as Finland has a very long border with the Soviet Union and there are large, completely destroyed, areas bordering on Finland, in the Kola peninsula. But though this worries people, they don't know what to do about it. The army has no relevance to the threat, and I am highly sceptical about the propositions being put forward that it should have a role in dealing with the problem. I don't think you can tackle environmental problems by forcing people to go somewhere and clean up the mess. Action has to be taken before that point, and in this regard it is the economic structures which are crucial.

MR: Perhaps we can come back finally to the priorities of the peace movements in Finland. I gather from what you say that social defence is not a major concern?

Thomas Hackman: No. It might become so, but at the moment it is not. The goal of the peace movement is rather to break down the military structures and demand a change of security policy towards the idea of common security. Its philosophy is that the dangers people face come not from an external armed enemy, but from militarisation, threats to the environment, and threats to social and cultural life. The peace movement sees as its special duty the breaking down of military structures and in that way reducing the degree of threat in the world.

Postscript, January 1991. Thomas Hackman writes:

I would probably answer some of the questions a bit differently now that we have seen what has happened in the Gulf and the Baltic States. Concerning the Baltic States, the Finnish government has condemned the violence of the Soviet forces. But at the same time they emphasise that the Baltic States are a matter of internal Soviet politics, and by implication they criticise the Lithuanians in particular for being too provocative. The military is using the present crisis to promote its own demands for more armaments, even though it is hard to see the relation between the present crisis and replacing the existing sixty attack aircraft with new ones in the late 1990s.

The events have of course activated the peace movement which is critical of the Finnish government for taking a cynical approach towards the problems of the Baltic States, while – as a member last year of the UN Security Council – supporting military action in the Gulf. There have been many demonstrations both against the war in the Gulf and against the actions of Soviet forces in the Baltic States – sometimes with both issues being taken up in the same demonstration. The various peace organisations are working well together on these issues.

I have been mainly focusing on the Baltic States – especially Estonia – and trying to promote the following:

CO Rights. There are 8,000 – 10,000 conscientious objectors in Estonia alone and at least twenty of them have asked for political asylum in Finland. The Union of COs has had contacts with the Estonian COs, publicised their situation and counselled some of those who came over to Finland.

Social Defence in the Baltic states. Some specialists in this field will be going into the Baltic States mainly to document the social defence taking place there. I have been working with Jörgen Johansen and Steve Huxley – an American social defence researcher living in Finland – on this matter. Huxley has recently visited Estonia and is preparing a pamphlet on social defence especially for the Estonians, relating it to their own history and situation. The plan is to translate the pamphlet into Estonian and to send copies of it there this coming spring. Other classic texts on non-violence may be translated and shipped into the country. There are also plans for fifty Finnish and Swedish peace activists to go over to the Baltic States.

The situation in Estonia is somewhat different to that in Latvia. Estonia has a Home Security Force – an unarmed Civil Guard – but there are also some small groups who are collecting weapons, mainly hunting rifles. There are also rumours that weapons are being bought in Finland, whether for the Estonian mafia or for a guerrilla resistance is not clear. In Latvia, however, the authorities are relying less on the civil guard, but instead, in Riga especially, are encouraging the people to play a greater role and to take to the streets. This reflects a different approach also to the crisis by the authorities. In Latvia they are putting greater emphasis on negotiations with Moscow, and they also better placed to negotiate.

One important factor is that the relations between the ethnic Russians and Balts is worse in Estonia than Latvia. In Estonia, the Russians are mainly either working class people, employed predominantly in military industry, or actually members of the military. But in Riga there exists a long-standing Russian cultural tradition. Many of the Russians living in the city are highly educated, and there has been much more interaction between them and the local population. Nevertheless even in Estonia, the proportion of conscientious objectors among the Russian population is quite high – in the region of 30 per cent. So even in Estonia the divisions are not entirely clear-cut.

Marco Hren

Interviewed on 22 July 1990 in Berlin. Marco Hren is from Slovenia, Yugoslavia. Born in 1959, he is now a peace researcher in the Faculty of Philosophy, University of Ljubljana. The subject of his research is *Non-violence in the European Heritage from 15th-19th Century*. He is the founder of the Peace Institute of Ljubljana.

MR: What, in your judgement, were the key factors leading to the political shifts in your country?

Marco Hren: Yugoslavia is not one country but several. We have to recognise therefore that as far as the process of transformation is concerned, each region has its own dynamics. In general, however, the process throughout Yugoslavia had its roots in the late 1970s.

First, after the twin-track decision of NATO, Yugoslavia no longer played the same role strategically as before. Following Tito's break with Stalin in 1948, it had assumed the role of a non-aligned buffer state and was supported as such by the West not only morally but financially. But after the twin-track decision, the enormous credits Yugoslavia had been receiving dried up and its economic position rapidly worsened. This brought social unrest, especially in the country's southern republics.

Second, the death of Tito in 1980 ended the dominance by one man of the military, the state and ideology – that Holy Trinity of Yugoslavia's post-war political life. His death represented a symbolic and substantial break with the past. After him, power was no longer centralised in one strong national and international figure. There was greater possibility for diversity.

To simplify somewhat, then, there were two dynamics at work.

One was rooted in the worsening economic situation, the other in the enlarged space for democratisation after the monopoly of centralised power had been weakened. In the west and north, where the economic crisis was less severe, the pressure for democratisation played a greater role. In the southeast poverty was the decisive factor and shaped the new politics. There poverty, as well as certain cultural factors, made for a new political homogenisation and the growth of a strongly nationalistic sentiment which was exploited by those in power, particularly in Serbia. People looking for a scapegoat for their situation were encouraged to find it on the one hand in the indigenous Albanian population, on the other in the demand for pluralism and democratisation - strongest in Slovenia – which threatened the unity of Tito's Yugoslavia.

In Slovenia when the space opened up, independent activity flourished. There were social movements, cultural, sub-cultural, and alternative cultural groups. The first large sub-cultural movement arose among young people and was associated with punk and rock music. This was immediately attacked by the state and accused of fascist leanings. Many independent writers and intellectuals came to the defence of the movement for human rights reasons, thereby creating an atmosphere of solidarity which extended also to some political bodies, especially official youth organisations in Slovenia. This was the beginning of the independent social struggle for people belonging to minorities to self-organise.

After that the development was very rapid. Social movements had a stronger and stronger voice. There were more and more independent papers and writings in 1983 and 1984, and the peace movement raised the issue of the militarisation of society, and the dominance of military ideology in the education system and public life. The Federal state hit back very strongly, accusing the movements of being counter-revolutionary. But the greater the efforts to suppress the movements, the more support they received.

It was at this point that the divergence between Yugoslavia and the Republic of Slovenia opened up. Some politicians in Slovenia took the side of public opinion in favour of democratisation; others continued to support the stance of the Federal government because it was they who provided the jobs. Politicians in Slovenia found themselves between hammer and anvil. In Belgrade they were attacked for allowing counter-revolutionary criticism and activity. In Slovenia they were accused of making compromises and of not putting a clear position to the Federal government. By 1986-87 some politicians were changing their position, some remained hard-liners.

In July 1988, the confrontation culminated in a trial before a closed military court of writers who had published articles critical of the military, mainly in the youth magazine *Mladina* which I helped to edit and to which the peace movement contributed. The magazine took a strong line against the army, the arms trade, the war in Ethiopia, and so forth. At the centre of the trial was a top-secret military document; this was found in our office where a couple of activists were employed. One of them, incidentally, Janez Jansa, is now Slovenia's Minister of Defence, the other is Minister of the Interior!

Janez Jansa was one of four people arrested. I escaped arrest because I was in the United States at the time, but part of the prosecution case was an accusation that I was taking this document abroad. We also discovered afterwards that the Intelligence Service tried to prevent my return to the country by cancelling my flight. It seems that the intention was to present the case as one of espionage.

This military document is very significant. It predicted social unrest – indeed the kind of unrest that later occurred throughout Eastern Europe. They knew already in February 1988 that something like this would happen. The document predicted there would be demands by the people for pluralism and democracy in Slovenia and they regarded these demands as counter-revolutionary.

The paper set out the possibility of military intervention in civil affairs to meet this threat. It is still a secret document – so now I am revealing military secrets! It spoke of how the military should secure their objectives, how they should be ready to fight against peaceful demonstrations and so forth. We tried to publish not the military document itself but information about it. We knew too that the military were planning to arrest people active in the alternative scene, and attempted to publish warnings about these plans. But that issue of *Mladina* was confiscated, and a couple of days later four people – well known writers and editors – were arrested and imprisoned. They were held in solitary confinement without access to lawyers or any legal help.

Their imprisonment led to the mobilisation of all levels of society in May-June-July 1988. A Committee for the Protection of Human Rights was founded in connection with the case which had 100,000 members, and was backed by trade unions, cultural organisations, and political groups. This put great pressure on the Slovenian government to change its position. It was forced to decide whether it would align itself with the Slovenian struggle or with the Federal government. There was no in-between position.

The communist party split on the issue. Towards the end of 1988, the hard-liners were kicked out of power, and the more liberal wing of the party took over. Events then moved rapidly. The basic ideas for political reform over the next two years were formulated: sovereignty for Slovenia because its rights were being violated; reform of the military and the constitution to allow for democracy; the free organisation of political parties. By 1989 a dozen or more parties were formed all with very similar programmes. This year, 1990, we had our elections.

The struggle in 1988 was purely non-violent – not a single drop of blood was shed, there was not a single baton charge by the police, not a single window broken, though we had tens of thousands of people on the streets. The Committee for the Protection of Human Rights consciously led the struggle in a non-violent way. There was a planning committee run collectively by twenty-four people consisting of prominent people from all sections of society, amongst them also some people from the peace movement like myself, Tomaz Mastnak and some others. The peace movement organised workshops on non-violence throughout the period. Women had their non-violent actions, and there were dozens of small actions which were purely non-violent such as offering flowers to soldiers – 'bombing with flowers' we called it.

We held negotiations also seeing these as an important part of our non-violent struggle – negotiations with politicians, with the army, with the government, with the President of the Republic. It was a cautiously non-violent struggle supported by international public opinion. One of the main activities of the committee was keeping international public opinion informed. Thus we made several tours around Europe to inform people of the dangers confronting Yugoslavia. Non-violence was the conscious basis for our whole activity.

It is important to stress here that the commitment to non-violence was rooted in five or six years activity by the peace movement which was very strong – I would say the strongest movement in Slovenia, but limited to Slovenia. It engaged in civil disobedience, and took up issues such as conscientious objection, education for peace, anti-militarism.

As to whether the non-violence was essentially pragmatic or 'principled' – that is a difficult distinction to draw in relation to the Slovenian struggle. It was pragmatic in the sense that there was in fact no other way in the conditions we faced. This point applies to other socialist countries which underwent a political transformation. But it is important to take into account the Central European tradition of what we could call 'oppositional intellectualism' exemplified by Charter 77 in Czechoslovakia, the Peace Group for Dialogue in Hungary, the Praxis group in Yugoslavia. The struggle in the 1970s and 1980s was conducted chiefly at the intellectual level, using argument and analysis rather than weapons. Students, writers, intellectuals – these constituted the leading force; it was not proletarian or rural based. In Romania, of course, the situation was very different.

In Slovenia there was another factor. The wave of peace movement energy from Western Europe had an important impact on Slovenia. Other parts of Yugoslavia were less affected but Slovenia was definitely influenced by the social movement against nuclear weapons in the West. There was good contact and co-operation from the beginning with the European Nuclear Disarmament campaign, indeed the first actions of the group I was working with were in support of Dutch demonstrations against missiles. In Brussels in 1983-84 I assisted in the organisation of the demonstrations against Florene. So we had good links with the Western movement and publicised the anti-missile campaign. The Committee for Human Rights recruited largely from social movements including peace movements, and was influenced by peace movement ideas.

MR: Why do you think events took such a different course in Romania?

Marco Hren: One of the significant differences between Romania and Bulgaria on the one hand and the rest of Eastern Europe on the other is that they were not in touch with the European movement. For one thing, the Western media did not reach either Romania or Bulgaria and it is clear that the media was an important factor elsewhere – in Poland, Czechoslovakia, East Germany, the Baltic States. This lack of information flow was one factor. Another is the fact that Romania is still largely rural, not as urbanised as other countries in the region. Finally the Romanian dictatorship was a totalitarian one; as a result almost no information could get through. Civil society in Romania was by far the weakest anywhere in the area. There was at least some room for manoeuvre in Hungary, for instance for the Dialogue group, some room in Czechoslovakia where lots of information passed in and out; similarly in Poland, East Germany and, of course, Slovenia. Yugoslavia as a whole was relatively free, and there was a lot of tourism which increased the contact with the outside world.

The growth of civil society was a crucial factor in the transformation of Eastern Europe; in Slovenia I would say it was the most important factor in the struggle both at a theoretical and practical level. There was a lot of discussion in Slovenia about civil society. One of its leading theoretical exponents in Europe, Tomaz Mastnak, was living in Slovenia and a leading activist. It became an important topic in discussions and influenced the strategy and development of the opposition movement.

MR: Do you see the grassroots movements continuing to play a central role following the demise of the old order?

Marco Hren: Obviously the situation has greatly changed, in Slovenia as elsewhere in Eastern Europe. Nevertheless civil society, and people power continue to be important, certainly for Slovenia; it must be left to others to talk about their own countries. But we in Slovenia see people power and the strengthening of civil society as of crucial importance.

The essential point is that the government cannot solve the problems facing the country. They are not experienced, and they lack the power to make the necessary changes. The new government is very weak. The structure of the government is not a natural one; it is an artificial democratic structure because it was put together in haste, in panic. You have to take into account the fact that some dozen or more parties arose in less than half a year. People had to make up their minds on an *ad hoc* basis in a couple of days and thus there was insufficient time to identify diversities of interests and policies. In this sense, the democratic system has yet to settle down.

Civil society is the bedrock on which a democratic system can be built. What will happen with parties and governments is unpredictable; it is civil society which provides the guarantee of participation and at the same time of security.

MR: Some former opposition activists from East-Central Europe I have spoken to seem somewhat demoralised and say the wind has been taken out of the sails of their movement. Support for the kind of networks they belong to has declined – in Poland, for instance, since the formation of a Solidarity-led government. Is it different in Slovenia? Is there still a dynamic behind the movements you have been associated with?

Marco Hren: Our situation is hardly comparable with that of Poland. We in the peace movement in Slovenia insisted from the start on maintaining a dialogue with the political parties. Our aim was to ensure support not only from the population for our projects and ideas but also from political parties. We consistently worked with the government and with political parties to introduce our ideas into political programmes and into the orientation of the government. We have been developing a global strategy for peace politics in which people power would play a central role.

It is true that people in Slovenia are somewhat disoriented because of the new polarisation that has developed and because of the difficulties that have arisen at the parliamentary level. Most of the discussions are blocked by this polarisation. The key issues in the debate are Slovenian sovereignty, and relations with the Federation. The democratic opposition won the elections and formed the government; but there are still the liberal, communist and socialist parties. These are treated as a red bloc but still have quite a lot of support.

But I would agree that the ecological movement has rather lost its identity. It has been absorbed into the Green Party which is a member of the ruling coalition. In general, it is too soon to give a final answer to your question. But for the time being at least the peace movement has managed to maintain its rhythm and enthusiasm.

Actually it is an advantage for civil society if conditions are bad. For example, in our case one of the results of the sovereignty euphoria is that in the field of culture the notion of a mainstream national culture is being strongly promoted. The result is that alternative and minority cultures are undermined. This has sounded the alarm for all kinds of minority groups and cultures to mobilise and join the network. In this respect I would say we are experiencing a strengthening of social activity at the grassroots.

The parliamentary discussions in Slovenia now are ridiculous. People watch them on television and laugh because some of the discussions are so stupid. The debates are shown live on television and the television crews and directors are still part of the old regime and like to underline the stupidities of the new government; they like to show how clumsy and inexperienced they are. For instance the Minister of Law and Justice angrily asserted in Parliament he would not listen to the Serbian language. That's really not something a Minister of Justice should do at the end of the twentieth century. He should at least be polite and say that he would like to have interpretation. It's a bizarre situation and people have distanced themselves from this parliamentary democracy; they see that it is all spectacle.[1]

MR: To return to the dynamics of civil resistance, what in your view moved people to overcome their fear of repression and openly oppose the old system? What were the factors that led to the extraordinary mobilisation throughout Eastern Europe?

Marco Hren: In Slovenia, it was a gradual process. With the opening up of the media in the early 1980s, people could express their ideas more freely. Of course there were some people who were particularly brave, others who held back. But when the four people I mentioned earlier were imprisoned there was an explosion of popular protest. Everyone was on their side.

One important factor in Slovenia is that the police forces were never violent. People were not afraid of police violence. They were perhaps afraid of a military coup, but nobody could imagine how this would work in practice. For myself, I was afraid that the Yugoslav military leadership might take crazy, irrational decisions. But I knew that if there was a coup, this would mean the end of Yugoslavia in two or three days. Because of its mixed composition, the army would dissolve if it intervened in any of the republics. It would be the end of the Federation, but a very bloody end.

However, there was no realistic fear of street repression. It was not like in Central America, not like in China, not indeed like Czechoslovakia where people were beaten. In Slovenia such attacks on the population never occurred during the struggle. But this is not the case at all in Kosovo, in Serbia, in Bosnia or in Macedonia. There people required 'civilian courage' to speak out or to go on the streets; even journalists have been beaten up in those areas.

Technology was extremely important in the development of the

---

[1] Marco Hren in a discussion with Michael Randle in December 1990 said that in the period since this interview was recorded the media in Slovenia had aligned itself more and more closely with the new government.

opposition in Slovenia. We had an independent radio station, Radio Student, one of the lasting achievements of the 1968 movement. It played a most important role. Other important means of communication and developing ideas were the weekly youth newspaper *Mladima*, and *Casopis a Kritiko Znanospi* (*Paper for a Critical Science*). A third important element was *Microada*, an independent publishing house and hi-tech business venture, where I worked. It was started by some friends of mine in 1985 to provide technology for oppositional activities. It was a self-managed company with a desk-top publishing department. It provided rooms for meetings, and telephone lines, modems, telefax machines and so forth for use by the movement. And because it was also a successful business venture it was able to provide funds for the activities. Slovenia is a very rich country, comparable to Western Europe; this made it much easier to organise there and to provide such facilities.

Cultural activities, including rock concerts for human rights, were an integral part of the opposition movement. During the two months that the four people were being held in solitary confinement, there were continual cultural activities. For instance at the Pen Club there was some event or other every day, whether a poetry reading, drama, or concert dedicated to these people in prison. Nor should we forget religious activity. For the first time the Catholic Church appeared as a political factor. There were prayers all over the country for the people in prison and for the peaceful solution of the conflict.

In 1988 people were not at all aware of where their activities might lead – i.e. to the main actors in the struggle becoming members of the government in 1990. Events in other East European countries were influential. The energy and enthusiasm for change spread from one country to another; there was a will for change. In addition as the momentum for change gathered pace, and began to show results, it became a must for Western Europe to accept the individualisation of certain states in the Eastern bloc, and a must that the Berlin Wall should fall. Thus the situation in Europe, East and West, helped but did not dictate the course of events. In each country there was a local struggle and it is important to be aware of this.

Clearly in many countries of Eastern Europe – though not so much in Yugoslavia – the changes in direction in Moscow were another important factor. Gorbachev was unwilling to send in Soviet troops to suppress the movements for change. In that respect he played a significant role. Nevertheless Gorbachev did not design the changes;

people did. There were decades of struggle before he came to power – in Hungary, in Poland, in Czechoslovakia, in Slovenia.

MR: How far was there any notion among people that the method they were using to overthrow the old regime could form the basis for the defence of society in the future?

Marco Hren: I would not say that the majority of people were even thinking that they could take power and form a new government – though perhaps a few people did. So the issue of social defence for a new democratic country did not arise at that point. Speaking for myself, however, I did follow discussions on social defence going on in other parts of Europe, so I was thinking in those terms and was in touch for instance with people in the campaign in Switzerland to abolish the army. But I don't think most people gave much thought to the security issue.

Personally I was very happy to participate in what I would say was a Gandhian struggle. I am extremely grateful for the opportunity this struggle provided – to see for instance 50,000 people, each one with a flower in his or her hand, in front of the military barracks demonstrating in silence. This was an experience of silent power which one never forgets. It represents a credit in hand for developing any kind of alternative security concept. We can use the experience now as an argument for alternative defence, even if at the time people were not thinking in those terms.

Civil resistance, and social defence, clearly do have a role in the situation we now face. We are working on this idea at the state level, not just at the level of civil society. There were several instances of civil resistance during the emancipation of Slovenia. For instance in September 1989, Serbia initiated an economic blockade. 1,000,000 Serbs also declared that they would come to convince Slovenes of the truth of their side in the dispute. In response, civil resistance was organised in Slovenia. It was an instance of civil society in one country against civil society in another, of social defence against social attack. Here again there was self-organisation by civil society, supported by the police, by local authorities and by the Republic's authorities and politicians. So a new concept of security was exercised on a social level and on a political level. Politicians from Slovenia – at that time communist politicians – negotiated with Serbia and with the Federation while civil society organised itself. These were parallel moves which achieved a brilliant result. The Serbians did not come.

MR: In what form were they threatening to come? Armed, for instance, or unarmed? How was it going to be done?

Marco Hren: They said they would come armed if necessary. But it was still civil society that would be involved; people would come as volunteers in trains, in taxis, in whatever transport they could muster. The Serbian government remained completely silent – which is to say that they were supporting the move. It was a serious matter, but an important and significant experience for the prospect of developing social defence.

Slovenia is now considering new security concepts. I have inside knowledge of this because I am a member of the Council of the Presidency of Slovenia for defence affairs. There are fourteen people involved including seven generals, and a couple of ministers. The Council have put forward an option for a demilitarised Slovenia, with social defence forming part of new security concept. It has been decided to present this option – in which Slovenia would not have an army – to Parliament. It is one of a number of options that Parliament will consider. And in presenting this proposal, we drew upon the recent experiences of civil resistance. We also pointed out that we have a very good police force in Slovenia which I would say is a non-violent force, well-educated and civilised.

Another helpful factor is that the official Yugoslav defence system has rested on three pillars, the standing army, the Territorial Army and Civil Defence. The permanent, standing army comprises 25,000 troops under the command of the Federal Yugoslav government and is maintained by a system of conscription. Territorial Defence relies essentially on preparations for the rapid mobilisation of previously trained units and is under the control of the individual republics. Civil Defence also comes under the authority of the individual republics and is designed to deal with natural disasters and measures for civilian protection. It includes the fire brigade and other emergency services and is already well organised with its own infrastructure and doctrine.

The peace movement strategy is to use existing frameworks like Civil Defence which are relevant to building an alternative security strategy, and to draw upon the experience of civilian resistance to show how the concept could be developed. Social defence in the context of an alternative approach to security is being discussed at presidential and government level in Slovenia and we are founding a peace institute which will research this approach. The Slovenian

Parliament too has established a commission on peace politics. These are all achievements of the past few years.

We were cautiously working in this direction before the elections, before even the constitution of political parties. When the first party was constituted in Slovenia in November 1989, we in the peace movement presented them with the concept of Slovenia without an army combined with social defence and a global approach to security. The new party accepted this as its strategy. It calls itself a liberal party but is different from liberal parties elsewhere. It now occupies a position in the centre of Slovenian politics, and is not a member of the ruling coalition. The Greens too have partially accepted it.[2]

MR: Is social defence relevant to ethnic violence such as one is seeing in Azerbaijan and Armenia, or for instance in the clashes between Serbs and Albanians in Kosovo?

Marco Hren: The question is partially answered in the example I gave of the threat by 1,000,000 Serbs to invade Slovenia. It is a very relevant question, however, for Slovenia, because if you ask people why we need defence, they would say – 'to defend ourselves against the southern Yugoslav nations'. Some people even say Slovenia should join NATO and that this is the only sound security approach for Slovenia. Our strategy in the peace movement is peace politics as an alternative way of solving this problem with Serbia – active peace politics, including negotiations, dialogue, and establishing good links. We try to strengthen civil society links with progressive groups in Serbia. Social defence must be linked to the internationalisation of civil society and we want to use the framework of the Helsinki Citizens Assembly for this as well as Green networks and others concerned with various specific issues such as human rights and peace.

We see the Helsinki Citizens Assembly as a framework for organising ourselves on an international basis. In essence it is a communication project. Strengthening communication – both at state and civil society level – between areas which are in conflict is the ABC of a new security approach. There has to be the will

---

[2]At their October 1990 Congress the Greens adopted the policy of Slovenia Without an Army. They form part of the ruling coalition government and their former president, Dusan Plut, is Slovenia's Vice-President.

to negotiate at the political level, with the assistance if necessary of international mediators, and there have to be sparks of light, of connections, between people of goodwill at the civil society level. We are working intensively on both concepts. We are trying to build on experiences and theory.

The Helsinki Citizens Assembly we see as one of the important frameworks – provided of course that it works! It is a project which has some strength if for no other reason than that it has support of people in so many countries.

MR: Is there a clear common ground between all the people and networks participating in the Assembly?

Marco Hren: The Helsinki Citizens Assembly project is still at the level of an idea and not yet a practical project. Thus far it is nothing but a small bunch of people with an idea. But it is a worthy idea which arouses enthusiasm and hopefully will achieve something. The vision I have is that it will use existing networks, opening up doors between them. When I was in Canada last March they told me that the HCA had already linked groups which had not been in contact before. This is the function it can perform both within and between countries. But it will only have a future if it builds on existing networks, existing potential.

The difference as I see it between the HCA and the European Nuclear Disarmament, is that the HCA should be a continuous process. Modern means of communication should enable us to do continuous work in this way in commissions.

MR: You have spoken of the threat which many people in Slovenia see as emanating from Serbia and the other southern republics. What other threats do you think people feel the need to guard against?

Marco Hren: They want to guard against threats to Slovenian national culture and independence. This matter needs to be put into perspective, and is chiefly a problem of psychology. Slovenia's situation is relatively good. The economy is quite strong and there is no serious problem of repression. The danger indeed is that Slovenians may become egotistical and behave in a narrow-minded way, closing gates to the south rather than opening them. Democratisation, in short, could bring selfishness.

The disputes with our neighbouring states can be solved with goodwill and wise peace politics. We are trying to develop this active approach towards politics and not to ignore the problems with our neighbours or actually create new divisions. But if the selfish approach to nationalism wins out, there could be serious problems. There are for instance those who call for the formation of a Slovenian national army and for the country to become a member of NATO. Such a move would be highly dangerous.

MR: It seems that the concept of social defence is being taken seriously in political and governmental circles in Slovenia. How far do you think this is true of other countries in East-Central Europe?

Marco Hren: I prefer to speak about an alternative security concept rather than social defence – but it's risky for me to say very much about other countries. I think the option is a relatively realistic one for Slovenia. But as far as I am aware, no other East European country is seriously working on such an alternative concept of security. The only hint of such an approach comes from Czechoslovakia, but even there no-one has been working seriously on the concept. In Slovenia, we devised, as I told you, a global strategy which included the setting up of a Parliamentary Commission. Slovenia without an army is now an option, though only one option amongst several. It will be elaborated and we will see what happens. As a protagonist of this option, I am quite optimistic about the prospects for its success.

MR: If in the main the new governments show no great interest in developing social defence, might the movements and individuals whose civil resistance helped to overthrow the old regimes develop and organise it from below?

Marco Hren: In our case the government is interested in the concept; some ministers might not be convinced and would argue that we need a Slovenian army, but they would at least be interested. I have spoken to the Minister of Finance, the Prime Minister, the Foreign Minister, the Interior Minister – and they would all support the elaboration of this idea, and support funding for the work involved. We have to use such official channels; that's my main strategy. I am personally not very happy to be running after these people who are busy with other things and who don't take the time and effort to listen, but still I think it is necessary and worthwhile. We have to try and work with these people who in fact are getting lost in governing the state – it's a new experience for them and not an easy task for these mainly young people. It is also psychologically very demanding for them. My strategy is to use these personal friendships and links and try to stimulate optimism among them that this kind of concept is realistic.

We have to be aware of the problems that the new governments face. I went to see the Finance Minister in Slovenia on Friday, just a few days ago, and spoke to him in his office about government finance now for a peace institute to study conversion and non-violent conflict resolution. He replied that there was a very bad situation in the country and that there was no money available. At the same time he said he very much supported the idea of setting up an institute and promised to include provision for it in next year's budget.

Then the telephone rang. It was the director of one of the biggest companies in Ljubljana to say that all the workers – thousands of workers – had had no salaries for two weeks and had called a strike. He said if they did not get their salaries by the next day he could not guarantee that the peace could be kept. But the Finance Minister replied that he had no money to give them, and to try another department. I experienced then the daily problems they face. I came there to ask for one hundred thousand dollars for an institute whilst he has dozens of factories every day on strike because the workers have not received their salaries.

I don't want to appear to be an apologist for the politicians, but at the same time it is important to understand the problems government ministers face and not to dismiss them as useless bastards unwilling to invest in peace politics simply because the money is not forthcoming straight away. I am sure that within six months I will get the money for the institute. Patience on our part is also necessary; that too is part of a non-violent strategy.

MR: What do you think might be the input of government on the one hand and civil society on the other in developing a system of social defence?

Marco Hren: I would not answer the question in terms of proportions. Government and civil society are different in kind and not directly comparable. However, I do think that the input from both must be strong. The government must invest in peace research and take seriously the development of an alternative security system including the notion of social defence.

But social defence cannot work without strong civil society and active public involvement in the evolution of a new approach. In Slovenia our efforts are also directed at mobilising society in favour of alternative security – through discussions, for instance through joint projects to secure the conversion of military barracks for socially useful purposes. There are now thirty five different groups in Ljubljana, from cultural groups to socialisation groups, which we are trying to bring together to demand the conversion of military barracks. In the cities, sites occupied by the military could be used for social welfare and community projects, and perhaps in the countryside, for starting organic farming ventures. Clearly it would be pointless trying to interest people in conversion without taking into account the needs of a given locality.

MR: But do you think social defence can provide an adequate deterrent against aggression?

Marco Hren: This is a relevant question but also in my view a secondary one. A point I always insist upon is that each country requires a separate case study to examine what possibilities for social defence exist there. We cannot speak of social defence in say Slovenia and Guatemala as if their problems were the same.

Concerning Slovenia, I am convinced that social defence is a realistic option for securing the country against aggression. I am not speaking here about immediate aggression, for there is no immediate threat of this kind. This is a concept which does not deal with the outbreak of aggression but with predicting aggression, and studying the causes of a dispute. People in Slovenia will not accept the notion of security based on peace politics if they feel there is an immediate danger and if there appears to be no alternative to military defence.

Parallel to introducing this new security system, we have to have guarantees from neighbouring states, and to have good links and communication with them. We have to present people with the problems and conflicts in the region, and to work on finding solutions to them. This is a realistic approach in Slovenia because although there are disputes there is no immediate danger; the disputes can be settled with patient work. This is why our peace institute will deal mainly with conflict resolution. They will study the problems in the Balkan area and try to discover their roots.

Of course it is not realistic to think we can jump from military defence to a non-violent defence overnight. There cannot be a jump because of the problems of conversion from military to civilian production, because of problems of political decision making, because of the time it takes to develop social defence, theoretically and in practice. Thus in reality there has to be a transition period during which military and social defence preparations will by default exist alongside each other. I would not say that the military and non-violent approaches are complementary, but I recognise that because of the nature of the process involved they must coexist during a period of transition.

MR: You spoke earlier of each country having to develop social defence for its particular situation. But within the region of Europe can one imagine the development of a common strategy or approach, and of co-operation across national boundaries? Thus on the military side you have alliances and the notion of strengthening the defence of small countries through collective security. It there something equivalent to that, or analogous to that, in the area of social defence?

Marco Hren: Clearly there has to be a degree of international co-operation to establish an alternative security system – for instance in the area of economic conversion and in negotiations over disputes. Peace politics, in fact, requires multilateral and bilateral approaches. My point, however, is that each country has to make an analysis of its particular situation and conditions. Thus while conversion throws up many similar problems from country to country, there is a big difference between the problems facing a country which invests say ten per cent of its GNP in military expenditure and one which invests fifteen per cent. Similarly changing to a system of social defence is very different for a country of 2,000,000 than for a country of 20,000,000 people.

Of course, in addition to studying the particular problems of a given country, it is also important to note the points in common with other countries and other struggles – in other words to conduct comparative research. Studying the experiences of different countries can give us a deeper understanding of the potential of social defence In Slovenia, for instance, I would like to see us making a thorough analysis of our own situation and then inviting for discussions people from outside with experience in organising civil resistance and social defence, and also people who have made theoretical studies of these concepts.

Transnational co-operation is important also in the campaigns to shift defence thinking in new directions. Thus we in Slovenia work closely with the campaigns in Switzerland and Austria to abolish the army, thereby giving each other security and jointly developing the case we are putting forward. There is also the global strategy of creating peace zones. A peace zone is by definition an international project. If you want to make Slovenia a peace zone, this cannot be simply a Slovenian project. It must of course have the support of the

Slovenian population and government, but the project itself has to be an international one.

In Slovenia at this point, we are struggling not so much for the abolition of the army as for this to be an option which the country seriously considers. We have to elaborate the project and seek support for it in our society. It is also necessary for there to be parallel negotiations with our neighbours and with the international community. We have to seek partners for our approach – and indeed we have partners. Hungary, for instance, has proposed a demilitarised zone. Demilitarised borders and demilitarised towns could be an important step in the process. It has to be a project of international civil society and of international diplomacy. It cannot be local only, but nor can it succeed without being local.

There was an argument at this year's END convention in Helsinki where someone was saying that a peace zone in Estonia is a selfish project – they want to get rid of the army and profit from that. Consequently some people argued that peace zones could only work on a regional basis – from Scandinavia to Greece for instance. But that idea is not realistic. We cannot develop peace zones from above only and impose them without the active support and consensus of the populations concerned.

Stretched resources at the Independent Information and Press Centre, November 1989. *Jan Kavan*

Jan Kavan

Interviewed in London on Monday 10 September 1990. Jan Kavan was born in 1946 of a Czech father and English mother and was one of the student leaders in Czechoslovakia during the period of the Prague Spring and the Soviet-led invasion of 1968. He participated in, and helped organise the non-violent protests against the Soviet occupation, and from 1970 onwards worked from London providing information, literature, and equipment to the opposition movement inside Czechoslovakia as well as supplying the British and other Western media with news and documents about the opposition inside his country. A co-founder of Palach Press (1974), the Jan Palach Information and Research Trust, and the East European Cultural Foundation (1985). A founding editor, and frequent contributor to, the *East European Reporter*, first published in 1985. Co-editor, with Zdena Tomin, of *Voices From Prague*, 1983.

Jan Kavan returned to Prague in 1989 and was elected to the Czechoslovak Federal Assembly as a Civic Forum candidate in the elections of June 1990.

Jan Kavan: I come from a country and a generation which did not have the luxury of deciding whether or not to be political. We had politics thrust upon us. In my case more than most because of my family background.

During the war years my father was one of many people in Czechoslovakia who believed that when the war was over the social system should change to prevent any future Munichs and also to prevent the kind of social injustice which existed in the first Czechoslovak Republic from 1919 to 1938. Although Czechoslovakia was during that period the most democratic country in the whole of the region, surrounded by fascist or semi-fascist regimes, it – in common with other civilised, advanced capitalist countries – had not solved all social problems. It was therefore understandable that my father joined the communist party. My mother was English and came from a middle class family which supported the Labour Party and believed in a kind of democratic socialism. This implied a just social and economic system implemented by democratic methods.

During the 1950s, my father and others who genuinely believed in communism, were imprisoned in the Stalinist show trials on trumped-up charges of espionage. I was therefore brought up in a strangely paradoxical atmosphere. The country was run by a communist party which was explaining to me that my communist father was an imperialist agent, a traitor, and that my mother, coming from an imperialist country, was an enemy of the society. The communist party claimed to have got rid of all class-hatred, race-hatred, social divisions and so forth, yet at school teachers, encouraged by the party, promoted an anti-semitic atmosphere. It was at school that I realised for the first time that my father was a jew when it was used against me as a small kid. At home, my mother explained to me that I shouldn't equate what the communist party said with the ideals of socialism and that my father was innocent of all the charges; in short what the school said was black was white.

It was not easy to make up one's own mind under such conflicting circumstances, and it probably encouraged me to think about political issues at a very early stage. I did in the end endorse my mother's perception of these issues and became convinced that one could fight for a just democratic socialist society by opposing the practical policies of the communist party. I concluded too that only by fighting for the implementation of civil and human rights, and respect for democracy, could one hope to bring about conditions for the introduction of genuine socialism. This placed me in a minority within my own country. Most people did not of course approve of the injustices of the system, but only a minority were prepared to speak out. In a country run on classical totalitarian lines, expressing any disagreement, however mildly formulated, made one immediately a pariah, someone with no future, existing on the fringe of society. Once the black mark was put down against you in your personal file, it went with you from job to job, from town to town. There was no escape.

MR: To what extent was there a black mark against you anyway because of your father having been in prison?

Jan Kavan: True I started already on the wrong side. Nevertheless my father was among the first people to be released and rehabilitated; this occurred in 1956 after he had spent about four years in prison. (I should add that the authorities continued to treat him, until his early death, with suspicion because of the bitter experience he had been through). Yet I was given a chance. I was after all only ten years old when my father was released and so I had the opportunity of accepting what the government was saying. I was only fourteen when he died. By endorsing the government's view, or behaving in a conformist manner, I could have broken out of the not-quite-closed straightjacket of my origin.

I became part of a double-minority. First, I was part of the minority who decided to be activist, despite the obvious dangers. Second, within that minority, I was part of a further minority who continued to believe that some of the socialist ideas were viable, and who continued to differentiate between communism and socialism, which government propaganda tried to equate, and between the practice and some of the theories. Some of the activists maintained that one had to combat everything to do with communism. However during the sixties we were, as young students, united predominantly by our commitment to fight against all injustice, and to bring about democratic procedures within the Youth Union, the Student Union, and the country as a whole. This commitment to civil and human rights was the common denominator amongst all of the student leaders of the sixties, irrespective of their ideological differences which in any case were not all that clear to us at that time, and developed much later.

The Prague Spring was very much the result of a *coup d'etat* from above, when the reformist communists took over the levers of power of one of the most Stalinist communist parties in Eastern Europe. But it is important to stress that the atmosphere in society was optimal for the reform communists to do this, in part because of the activities of the students, the most active and radical group at that time within society, and the only one, outside the reform communists, able to put forward a set of political ideas for change. Our clash in 1966 – and more especially in 1967 – with the leadership of the Party helped to create the atmosphere of autumn 1967. We, and the writers' community which supported us, were a kind of catalyst, if you like, for the major reforms of the Prague Spring.

During the Prague Spring, although we supported the reform communists in their attempt to democratise the country, and in their clash with the remnants of the Stalinists, we were also very careful not to give the impression that we endorsed all their ideological arguments. We argued even then that it was not enough to demand just democratisation – the slogan of the reform communists – and that what was needed was democracy. We were therefore critical, even during the Prague Spring, of some of the half-hearted steps taken by the reform communists; we wanted to change society faster and more radically, and to decentralise the decision-making process. I found myself being critical of Dubcek and company, in particular because they showed great reluctance in the first few months of 1968 to trust the people, and to endorse and support the calls for the establishment of enterprise councils or workers' councils. That kind of grassroots democracy they regarded with a certain distrust and apprehension.

After the invasion the students and the workers were again in the forefront of organising passive resistance. I was very much involved in an initiative which resulted in students and workers signing mutual political agreements supporting each other and supporting a minimal programme of reforms which we wanted to preserve at all costs. We suddenly found ourselves backing the minimal programme of the communist party against the very authors of that programme, the leaders of the communist party. Some of our minimal programme was taken from the April Action programme of the communist party which we had disagreed with at the time it was passed on the grounds that it was too much of a compromise, too half-hearted. After the invasion we said, alright let's keep at least the basis of that.

But by then Dubcek and company, the authors of the programme, were no longer prepared to support it. They went from one compromise, one concession, to another. It is a slight simplification, but only a slight one, to say that at that time they were probably more afraid of their own people than they were of the Soviet Union, even though the latter was already occupying the country and making clear that they would use salami tactics to remove one reformist leader after another. This is eventually what happened in 1969, despite the sacrifices some people made, Jan Palach in particular. Jan made the greatest sacrifice a human being can by giving his life, and emotionally I was deeply affected by that.

MR: Did you know him personally?

Jan Kavan: No, I didn't. I was at that time one of the student leaders and was in the office of the student union when we received a telephone call to say that a young student had poured petrol over himself and burned himself alive in Wenceslas Square, which was only about ten minutes walk away from our office, and that he had left a note with two demands which we immediately, as leaders of the student union, accepted as our demands and began to put pressure on the government to implement.

Next day we received a call from the hospital where Jan Palach was dying, very badly burned, to say that he wanted Lubos Holecek, a very close personal friend of mine, to go to the hospital. Lubos and Jiri Muller were the two main student leaders in the country at that time. I went with him but stayed outside the room when he went in. Jan Palach – with great difficulty, in terrible pain, his lips burned – gave Lubos a message for the other students who were prepared to be human torches following his example. He said they should not do it, but should continue in the struggle aligned with us. The fact that out of the whole society he picked out the students, and the radical students in our group specifically, gave me a great feeling of responsibility and at the same time a feeling that there must be something we were doing right.

Jan Palach tried to halt the process of increasing apathy in the nation, to shock them out of the apathy. He managed to slow down the process, but he didn't manage, unfortunately, to reverse it. However, he did instil in the hearts of some people even greater determination to continue the social resistance by any means available. Those means began drastically to change as new restrictions were introduced in the course of 1969.

I was eventually forced to become an emigré in 1970. When I was discussing whether or not to risk imprisonment in Czechoslovakia, or to become an emigre, Jiri Muller, whom I mentioned earlier and who again was a close personal friend, told me that if I decided to stay abroad, I could be very useful to the emerging Czechoslovak opposition, but only if I accepted the discipline of meeting their needs as they defined them, and as these might change over the years. I accepted this discipline and that has been the main criteria for my work over the last twenty years. However, I have to say that when I made that decision in 1970 I did not expect it to take twenty years before I could return. Had I known that, I would probably have chosen to risk imprisonment in Czechoslovakia rather than twenty years in exile. I thought it would be a much shorter time, drawing on the Hungarian experience when people who had been expelled, or people who became emigres after 1956, were allowed back in the 1960s.

The needs the opposition defined were on the whole very straightforward. They needed literature, both Czech and Western, both political analysis of and information about what was happening in their own country. They also needed some material of a more academic nature, about developments in different fields of science, since many of the dissidents had been excluded from following their chosen profession. They needed financial help and technical help, duplicators in particular. Eventually, in the 1980s, as the opposition made greater use of technology, they needed video recorders and cassettes, personal computers, printers and modems. But in the seventies, the first thing I was asked to send in was an electric gestetner duplicating machine, and of course lots of books. I basically devoted the last twenty years to this kind of work, co-operating in the UK primarily with individuals who were clearly on the left of the political spectrum or associated with the peace movement.

I did not change my general political views and this placed me, in Britain also, among a minority. It made it more difficult for me to raise money for the work of the Czechoslovak opposition. Nevertheless we were fairly successful. We were able to get the machines and books into Czechoslovakia throughout the seventies, and the group I established in Britain was clearly the most successful of all the groups of this kind in the West, at least up to 1980. We were able to get literature in on a much larger scale than anyone else, and this led eventually to us receiving an enormous amount of information, samizdat books and periodicals from Czechoslovakia, with requests to publicise what was happening there. We did this by contacting newspapers, radio and television stations, as well as finding publishers for samizdat books.

When the quantity of this information became very large we tried to institutionalise the work. At the end of 1974 we established an agency called Palach Press whose main job was to inform the Western media, human rights organisations, universities, organisations concerned with political prisoners such as Amnesty International, and other international organisations as to what was happening in Czechoslovakia, and also making available copies of samizdat literature. Eventually Palach Press had to concentrate on this work whilst the work aimed more towards Czechoslovakia – supplying literature, finances and equipment – was carried out by another charity I helped to establish called the Jan Palach Information and Research Trust.

We also began to co-operate very closely with groups in the West doing similar work in relation to Poland and Hungary, and with their help established close contacts with democratic opposition groups in these countries. This led in 1985 to the establishment of yet another charity, the East European Cultural Foundation, which had aims similar to the Jan Palach Trust, but which covered the whole of Central and Eastern Europe.

It eventually concentrated on two things. One was the publication of a quarterly journal, *East European Reporter*, which offered its pages almost exclusively to East European activists and scholars living in Eastern Europe. It was the first English language journal which continuously and systematically treated the area as one having a clear political common denominator, whilst fully respecting the historical, cultural, and other differences between individual countries. It allowed the leading activists of that area to spell out this common denominator to their Western audience, and also, because we smuggled a certain number of these journals back to Eastern Europe, to increase contact between opposition groups within the Soviet bloc. Ironically the regime was so afraid of such contacts being established, that it was more difficult, for instance, for the Poles to find out what was happening in Hungary or Czechoslovakia, than it was for them to find out what was happening in Britain or the United States.

This brings me to the second thing the EECF concentrated on – namely facilitating greater contact between opposition groups within Eastern Europe. We started with the Poles, Hungarians and Czechs, but eventually also involved activists in East Germany, Yugoslavia and, in the last years, Bulgaria and the Soviet Union – both from Moscow and from some of the Baltic States. The EECF was in fact the first organisation which helped to put together joint multilateral statements by leading activists in several East European countries. The first such statement was issued in October 1986 on the thirtieth anniversary of the Hungarian revolution of 1956. We continued to work in this way for several years, until 1989 when the activists began slowly to establish contact directly themselves and no longer needed the services of the EECF, or at least not on such a scale. However, some services of EECF in this respect were used right up to the time of the 1989 revolutions.

MR: During this period, was your analysis of the structural weakness of the Czechoslovak regime such that you felt confident things would eventually change there and in other parts of Eastern Europe? Did you ever lose hope of seeing radical change in the area?

Jan Kavan: That's a very difficult question. I obviously believed throughout that things would change. I never accepted that such repressive regimes could survive anywhere for ever. I also believed that one had a moral and political duty to carry out this work irrespective of whether or not these changes would take place – or would take place in my lifetime. One had a duty to help the activists in those countries. Obviously if there had not been any opposition in the Eastern European countries, one would not try to create it artificially from the West; my main motivation and desire was to help the active groups and to meet their needs as they defined them.

At the beginning many of the people in the opposition were my personal friends, but later as the years went by, a younger generation became very active. I was then helping people whose names and personal friends, but later, as the years went by, a younger generation became very active. I was then helping people whose names and that I was a useful and reliable contact to whom requests could be sent and who would try his level best to meet those requests.

The fact that these new young people joined the opposition – a generation that grew up under Husak – showed that Husak's normalisation project had failed. I remember a meeting in 1969 at which Husak said that my generation was lost and corrupted but that a new generation would be brought up and educated in such a way that our ideas would never fall on fertile soil. But he was being proved wrong, and this gave me renewed hope. Husak's normalisation produced some very conformist people, but not people who were pro-regime. They were conformist as a result of fear or opportunism. Such people are hardly reliable supporters of any regime. Once they believed they could get away with it, they would turn against the regime and punish their masters for the humiliation they had endured. Indeed they would be keener to see them punished than would those who had actively opposed the old order.

But normalisation also produced, among Husak's so-called younger generation, new activists. This was a generation which had not experienced the Prague Spring and the invasion, and who had been brought up in the 'normalised' schools, yet they still found reason and motivation to oppose the regime. That gave me tremendous hope, tremendous encouragement.

Still it is true, to answer your question, that there were occasions throughout the twenty years, when I felt that the changes would take place but that it would be much, much later than I had originally anticipated. It might not even be in my lifetime. I got a great deal of personal satisfaction and encouragement every time I received a letter from friends of mine thanking me for what I was doing, but it was hard and exhausting work, and frequently very frustrating. So I had moments – not of hopelessness, because I never lost hope – but of sadness and depression. These were times when I had to gather all my strength to continue. But then I thought of some of my friends who paid an even higher price by languishing in prison for years – some for five, six years, some even for nine – and who came out and continued the very work which had put them in prison in the first place, and I said to myself – If they can do it, I should be able to. If Jan Palach was prepared to pay such a high price, I should be prepared to pay the price of major discomfort. As the years went by, hopes rose and fell by turns. One's hopes rose obviously when Solidarity was launched in Poland in 1980, but they were dashed, or suffered a great setback, with the introduction of martial law.

I also found it very frustrating trying to convince socialists and social democrats and almost anyone left of centre in the West that they should devote a lot of time, energy and resources helping the dissident and activist groups in the East. It was hard to convince them that this was not a struggle which in the end would help the Reagans and the Thatchers and the right wing circles in the West, but that on the contrary it would, in the long term, create an atmosphere in Europe in which one could discuss socialist ideas without feeling guilty, without having to suppress information about how these ideas were misused in one half of the world. I found it frustrating that many people on the left found it so difficult to accept this, and that many of them subscribed to the old fashioned and dangerous idea that the enemy of my enemy is my friend. This black and white thinking throughout the last twenty years was a source of my scepticism and growing disillusionment, and occasional bouts of depression. However none of this prevented me from continuing with this work, and I always believed it was the only possible way forward if one wanted eventually to live in a Europe free of fear and repression, and free of injustice of all kinds – free too of the danger of military confrontations. This was the kind of Europe I wanted to live in, and I believed the work I was doing was the only way I could personally contribute to the eventual realisation of such a dream.

MR: When things started to move in Czechoslovakia they moved with extraordinary speed. What brought the situation to a head in 1989, there and elsewhere? How important a factor was Gorbachev?

Jan Kavan: The dire economic situation and the need to change it, has been at the back of all the changes in Eastern Europe, including those within the Soviet Union. Allied to this was the need to free political forces capable of dealing with the economic problems. In Czechoslovakia there was also the shock of the twenty-year-old occupation and the desire to regain independence and restore sovereignty.

Once radical change was shown to be possible in one East European country, the pace of events quickened. By the autumn of 1989, one communist regime after another began to topple. The final collapse of the old order in Czechoslovakia occurred with such breathtaking speed partly because the population were determined that the country should not be left behind as a kind Stalinist enclave in the centre of Europe.

Gorbachev was important in the wider process of change throughout Eastern Europe in the sense that his reforms created a favourable atmosphere and helped set the process in motion. Certainly without him, those revolutions would have been postponed; he created the possibility, and that was important. But Gorbachev didn't carry out those revolutions and nor were they carried out by Czech or Hungarian or Polish Gorbachevs in those countries. They were carried out primarily by those who had organised the civil resistance throughout the previous few decades, many of whom were highly sceptical of Gorbachevian or other communist reforms, regarding them as half-hearted and incomplete. They pointed out the failure of *perestroika* in the Soviet Union which hadn't brought about the required economic changes, and the failure of *glasnost* which hadn't brought about – at least up then – a truly democratic society. Nevertheless both *perestroika* and *glasnost* opened up the possibility of finding solutions; they broke the chain and spelled out the end of the Brezhnev doctrine of which all the Eastern European countries were victims. As a catalyst, the Gorbachev reforms were very important, but if it wasn't for the movements in those countries we would probably have today semi-Gorbachevian, semi-reformist societies run still by some kind of reform communist parties.

MR: Wasn't Gorbachev himself pushed more and more in a radical direction, not only by the economic problems but also by the demands that were being made within the Soviet Union and outside?

Jan Kavan: Of course – and he continues to be even today. I think in time he will sound even more radical because he will continue to be pressurised by Yeltsin and more radical reformists on the one hand and by nationalists in the non-Russian republics on the other. The continuing failure of the half-hearted reforms up to now will force a decision as to which way to go. The objective situation will force him to be more radical. So too will the political and economic developments in Eastern Europe which, although they started later, are now well in advance of those in the Soviet Union. So I believe he will have to ally himself with Yeltsin against the neo-Stalinists and nineteenth century nationalists.

MR: The opposition movements and groups clearly played a crucial role, as you say. But isn't it the case that the number of people actively and openly involved in them remained quite small until a very late stage – except in the case of Poland?

Jan Kavan: In fact even in Poland, where indeed you did have quite large numbers of people involved after the formation of Solidarity, the process was the same. KOR which was set up in 1976 comprised a very small group of intellectuals defending workers, but they provided the catalyst for the emergence of the mass movement. Subsequently, however, even after the introduction of martial law, you had a very large section of Polish society taking part in different opposition activities.

In Czechoslovakia, the development of the opposition occurred in a similar way to Poland, but the number of people involved was infinitely smaller, and the percentage of workers involved was smaller still. Nevertheless the human rights movement, Charter 77, and later some of the peace and human rights groups set up by the younger generation, for instance the Independent Peace Association, formed a crucial network of pressure groups – of activists working within an informal structure. If these networks had not existed, the revolution would either not have taken place, or would have taken on very different forms, including unfortunately unpleasant outbursts of spontaneous violence. All these different groups within the opposition had in common a desire to see change by non-violent means. And the imprisonment of their members, their suffering, the courage with which they continued throughout those years to put forward ideas on non-violent change, earned them a certain moral credit which was payable when people felt – 'it's now or never'.

Once again, the protests of the youth – as in 1967, and several other times in Czech history – proved to be the catalyst. But the revolt was not expressed in spontaneous violent outbursts because people turned to the already tested informal leaders of civil society. And the civil society structure, however small it was, was capable of providing both the leaders and ideas which were at the core of the revolution. These ideas then became widened and clarified in discussions between previously existing political forces and new ones. But the basic principles, which for example underlay the foundation of Civic Forum in Czechoslovakia, and the first programmes of Civic Forum, didn't fall from the sky. They could all be read in the Charter 77 programmes. If you today read some of the foreign policy documents put forward by the Foreign Secretary, Jiri Dienstbier, you get a feeling of *deja-vu*, of reading old Charter 77 documents.

Civil society and resistance groups provided the infrastructure necessary to ensure the revolution was carried out peacefully and with a focus on important political principles. In 1989 the enormous mass support, which had not been forthcoming earlier, enabled the Chartists to implement those principles. The popular enthusiasm could be translated into political action only thanks to the existence over many years of the civil society structures. Otherwise it could have been easily manipulated, diffused, or even betrayed – as unfortunately we may be seeing in Romania, and possibly Bulgaria.

I also think it is crucial that some such groups as Charter 77 continue to be active in the current situation, because this has produced new problems. We no longer have human rights violations, but we don't yet have a society where people can make decisions, and participate actively in all decisions which affect the quality of their lives. We don't yet have a situation in which social justice is guaranteed. There are so many remaining problems, some

. subjective, some objective, none of them easy to solve. Therefore it is important for the bodies which constitute civil society to continue in being, and in fact to become stronger.

One positive factor is that people whose personal inclinations are not to risk imprisonment, but who still feel strongly about a number of political and social issues, now have an opportunity to engage actively in civil society. Civil society, in short, is no longer the preserve of the courageous. More conformist people can also participate if they feel strongly about certain issues and about the way in which their country will develop, and the shape in which it will eventually join Europe.

MR: You cooperated closely with the peace movement in the West. Perhaps you could say something about both the problems and satisfactions of this collaboration, and also of the difficulties you must have encountered at times within Eastern Europe among people who viewed the peace movement with suspicion, and for whom the very word peace was associated with official propaganda.

Jan Kavan: Working with the peace movement here only reinforced the feeling that I am frequently – within both East and West – part of a double minority. With everything I do, I seem to go from one minority to another. Despite this I have an unshakable conviction that many of my beliefs are actually based on a correct and true interpretation of reality. I believe that eventually people will endorse these ideas in much larger numbers.

In the West, many peace movement people, in CND especially but not only there, had, in my perception, a very narrow view of what the whole peace issue is about. To start with, they believed in single-issue campaigns and concentrating on getting rid of particular weapons; the campaign against Cruise and Pershing missiles was a good example of this. They campaigned for the removal of nuclear weapons without taking into consideration what always seemed to me to be an axiomatic truth, namely that the missiles were placed there by politicians and the decision to deploy them was the result of a certain political situation, and a certain kind of political thinking.

Unless you solved those conflicts, attempting to remove particular weapons would be unlikely to succeed, and if it did so, would not end the danger of military confrontation. Therefore I always argued, as did my Charter 77 friends in Czechoslovakia, that the struggle for peace has to be a combination, on the one hand of a struggle against militarisation, the deployment of weapons of mass destruction and the growing influence of armies, and, on the other hand a struggle for human rights and democratic decision-making. In short, it was necessary to remove the political causes of confrontation, including the division of Europe into two military and political camps. This idea, which seemed to me so obvious, wasn't easily accepted either in the East or the West.

Many Western peace activists felt that once you linked peace issues – which in their minds meant disarmament issues – with human rights issues, you made the task impossible. The Soviet Union would not accept this linkage, and there would be no hope of ever succeeding. Trying to secure the removal of particular weapons, they argued, was at least realistic. Others went even further and argued that once you introduced human rights issues, they would be used by Western politicians primarily against the Soviet Union and this would undermine the whole struggle for peace. Some of these people did actually perceive the Soviet Union as a peace-loving country, despite the occupation of Czechoslovakia, despite the war in Afghanistan and all the other clear evidence that it was a very strange peace-loving country indeed!

In the East, many of my friends responded with great allergy even to the term peace, because peace was, in the day to day propaganda to which they were exposed – in the media, in schools, everywhere – the peace imposed by the tanks. Peace was something you were urged to struggle for against some enemy defined in Cold War terms. Therefore peace was perceived as a propaganda weapon of totalitarian regimes. The original meaning of peace had been hijacked by the state propagandists.

That was one reason many of my friends were mistrustful of the peace movement. The second reason was that the only Western peace activists they met were those who enthusiastically travelled to the 'peace-loving countries' of the East, including Czechoslovakia, and spoke there on television endorsing the Soviet so-called peace offensives and Soviet foreign policy. They were perceived as at best naive, and at worst as a kind of Soviet fifth column in the West. Thus my co-operation with the peace movement created distrust among some of my friends towards me, and I had to spend a lot of my time trying to explain that not all peace activists are the same, that there are people among them who analysed the problem as we did, and that it was important to be patient even with the naive ones and open their eyes to the reality of the situation.

However, it took several years of this thankless work before the human rights activists in the East began to engage in serious discussion with peace activists here, and vice-versa. Retrospectively I feel very proud that I was among those who helped to start this dialogue, even though it wasn't an easy dialogue and wasn't always fruitful dialogue. It led eventually to a much greater understanding of the issue on both sides. In the late eighties it led to the emergence of a kind of informal network, almost a coalition, of human rights activists in the East and peace activists in the West who finally understood that they had much more in common than they have with the opposing governments.

This laid the foundation for the Helsinki Citizens Assembly whose founding conference, symbolically, will take place in Prague in October this year.[1] This movement is determined, in the much more conducive atmosphere of Europe today, to implement the ideas discussed between those groups in East and West in the worst years of repression, expressed for instance in the Prague Appeal of 1985. In this appeal, the Chartists talked about such taboo issues as the right of all Germans to self-determination, the withdrawal of foreign troops from Europe, and accepting the principles of the Helsinki Final Act as providing the foundations of European integration.

The Helsinki Citizens Assembly is an authentic continuation of the nascent civil society structures in East and West of those years. The fact that these principles have now been accepted by some politicians today, and that some of the activists who fought for them are now in government, does not make the movement any less important or less worthwhile. I am convinced the movement will play an important role in the whole process of the integration of Europe and of ensuring that eventually it will be the ordinary people, the ordinary Europeans, who will decide about the quality of life on their continent. Issues such as the environment, demilitarisation, and the securing of social and economic justice are too important to be left solely in the hands of professional politicians. There must

---

[1] The Helsinki Citizens Assembly took place in Prague from 19-23 October 1990. Seven hundred people from 25 CSCE countries participated and established permanent working groups on a variety of issues ranging from human rights to demilitarisation. The opening address to the Assembly was given by President Vaclav Havel.

be a grassroots movement, especially a movement with the kind of history which the Helsinki Citizens Assembly has, going back to the tentative dialogue between peace and human rights activists established in the early eighties. The last nine years, a relatively short period of time, have seen a major change in people's approach and in their ability to overcome their own prejudices and illusions.

MR: Turning to the issue of social defence, do you think that the success of civil resistance has led any of the new governments to think seriously about this as a way of contributing towards the security of their countries and towards the demilitarisation of Europe?

Jan Kavan: I have not so far seen any convincing evidence that the governments in Eastern Europe are thinking along these lines, though it is possible that some of them at least will do so in the future. I think the governments primarily perceive the civil resistance of 1989 as the desperate response of a repressed society determined to achieve change. They believe that they themselves now represent and embody this change, and so some of them don't even see the need for such movements to play any political role in the future.

Others may see a role for them because they are aware that many problems have not been solved. On the one hand the old structures remain powerful, though operating in different fields. For instance, in some countries the former office holders and party bureaucrats have substituted a new economic power for their old political power and are using their great experience of the system, and their knowledge of the bureaucracy, to create formidable obstacles to genuine long-term democratic change. On the other hand we see an upsurge of national and social conflicts which were always there under the surface but which previously were suppressed by force. Therefore some of the old activists now in government do recognise the need for pressure from an independent people's movement to find a democratic solution to these problems, a way to resist the tendency of some groups to resort to violence or to authoritarian and totalitarian measures. The movement, in short, could be used to carry out a kind of permanent, second revolution.

That is still quite a long way from the notion of the movements playing a role in social defence as part of the security system. But I do believe that this will eventually enter into the consciousness of some of the political leaders. They are not necessarily unsympathetic to the idea of social defence, or opposed to it on ideological grounds; it is rather that developments in that part of the world have not placed the idea at the top of the political agenda. I think it will be put on the agenda relatively soon as governments and politicians have to discuss the role of their countries within the new Europe, and within the new European security system.

As more and more ideas are emerging about such a new security system – what it should be based on, what the relationship of individual countries and regional groupings should be to each other, and how within such a new Europe you could structure your own internal security – there will be increasing pressure to consider social defence. I think it would be considered with sympathy, especially by those new politicians who have not yet become alienated from the ideas which motivated them while they were still active in the movements.

In the Helsinki Citizens Assembly, we are now putting forward ideas which range from European wide ecological measures to demilitarisation, and the notion of a second Helsinki Conference. One aim of the latter would be to conclude a peace treaty taking in all the countries involved in the Helsinki process to put a final stop not simply to the Cold War but to the tense No Peace/No War situation which has prevailed in Europe since the last war.

This inevitably raises the question of how to ensure that none of these tensions and conflicts will re-emerge. And again in that context – no doubt introduced in the first instance from below by movements such as the Helsinki Citizens Assembly – the idea of social defence is likely to receive serious consideration both on a national and a European-wide level, especially in a more integrated, more democratic, and less militarised Europe.

MR: You obviously see both the deepening of democracy and the process of demilitarisation as depending to a large extent on continuing pressure from civil society, and from the co-ordination of this pressure across national boundaries through movements like the Helsinki Citizens Assembly. But how strong are those movements within individual countries in Eastern Europe now that the common enemy of a totalitarian system has been overthrown? Is there a feeling among people that they can now go back to their daily lives? Or is there still energy and dynamism in those movements?

Jan Kavan: That again is a very difficult question to answer because there are few criteria you can use to establish the strength and vitality of these movements. Probably in a year's time I could answer the question more clearly, using the viability of the Helsinki Citizens Assembly as one of the criteria. We are now only starting.

It's not going to be easy at first, and nor can we expect at the beginning a homogeneous, strong movement, primarily because the common enemy has been removed. Now individuals have differing preoccupations, partly related to their own personal histories, partly related to the history and situation of their nations. Obviously people living close to the borders between Poland, Czechoslovakia and East Germany will be preoccupied with ecological measures; unemployed people will be preoccupied with creating an economic system which would diminish this kind of social injustice. But both sets of people would be prepared to join in European-wide discussion as to how you build an efficient economy, even a market-based economy, while still respecting the need for economic justice, social justice and maintaining an ecologically safe environment.

Even on these issues there will be differences. Many people coming from Eastern Europe, subjected for forty years to bureaucratic, inefficient centralised planning, will have exaggerated perceptions of the beneficial impact of a market economy, perceiving it as a panacea for society's ills. This might apply even to people living in highly polluted areas. Many people coming from the West will stress the primary importance of ecological factors, and would be very sceptical of the attempts to introduce even commonsense market criteria into the East European economic mess which prevails today.

However, I believe that the majority will come to accept an approach that lies in the broad spectrum between these two extremes, and that there is sufficient common ground for a productive dialogue to take place. I hope, therefore, that the Assembly – along with other non-governmental organisations – will emerge as a strong and influential movement within the next two to three years. There is a shared determination to create a framework which would allow individuals and non-governmental groups – what we used to refer to as the informal structures of civil society – to determine their own future and their own quality of life. Above all, there is a determination to find non-violent means of solving outstanding problems, and a commitment to non-violent change towards a freer and more just European-wide society.

Alexander Karackachanov, secretary of Ecoglasnost, speaking to Sofia deputy mayor Popov during October 1989 demonstration.   *East European Reporter*

Elzbieta Rawicz-Oledzka

Interviewed in Berlin, 23 July 1990. Elzbieta Rawicz-Oledzka is a Lecturer in Sociology at the University of Poznan, and has been active since its foundation in 1985 in the *Freedom and Peace Movement in Poland* – known by its Polish acronym WiP (Wolnosc i Pokoj).

MR: What in your view were the key factors that led to revolt and political change in Poland?

Elzbieta Rawicz-Oledzka: The economic factor was the most important one. The Round Table talks between representatives of the government and Solidarity in early 1989 opened the way to a new political and economic system; they also set a precedent which was followed elsewhere in Eastern Europe. But it was largely the economic situation which forced the government to take this unprecedented step. The government needed a compromise at home to get the economy moving again; and it needed international legitimacy to encourage other countries to assist Poland in a period of economic crisis. Back in 1981 the government had tried to crush Solidarity through brute force. But this did not touch the root of the problem, and by the mid-1980s the economic crisis had become so acute that it was clear that a new initiative would have to be taken.

There were, of course, other factors, notably the changes in Soviet policy under Gorbachev. But the economic factor was central.

MR: How important was non-violence in the struggle for change?

Elzbieta Rawicz-Oledzka: For the movement I worked with, Freedom and Peace (WiP), non-violence was crucial right from the start. This is clear from WiP's founding statement in 1985. Contact with the Western peace movements was also of central importance both tactically and in terms of the exchange of ideas. Tactically it enabled us to put pressure on the Polish authorities to avoid extremes of repression in dealing with our movement. Thus we distributed our founding document to friends in the Western peace movements and as widely as possible both within Poland and outside it. As a result when all the participants in our first action were arrested and faced the possibility of long prison sentences, protests from the Western peace movements, publicity on Radio Free Europe and the Voice of America, and so forth, prompted the Polish authorities to release all of us involved in the action quite soon.

MR: Nevertheless when you and others openly protested against the policies of the government, you knew you faced serious risks of being beaten-up or spending years behind bars. What led you to overcome your fears and take to the streets?

Elzbieta Rawicz-Oledzka: I and many from a still younger generation had been at school or university during the period 1980-81 when Solidarity emerged as a major force in Polish society, and at the time of the crackdown in December 1981. In a sense we felt that it was our turn to do something to change an intolerable situation.

It is true that at first the arrests, searches and imprisonment have a traumatic effect. For instance, when your home is searched for the first time, it feels like a violation of your person and privacy. But after a few times you know what to expect and the impact is less. Speaking for myself, I can say that there came a point when I felt that the situation in the country was quite unbearable, and that I simply had to do something to try to change it.

MR: WiP adopted, I understand, a very different style of protest from Solidarity.

Elzbieta Rawicz-Oledzka: That's true. Since the imposition of martial law in 1981, Solidarity had been operating underground. By 1985, however, it had largely lost momentum, and we in WiP decided that the time had come to act openly. As I told you, we informed as many people and organisations as possible about our intentions in advance of an action. We even wrote to the police giving them details of our plans. I should mention here that the underground press was very important in spreading the word within Poland. It was a flourishing industry at that time, with many factories producing two or three underground papers. The publicity afforded us a measure of protection as well as encouraging people to speak their minds.

Humour soon became an important element in our protests. One man in Wroclaw was largely responsible for this, launching a series of happenings which he called the Orange Alternative Theatre. These demonstrations were often so amusing that people watching would all be laughing and enjoying themselves and the police would stand round embarrassed not knowing how to react or what to do.

Sometimes these demonstrations were timed to coincide with significant anniversaries. For instance we held a demonstration to 'celebrate' the anniversary of the 1917 Russian Revolution, with groups of people representing the Bolsheviks, the Mencheviks, the Czarist forces and so forth. The atmosphere was relaxed and good-humoured with onlookers laughing and joking. At first the police did not even realise that this was an action aimed against the authorities and for some time they did not interfere, even though all public demonstrations were banned. When finally they did realise what we were up to, they moved in and arrested us all. But then down at the police station they charged us with the offence of 'Celebrating the Russian Revolution' – and these were the words which actually appeared on the charge-sheets of many of the demonstrators and were solemnly read out when they appeared in court!

On another occasion, one group of demonstrators dressed up in imitation police uniforms carrying French style baguette loaves instead of truncheons, and used these to stage a mock attack on the rest of the participants. The bystanders were all laughing, and again for a while the police did not know what to do.

This style of demonstration spread from Wroclaw to other cities, and humour became a feature of many WiP demonstrations.

MR: Did Solidarity follow this lead at all?

Elzbieta Rawicz-Oledzka: No, not to my knowledge. I think the Solidarity leaders were too old and rather too serious to adopt this style of protest.

MR: But did they follow your example in other ways – for instance in organising and demonstrating more openly?

Elzbieta Rawicz-Oledzka: I don't think we influenced them in that way either. However, after the opening of the Round Table Talks in early 1989, Solidarity were in a curious situation of semi-legality. Formally they were still an illegal organisation; but their leaders were sitting down with government and Party representatives to try to reach agreement on a new constitution for Poland. By this time Solidarity had their own offices and were able to organise quite openly and without interference.

But of course there was a considerable degree of interaction between WiP and Solidarity especially in the late 1980s. At the invitation of Solidarity, some WiP people joined the Solidarity National Committee. It was largely due to WiP influence too that Solidarity eventually took up the issue of Alternative Service to conscription.

MR: What in fact is the position of conscientious objectors in Poland today?

Elzbieta Rawicz-Oledzka: Conscientious objectors can choose to do alternative service, but their situation has been very bad. They were paid extremely low wages – not even enough to live on. However, this year (1990) following a demonstration by objectors in front of the Parliament Building, the wages were increased and the situation has improved. We were helped here by friends on the 'inside'. Jacek Kuron, for instance, the Minister of Labour is a good friend of ours from the period when we were all active in opposing the communist government. We also have one – though only one! – WiP member in Parliament.

MR: Has there been much interest, arising out of the success of civil resistance in Poland, in the notion of social defence?

Elzbieta Rawicz-Oledzka: Not as such. For a while after the end of communist rule, there was a lot of interest in the idea of Polish neutrality, and of drastically reducing the size of the armed forces and the level of military expenditure. But the ambiguous statements by the West German Chancellor, Helmut Kohl, on the issue of Poland's borders alarmed people. They have been alarmed too at the pace of German unification.

Now the government is trying to raise the prestige of the army which had fallen very low. For instance, they have appointed someone from the navy to be Minister of Defence. This was a clever move because the prestige of the navy has remained high; unlike the army and the militia, the navy was not involved in the repression of popular movements under the old regime.

The more conservative members of the government are talking of retaining the old structures, and some even support continued Polish membership of the Warsaw Pact. There is still wider support, however, within the government, for the effort to raise the prestige of the army and make it technologically more efficient.

MR: How strong is WiP at this stage?

Elzbieta Rawicz-Oledzka: Unfortunately the end of the old system has left many WiP activists feeling unsure of their role; there are disagreements about what to do, and some people have become demoralised. Numerically WiP was never strong – it had no more than a few hundred active supporters at the height of its activities. However, because of the style and daring of its demonstrations it had an impact out of all proportion to the numbers involved. It succeeded in particular in making conscription and alternative service a major issue in the country.

With the emergence of the Solidarity-led government, and the move to a more democratic system, there is no longer the same sense of urgency and purpose about mounting demonstrations. There is also within the country as a whole a degree of disillusionment as the economic crisis deepens, and living standards continue to fall.

Albanian dictator toppled – Tirana demonstrators pull down statue of former dictator Enver Hoxha. Reuter/Popperphoto

Jirina Siklova

Interviewed during a visit to the Netherlands, 1 February 1991. Jirina Siklova was born in 1935 in Prague and studied in the Faculty of Philosophy at Charles University, finishing her studies in 1958, and then working as a member of the Faculty until 1970. From March 1968 until April 1969, she was head of the Communist Party in the Faculty, a post from which she resigned when Gustav Husak took power and, on Soviet insistence, overturned the reforms of the Dubcek period. After 1969 she was permitted to do research, but not to teach, in the Psychology Faculty, and in 1970 her work at the university was terminated.

She then worked as a cleaning woman and subsequently as a social worker in a hospital. She was one of the signatories of Charter 77 and collaborated with Jan Kavan of Palach Press in London in smuggling literature and equipment into the country. In 1981 she was imprisoned for one year for these activities, and after her release returned to work in the hospital specialising in social pediatrics. After another spell in prison in 1988, she was again employed as a cleaning woman until January 1990. In May 1990 she was re-appointed to the Faculty of Philosophy at Charles University where her field of study is methods of social work. She has a daughter now aged 30, a son aged 28, and four grandchildren. She is a member of the International Committee of the Helsinki Citizens Assembly.

MR: What were the factors that led to the revolt in Czechoslovakia, and what led you personally to become involved?

Jirina Siklova: The reasons behind the revolt are set out very clearly in Vaclav Havel's book *The Power of the Powerless*.[1] He explains them better than I could do. People were forced to live a lie, to pretend that things were exactly the opposite of what they knew them to be, and there came a time when they were no longer prepared to put up with this. I believe the personal factors behind the revolt were more important than the political ones. People came to hate the communist party and to see it as a stupid mother-in-law seeking to control and manipulate everything. Even actions which were not at all politically motivated were often interpreted by the Party as a political attack.

As to my personal motives, I became involved because I wanted to be able to look my own children in the face. If I had not acted as I had done, how could I now explain my inaction to them? This was not a matter of heroism. It was simply a matter of being able to live with myself and my family and to speak with other people without shame or blame.

MR: Why do you think the revolt remained so remarkably non-violent, earning it the nickname 'the velvet revolution'?

Jirina Siklova: The opposition was non-violent because this was the only way forward. Czechoslovakia has a population of 15,000,000 but only 1,864 people signed Charter 77. And even by the summer of 1989, with revolts taking place all around in the other Warsaw Pact countries, only 39,000 people had signed the appeal for democracy entitled 'Some Sentences'. It simply wasn't possible in this situation to contemplate using violence. The power of the opposition is explained in Havel's book. I think the Party and the authorities by their attacks upon us actually contributed to our power.

MR: Regarding the dynamics of civil resistance, what was it do you think that moved people in 1989 to overcome their fear of repression and to act openly against the system?

Jirina Siklova: I think what precipitated the revolt was the visibility of violence. During the 'Palach week' in January 1989, the twentieth anniversary of his death, the participants were prevented even from laying flowers on the spot in Wenceslas Square where

---

[1]Vaclav Havel et al, *The Power of the Powerless*, Edited by John Keane, Hutchinson 1985.

he died. A confrontation developed between the brute power of the Party and normal citizens. At 5pm on the evening of the first demonstration, as soon as it was dark, the police attacked the participants – and this scene was repeated every evening during the rest of that week. That was when it became clear that things would have to change – though how and when nobody knew. I, for instance, thought it would take longer to overturn the system, and that when it did occur it would be more like what happened in Romania.

What is important, however, is not only that the revolution started as a confrontation between stupid power and ordinary citizens but that the intellectual and ideological initiative lay from the outset with the opposition – the so-called dissidents. The latter were helped by the fact that the communist party itself was divided with one section wanting to see changes in the party leadership.

I can tell you a story to illustrate this. In the summer of 1989, Mr Jakes, the Party Secretary, gave a particularly stupid lecture to the top functionaries of the communist party. I received a tape-recording of it, which somebody had made unofficially, and I sent it to Radio Free Europe. The quality of the recording was poor, but they broadcast it with a good commentary. Then after one or two months there appeared in Prague an official video of the speech, professionally recorded. It is impossible for the unofficial copy to have been made without the collaboration of people within the Party, perhaps of one faction of the leadership who wanted to undermine the other. Of course these people within the party wanted only to change the leadership, not the system itself. But Civic Forum and its Slovak counterpart, People against Violence, and the people who took to the streets, changed the agenda.

Humour was a vital weapon for the opposition. For instance demonstrators would use some of the well-known slogans employed by the communist party but endow them with a new meaning. One slogan used repeatedly at communist party rallies from many years back was 'We are here! We are prepared!' And now when Havel and others appeared on the balcony overlooking Wenceslas Square, people took up the chant: 'We are here! We are prepared!' It was lovely. Everyone appreciated the irony.

To give another example, the former First Secretary of the Party in Prague was Miroslav Stepan. He is now serving a four year prison sentence, though he is the only one to have been imprisoned. On the day after Christmas, the feast of Santus Stepanus (St. Stephen's

Day), the crowd took up the chant: 'St. Stepan's day without Stepan!'. And then there was the cry: 'What do you want under the Christmas tree?' To which came the response: 'A new government under the tree, and the old government on the tree!' But it was a joke only, not a threat. Violence was completely absent.

MR: It is now just over a year since the 'velvet revolution' took place. What are your feelings about the present situation in Czechoslovakia?

Jirina Siklova: One thing that particularly concerns me is the attempt to exclude from public office and responsible positions anyone who was connected with the communist party or regime. This is stupidity and cannot work. Trying to find people who held responsible positions under the old regime who were not in some way connected with the Party or the secret police is like looking for virgins in a brothel!

I think many ordinary people in Czechoslovakia during the 1970s and 1980s regarded those of us in Charter 77 and so on as foolhardy. But still they sympathised with us. They would say to me – 'Why do you do these things? It is dangerous for you, for your children. You are responsible for your children. They will be against you because it is they who suffer for your actions; you have made them the victims.' But I could see that really they were trying to convince themselves, not me, and that they were having this same discussion among themselves.

Many of these people come from what has come to be known as the 'grey zone'. I have written about this in a paper published in the *Journal of Social Research* in 1990.[2] To quote from the summary: 'Journalists and politicians from Eastern and Western Europe use the same terminology – for instance communists, marxists, leftists and so on – but the content of the words is different. At present in Czechoslovakia there are only two politically clearly defined, though numerically insignificant, groups: the socialist establishment – Party bosses, some members of the security services, high ranking military people – on the one side; and so called 'dissidents' on the other. Nearly every professional group includes the so-called grey zone

---

[2]Jirina Siklova, 'The Grey Zone and the Future of Dissent in Czechoslovakia', *Journal of Social Research*, Vol 57 No 2, Summer 1990, pp.137-163.

which is composed of qualified but politically conforming people who support officially the regime while simultaneously favouring the opposition, the dissidents. In the event of the dissidents' bringing about political change, the grey zone will join them and will then represent the decisive force. Since the dissidents have not for a long time exercised their own professions, the grey zone people will be better equipped to be the future managers of society. Following the political take-over, the dissidents will lose their political unity, cohesion, special position and the goals for which they have fought. Consequently the people of the grey zone will be their competitors and the dissident movement will slowly disappear.'

In a postscript added in January 1990 I wrote that many dissidents frankly acknowledge their dislike of, and unwillingness to participate in, power politics. I am proud to say that this article was written in the summer of 1988, and first presented at a conference in France in September of that year – though of course I did not have a passport and was not able to present it personally.

I think this paper goes a long way to explaining the present situation in Czechoslovakia. Increasingly people from the grey zone are occupying the leading positions in society, while the dissidents for the most part are not doing so. For instance in the Philosophical Faculty where I am now working once again, there was a choice of two candidates for the post of Dean. The Senate of the Faculty elected the man who – though relatively speaking quite good, and better than the previous man from the *nomenklatura* – had been with the university these past twenty years and thus had been part of the old system. The Senate explained (very nicely!) that he was more familiar than his rival with the situation in the Faculty – and of course this was the case! It is the same story elsewhere. I think in any case that we so-called dissidents haven't the personal characteristics to be power holders as yet.

The country also faces many social and political problems which were hidden not solved under the old system. For instance there are sporadic outbreaks of violence – skinheads against gypsies and so forth – and tensions between Czechs and Slovaks. The fact is that we were not prepared for all these problems.

Of course problems such as prostitution and drug abuse existed under communist rule, but it was impossible to write about them or discuss them openly. Now I'm afraid that people will apply the principle of *post hoc, ergo propter hoc*; because the problems have become visible under Havel, it is Havel that has caused them! During the communist period, only the facade was repaired. This was true at a physical level in the cities. In Prague, for instance, the facade of the old town square was repaired for the sake of tourism, while behind it the buildings continued to decay. It was true too of the way the communist authorities dealt with political and social problems; behind the facade of the official propaganda lay the devastation we now see. And it was devastation at every level – the moral, the political, the ecological. The ecological devastation of Northern Bohemia, for instance, represents also a moral devastation for our nation.

Personally, however, I did not anticipate the national problem we now face between Czechs and Slovaks. I and people of my generation grew up believing that democracy would solve the problem of nationhood. Of course when freedom was lacking, there was no possibility of solving it. Moreover in marxist thinking, it was a transitional problem, a residue of the past, and so no attempt was made to confront it.

I fear that nationalism is being used as a substitute for genuine self-esteem. In other countries people define themselves in terms of their secondary social status – their acquired status as members of a profession or whatever. But in Czechoslovakia to acquire such status involved collaboration with the old regime. So people cannot take a straightforward pride in themselves and what they have achieved, being aware always of the compromises which were involved. However, when people say 'I am Czech! or I am Slovak!' they are referring to their first status, the status deriving from their birth. No-one can challenge them by asking 'How come you are a Czech?' or 'How come you are a Slovak?' – the way they might well ask 'How come you are the head of a university faculty?' or 'How come you are the director of an enterprise?'

I see in this the roots of the present wave of nationalism, and I hope that in the near future, if the people have the possibility of attaining their own secondary status without a sense of shame, that nationalism will ebb. You will observe that nationalism is stronger in Slovakia, where the resistance to the old regime was not so strong as it was for instance in Prague.

MR: Is anything being done, or could anything be done, at grassroots level to tackle the problem of nationalist tension and antagonism? For instance could Civic Forum and People against

Violence take joint action as they did in the struggle against the old regime?

Jirina Siklova: Both Civic Forum and People against Violence oppose nationalism. But what they can do about it in the near future, I don't know. They face a particular difficulty at the moment. The Commission set up by the Federal Parliament to investigate the events of 17 November 1989 has unearthed a register of 115,000 people who collaborated with the secret police under the old regime; of these the majority were simply informers, though 12,000 were actually paid agents. I am informed that many people holding top positions in Civic Forum are on the register.

Furthermore during the next two months the policy of *lustration* – literally bringing to the light – will be implemented. This is an initiative proposed by the Commission and adopted by the government with the support of Civic Forum and People against Violence. The plan is to approach privately all those on the register and inform them that their collaboration is known about. They will then have the choice of resigning from their posts on health grounds, or on some pretext, or face public exposure and disgrace. The consequences will be tragic for many people. I know personally, for instance, the new director of a hospital in Prague – a very good man – who faces exposure. He was never a member of the Party, but we now know that he did collaborate with the secret police.

I strongly oppose this policy. I am in favour of informing people privately that the authorities know about their collaboration since this could protect them against blackmail by communist party members or former members of the secret police, but I am against forcing them to resign. I believe people should be given the opportunity to change. Primarily it was the system that was immoral, and only secondarily the individual who, under pressure, collaborated with it. Moreover, we don't know the extent to which many of these people collaborated. We have the names, but we don't know exactly what they did.

It is now known that many members of the Slovak National Committee – the Slovak government – were collaborators of the secret police. There are also some former collaborators within the Czech government, though not so many. Now the Slovak Premier, Vladimir Meciar, says that the whole issue is one for the Slovak government to deal with, and I don't know whether the *lustration* policy will go ahead in Slovakia. But in the Czech Lands it will do so very shortly.

The *lustration* policy was applied in a limited way to candidates at the general election last July, after the Federal Commission first unearthed evidence about collaborators. At that stage, however, the Commission's list was incomplete; moreover the policy was applied only to well-known collaborators. Now the Commission has a complete list and the policy will be more strictly and extensively, implemented.

There are some people who want to go further and ban the communist party altogether. On Sunday, I will attend a meeting with colleagues in order to oppose strongly such a move. It is no way to start a democracy. And as you know I have certainly good credentials for fighting on behalf of the communist party!

I am opposed to the notion of collective guilt and the practice of collective punishment. We applied collective punishment to the ethnic Germans in Czechoslovakia who were expelled from the country after the Second World War – and this proved to be the starting point for further violence. In marxism, collective guilt is applied to whole classes of people, the bourgeoisie and so forth.

MR: To return to your work for the opposition during the 1970s and 1980s, how important was the contribution from the outside, of Jan Kavan from Palach Press, and others, to the movement?

Jirina Siklova: Extremely important. Jan was the one who first established a channel of communication with friends in the West, starting in January 1971 when the first van was driven to Brno. From then on we received regular help from Palach Press, from Amnesty International, and others. Jan's work was vital. For ten years he and his friends brought in material by van until in 1981 the secret hiding place was discovered by the border guards. After that other ways had to be found. Could you express our thanks to the many, many people, quite unknown to us, who helped us? They drove in the vans, smuggled in information, literature, equipment. I met many of them, but I didn't and couldn't know who they were. Just now in Holland, for instance, I learned for the first time the names and nationality of three Dutch ladies with whom I was in contact, with the help of Jan Kavan. So please, thank all these people for us.

MR: You are now, I believe, associated with the Helsinki Citizens Assembly which held its first international conference in Prague last October.

Jirina Siklova: Yes, I am a member of the International Committee. I think now that Civic Forum has become a regular political party, the work of this committee, and Charter 77, will be very important. At present it may not be so important for us – but in the future I'm afraid it will be.

MR: Finally, can I ask you if at any time over all those years, particularly when you were in prison, you ever lost hope?

Jirina Siklova: When I was in prison, people helped me and my family. I was aware of the help international organisations had provided to others, so I knew they would help my family too; I didn't have to worry on their account. For instance I received two postcards at the prison to say my daughter's wedding was being paid for by 'Uncle Wilhelm'! It was clear to me at once that someone was giving them the money they needed for their wedding. Help came from international sources, but also from the so-called grey zone. So I can't now be directly against these grey zone people. Finally I should say that the situation in Czechoslovakia was not so hard at any level as in the Soviet Union. It was hard, but still it was possible to survive.

Budapest October 23, 1989: Pal Malitar's widow, Judit Gigenes, front of the Kilian barracks. Plaque reads: In memory of the martyrs and heroes of the revolution and fight for freedom of 1956. Erected by the opposition of the 8th and 9th Districts.

Nagy Riroska

Thousands flock to Heroe's Square, Budapest, to pay their last respects to Imre Nagy. *Reuter/Popperphoto*

Peter Szasz

Interviewed in Berlin, 21 July 1990. Peter Szasz is a member of the Alba-Kor Katonai Szolgalatmegtagadok Szovetsege (Alba Society – Conscientious Objector League) in Hungary.

MR: What in your view were the principal factors behind the political and economic revolution in Hungary?

Peter Szasz: Hungary has experienced many uprisings during its history – against the Ottoman Turks, against the Hapsburgs, most recently, in 1956, against the Russians. These revolutions were bloody but unproductive. Thus people wanted this time to make a revolution without bloodshed. That is the first point.

Second, there was Gorbachev. He introduced widespread changes within the Soviet Union and relaxed Soviet control over Eastern Europe. Gradually it became clear that the Brezhnev Doctrine no longer applied. The Russians had enough problems of their own and were not likely to intervene militarily in an attempt to halt reform in Eastern Europe.

Of course the movement for reform in Hungary began long before Gorbachev came to power. From around 1977 onwards we had a very strong democratic intellectual opposition – akin to the Charter 77 movement in Czechoslovakia. Writers, artists, scientists of the highest calibre were involved in this opposition. They were not in a position to leave the country, but instead produced *samizdat* publications to spread their views. People were receptive to their criticisms of the regime because their daily lives bore little relation to the official propaganda.

I would say, however, that the person who really set things in motion in Eastern Europe was not Gorbachev but Reagan. Reagan exerted tough economic pressure on the region. Hungary and other countries were able to obtain Western credits but because of the restrictions on high technology transfers to Comecon countries, were unable to use them to obtain the equipment they needed to modernise their industry. They had to make do with older, less efficient technology, and hence produced goods of an inferior quality. These could not be sold abroad to obtain the hard currency with which to repay the credits. Hence the increasing indebtedness and the worsening economic situation.

Eastern Europe was, of course, able to obtain both credits and technology from the Soviet Union. But in many ways that made matters worse. In the seventies and eighties the Soviet Union itself encountered increasing technological difficulties; it was simply not in a position to supply the technology that Eastern Europe required.

Prices rose steeply and living standards fell. People turned against the system. In the main they were interested not in politics but in the economic situation they faced in their daily lives. Divisions opened up too within the ruling communist party; the availability of Western credits benefitted the top echelon of the party but not the rank and file members. It is true that Hungary was in a relatively favourable situation compared to the rest of Eastern Europe. After 1956 it did not have such a hard-line, Stalinist-type regime, and living standards were also relatively high. But still the trend was the same as elsewhere in the region.

In 1988 the authorities responded to pressure and criticism with cautious political changes. They thought they could open the door just a little while maintaining political control; there would be freedom to travel to the West and greater freedom of expression – but the one-party system would remain. However, once the door was open that little bit, people put their foot inside it and pushed it open further.

From 1980 onwards the annual official demonstration on 15 March to commemorate the 1848 revolution against the Hapsburgs had its counterpart in a rival demonstration organised by the democratic opposition, and each year the latter attracted more and more people. I first joined it in 1986, and that year the police attacked it with baton charges. They did so again the following year, but in 1988 though there was some intervention by the police, it was minimal. More importantly, the numbers of demonstrators increased dramatically. At the beginning in 1980 about fifty people took part. By 1986 there were 400 to 500 people; by 1988 somewhere in the region of 5,000 people. Towards the end of March 1988, following the success of the march, FIDESZ – the Federation of Young Democrats – was formed, the most outspoken and militant of the opposition organisations.

Several months earlier Imre Pozgay from within the Hungarian Socialist Workers Party – the communist party – had founded the Hungarian Democratic Forum. Initially it was purely a forum to discuss politics, a talking shop which was tolerated though not supported by the regime; later it transformed itself into a political party and is now the main party in the coalition government. In Hungary there were three categories of activities and organisations – those supported by the regime; those tolerated by the regime; and finally those outlawed by the regime. These categories applied in every field – politics, music, culture in general. The Hungarian Democratic Forum came into the second category. It attracted people who were not primarily interested in politics; they were not members of the dissident opposition but neither were they, for the most part, members of the communist party.

FIDESZ was founded by law students and young lawyers who carefully examined the Hungarian constitution and concluded that there was nothing in it which forbad the establishment of independent youth organisations. Soon after they set up the organisation they were summoned to appear before a court. They described to me what happened. The court consisted of three judges – one young judge who was very tough and arrogant taking the line that he knew everything and they knew nothing, and how dare they contradict what he said; and two older judges who took a softer approach, saying that if they dissolved the organisation their misdemeanour would be overlooked and they would not be punished.

The judges had three volumes in front of them on the table; one small, one medium, and one very large impressive tome. But the FIDESZ people quickly realised that these were three editions of the same book, namely the Hungarian Constitution; the three copies were there simply to impress. The judges asserted that the organisation they had formed was forbidden under the constitution. But when the FIDESZ people challenged them to point to the paragraph in the Constitution which stated this, they were unable to do so. It was an important moral victory – the foot in the door so to speak.

Young people spearheaded the opposition and alternative movements in Hungary; we did not have material possessions to lose and generally speaking were less fearful than the older generation. But once we had shown what was possible a much broader range of people became involved, joining existing bodies or forming new organisations and political parties. In May 1988 the first independent trade union, the Democratic Union of Scientific Workers, was formed, and the opposition groups set up an open political organisation, the Network of Free Initiatives.

From the autumn of 1988 onwards new political parties appeared on the scene. Some were 'memory parties' – like the Smallholders Party which had won most votes in the last free election in Hungary in 1947 but now had little to offer in the way of a programme. The Network of Free Initiatives formed themselves into a political party, the Association of Free Democrats, as did the Hungarian Democratic Forum. The Social Democratic Party was also re-formed and was subsidised by a grant of $2,000,000 from the Socialist International. Westerners do not seem to have grasped the fact that after the experience of the communist system there is no future for social democratic parties of this kind in Eastern Europe. Support for FIDESZ, however, declined as these new parties grew in strength. They patted us on the head and said we had done well; but we were still young, not yet ready for adult politics. FIDESZ is not represented in the new government and I think that is a loss.

The events of 1988 created an avalanche of political change in Hungary. Karoly Grosz, Prime Minister since the summer of 1987 and elected as leader of the communist party in May 1988, was forced to quit – first his post as Prime Minister, then, at the special Party Congress in October 1989, the leadership of the Party. He had come to power as a reformer but failed to keep pace with the changes in the demands and expectations of the population. The 15 March demonstration in 1989 was a truly mass demonstration, attracting around 80,000 people from thirty-one independent groups. In June 250,000 people attended the re-burial of Imre Nagy and other leaders executed after the 1956 revolution.

Bloodshed in Hungary was avoided partly because the reformers within the communist party persuaded it that change was essential. The hard-liners were defeated and there were a series of changes in the leadership of Party and government. In November 1988 Miklos Nemeth took over as Prime Minister from Grosz and introduced the changes that would lead to pluralism and a parliamentary system. The Party made concession after concession to its critics. Thus from having for decades denounced the revolution of 1956 as a counter-revolution, they first conceded that it should be regarded as a 'popular uprising', then finally agreed that it was a genuine revolution.

MR: You have indicated how bloodshed was avoided. But were Gandhian notions of non-violence at all prevalent within the opposition?

Peter Szasz: People knew that if there was violence the Russians would intervene as they had in 1956; the only hope of success lay in a bloodless revolution. In addition, some people within FIDESZ had a deeper commitment to non-violence. FIDESZ was a coalition of individuals and groups with very different views on this issue, but included peace movement people – for instance from the East-West Dialogue Group. It was mainly through their influence that the second congress of FIDESZ in September 1989 passed a resolution in favour of a law recognising conscientious objection. But for the most part people avoided violence for pragmatic reasons; any other course could have spelled disaster.

MR: What effect has the introduction of a parliamentary system had on the fortunes of opposition groups and movements. Are they stronger or weaker as a result of the changeover?

Peter Szasz: Once it became clear that there would be free elections in Hungary, the opposition sharply divided. Democratic Forum went in one direction to play a very dangerous, nationalistic game. The Free Democrats went in a different direction and developed a programme to change the system radically – not just the ideology but the whole system. Democratic Forum presented themselves as the patriotic party who would defend Hungarian identity and culture, and denounced the Free Democrats as a 'cosmopolitan' party which would destroy these things if elected. They argued too that the programme of rapid and far-reaching changes proposed by the Free Democrats would bring great hardship and misery to the people; their own programme, they said, was to change things gradually, step by step. In fact their goal was to change the ideology but not the system itself. Being Hungarian was for them the central issue.

Today the government dominated by Democratic Forum continues to play a dangerous nationalistic game in relation to neighbouring countries – to Czechoslovakia with respect to Slovakia, and to Romania with respect to the Hungarian population in Transylvania. It is a crazy game that is irritating neighbouring states and raising tension.

The problem dates back to the Versailles Treaty after World War I which established the Hungarian national territory in such a way that 75 per cent of Hungarian people lived outside it. Like the Germans, Hungarians felt they had been hard done by, and under the fascistic government of Horthy, Hungary sided with Hitler in World War II. The chief motivation for this was to incorporate Transylvania and Slovakia into the Hungarian state. The exclusion of Transylvania from the national territory under the Versailles Treaty was a particularly sore point because it was there that Hungarian people had lived for the longest period – for one hundred years in fact before they moved to present-day Hungary in 896 AD. Moreover, Transylvania was never occupied by other countries, never part of the Ottoman or Habsburg empires. There was no logic in the decision at Versailles to grant Transylvania to Romania; no-one in Hungary could understand it.

MR: Is there still today a widespread feeling among Hungarians that Transylvania should be returned to Hungary?

Peter Szasz: No, there isn't. Under Stalinism and the Warsaw Pact, the problems of Eastern Europe were put on ice but not solved. Today old fears have revived: the Romanians are fearful of our intentions, we of theirs. Similarly the Poles fear German intentions, Czechs fear Slovak intentions, Slovaks fear Hungarian intentions. This is what makes the game being played by Democratic Forum so dangerous. Every day you can see on Hungarian television reports of discrimination against Hungarians in Romania. The Hungarian government's position is that they do not want to incorporate territories where there is a large Hungarian population. But they press for the areas in question to be granted autonomy, or, if that is not possible, for special rights to be granted to Hungarians – for them to have their own schools, cultural centres and so forth.

The Romanians and Slovaks, however, fear that if they make such concessions their own national culture, in areas where Hungarians are in the majority, will suffer or die out. They fear, for instance, that children of mixed marriages would be brought up speaking Hungarian and attending Hungarian schools, and be cut-off from the national culture. The territory might remain under their jurisdiction, but the population would not be part of the national culture. This a fear shared by Romanians and Slovaks.

MR: Given these problems, what kind of security system is the government contemplating for the future?

Peter Szasz: Immediately after the 1989 revolutions, there was a wave of popular sentiment in favour of demilitarisation and neutrality. More recently there have been suggestions coming from some quarters in both the West and the Soviet Union to turn NATO into a pan-European organisation, to include also the Soviet Union. A united Germany is likely to be in NATO, and my fear is that when the Warsaw Pact is dissolved there will be pressure on Hungary and other countries to join it. Today people in Hungary are not talking of neutrality any more; all the talk is of joining NATO and becoming part of a European defence system. It is seen as part and parcel of joining the European Community.

We in the Alba Society continue to campaign for demilitarisation and neutrality, and for the government to abide by the national plan to abolish conscription over the next ten years. In Hungary there are at present two armed forces. One is the Army controlled by the Ministry of Defence; the other is the Border Security Force under the control of the Ministry of the Interior. The first step in the plan is to make the Border Security Force fully professional, without any conscripts. In the longer term this would be the only defence force in Hungary and the existing Army would be abolished.

MR: Is there, either within the government or independent groups, any interest in the notion of non-violent defence – i.e. using non-violent forms of resistance to deter or deal with outside threats or internal coups?

Peter Szasz: Nobody talks about it. In the new Hungary, economic questions predominate; all other questions are pushed to the sidelines.

Candle of hope in an East Berlin church.

Martin Argles
The Guardian

Knud Wollenberger

Interviewed in Berlin, 14 December 1990. Knud Wollenberger was born in 1952 and is a poet and writer. He and his wife, Vera, live in what was formerly East Berlin and were involved for many years in the East German peace movement. They have three children born respectively in 1972, 1982 and 1986. Vera Wollenberger was elected as an MP for the Green Party in the GDR elections in March 1990, and re-elected to the Federal Parliament in the united Germany elections of December 1990.

MR: Can you tell us first of all about the involvement of Vera and yourself in the peace movement in East Germany?

Knud Wollenberger: Vera and I first became involved in the peace movement in 1980. By chance we were at a meeting where a list was circulated to found the *Pankow Friedenskreis* – Pankow Peace Circle. We put ourselves on the list and shortly afterwards attended its first meeting. It was one of the earliest independent peace groups in East Berlin, and, like practically all groups during that period, was under the umbrella of the Church. In fact it wasn't until 1986 that the first group unconnected with the Church, the *Initiative fur Frieden und Menchenrechts* – Initiative for Peace and Human Rights – was founded in East Berlin.

The Church provided a measure of protection against interference by the government and a safe space for groups to meet. I can only recall one occasion when the authorities actually entered Church premises to interfere with the activities of an independent group. This was the well-known raid on the night of the 24-25 November 1987 by members of the Public Prosecutor's office and the security police on the Environmental Library, housed in the basement of the Pastor's house attached to the Zion Church in East Berlin.

From 1980 to 1983 we campaigned mainly against any new nuclear weapons being brought into Europe, and into East Germany in particular. But in 1983 the West German *Bundestag* voted in favour of accepting Pershing II and cruise missiles, and in response the East German government called for the deployment in the GDR of new Soviet missiles. This was a serious setback for us, a failure for the campaign we had been conducting.

The independent groups from then on began to devote more attention to other issues, especially to questions of ecology. Vera and I had been interested in ecological problems from 1980 onwards, but it wasn't until 1983 that the independent peace groups as such began to take them up in a serious way. It was about this time that the Environmental Library was founded, and by the mid-1980s there were many groups working here. In Berlin a veritable sub-culture developed. Often, for instance, Vera and I would have invitations to attend two or three meetings a day. Most of the groups were still under the umbrella of the Church and meetings took place either in Church rooms or in private flats.

It is important here to distinguish between the genuinely independent groups and government-sponsored bodies which were intended to promote the official line. However, even such sponsored bodies sometimes rebelled. For instance, the *Society for Nature and the Environment*, founded by the government, became a breeding ground for independent thinking because the ecological problems were so grave that even government-oriented people couldn't keep to the official line. One of the first rebellions within the system that we learned about occurred in 1987 or 1988 at an executive meeting of this *Society*. The executive stated bluntly that they could not endorse the government's economic plan because it did not pay sufficient attention to ecological issues. There was also, of course, some communication between independent and non-independent people, especially in the ecology area; it wasn't too difficult for us to talk to each other.

MR: Coming now to the more recent past, what do you see as the key factors that led to the widespread revolt of 1989 and the collapse of the system?

Knud Wollenberger: One important factor which has not been talked about very much is that most of the people who formed part of the governmental pyramid lost the will to retain power. Only at the very top did that will remain unbroken, amongst perhaps the top twenty or so people in the country. These were largely people whose biography and background were such that they were totally committed to maintaining the system, and to keeping power at any price – people who had fought in Spain, and been active in the struggle against fascism and Nazism. I would say almost nobody on the lower levels was prepared for the party to retain power at the price of bloodshed.

Everybody, in fact, could see that the system had to be altered. It couldn't go on as it was, especially when large numbers of people began to flee the country daily through Hungary and Czechoslovakia to West Germany. The government realised that it would be impossible to close their borders completely – to tell the population that now they were entirely confined to their own country and would not be allowed to travel even in Eastern Europe. People were simply not prepared to accept that. The authorities were losing control and the people realised this.

MR: How important were the changes that had been taking place in the Soviet Union under Gorbachev?

Knud Wollenberger: They were very important. In one sense everything that happened in East Germany was the result of the people making their own history. I don't think there was any direct Soviet influence in the developments in East Germany over the last three years. But the breaking down and rejection of the old centralised system in the Soviet Union had a major impact. A central tenet of communist ideology was that socialism was a system that worked. When it was clear that this was no longer true even in the Soviet Union itself, the hand of the reformers, and all those demanding change, was greatly strengthened. At the same time many people were feeling that – especially in a middle-European country which did not share Russia's long historical experience of despotism – there should be greater democracy.

MR: In other East-Central European countries, the breakdown of the economy has been identified as a major cause of the popular discontent. By contrast, the East German economy was, as I understand it, relatively strong.

Knud Wollenberger: Yes, that is right. The only other East European country that had a comparably high living standard was Czechoslovakia. The East German standard was comparable to that of a number of Western capitalist countries. But, people could see in the 1970s and 1980s that the situation was stagnating and that problems were accumulating. Moreover, there was the feeling that there was more to life than having a reasonable standard of living.

East Germany did, however, retain the elements of a social economy. There were almost no very poor people, and the social system worked rather well by comparison with the economy.

MR: What credence do give to the theory that there was a plot within the upper echelons of the party, with the support and connivance of the KGB, to get rid of Honecker and replace him with a more moderate reform-minded communist? Jens Reich, one of the founder members of New Forum, put forward this thesis recently on a British Channel 4 television programme – though stressing that it was a plot that misfired in the sense that the reformers were not able to hold the line at the point they had intended to hold it.

Knud Wollenberger: It's possible that this is correct – but I can't say how probable it is. Some of the older Party members were too set in their ways to be able to imagine living in a different system, but you can be sure that there were people in the top echelons, especially among the younger people, who could see that things could not continue to be run as they had been. However, I have no information about the internal moves and discussions that took place. Clearly it took a long time to oust Mr Honecker, and when it did happen it was much too late for the system itself to survive.

MR: Jens Reich, in the same television programme, said he was fearful of the social consequences that could flow from the tremendous disillusionment which he sensed among a large section of people in East Germany now that the old communist system had been overthrown and unification with West Germany achieved.

Knud Wollenberger: Let me talk first about the people I know best, even though they are not representative of the majority of the population. The people I know have the feeling that somehow things have rolled over their heads. In the beginning, around November-December 1989 – until the 19 December I could say when Chancellor Kohl came to Dresden – you had the feeling that you were the subject of history. Then things changed. Very quickly you were thrown into the position of being just an object of history. Naturally this is a disillusioning experience. In the beginning we had the feeling that we could really build up something new. We felt that the Western market economy was not the best solution for the problems of our world. But we soon learned that the kind of third way we favoured was not going to be realised.

However, for most people the disillusion springs not from a sense of having lost an opportunity to build a different kind of society, but from the disappointment of their expectations of becoming West Germans in the shortest possible time. The big boom in East Germany which many hoped for is not occurring up to now. Unemployment, on the other hand, is growing, and people will have to come to terms with the fact that it could be here for a long time.

The election results indicate that most people are looking to Chancellor Kohl to sort out the problems. However, I found it surprising – and reassuring – that the extreme Right wing – the Republicans – did very badly in the elections, gaining less than one per cent of the vote in East Germany. I had expected them to do much better. It seems that people are not so disillusioned as to turn to them.

MR: How well did the Greens fare?

Knud Wollenberger: The Greens got 6.1 per cent of the vote. Vera was one of the lucky – or unlucky – ones to be elected to the *Bundestag*. I say lucky or unlucky, because they are terribly overworked. There are only eight of them and they now have to represent the citizens' movements of East Germany and the East German Green Party – and somehow also the West German Greens. There are twenty-three committees in the Parliament, and when you are only eight people it means you can work from morning till night and still not get through all your papers. The Greens could have done better, of course, but at least they are there in the Parliament.

MR: Why do you think that New Forum in East Germany, which played such an important role in mobilising the population against the old regime, has been so marginalised – say by comparison with Civic Forum in Czechoslovakia? Is it the pull of the West German Christian Democrats?

Knud Wollenberger: First of all that. But I think the citizens' movements in Czechoslovakia were much stronger. They also had leaders who had been prepared to take serious risks down the years and to undergo imprisonment for their beliefs; they had to stand up to a more repressive government. I don't want to underestimate the problems we had to face, but the punishments meted out in Czechoslovakia were heavier. More importantly, if you look at the publications of Charter 77, the level of their thinking was very high compared to what we in East Germany were able to produce.

MR: To return to the conduct of the resistance in East Germany, how important would you say was its non-violent character? How, too, was it maintained?

Knud Wollenberger: The changes occurred without violence for two principal reasons. First, the demonstrators understood that it was not necessary to resort to violence to achieve their goals. Second, there was an unwillingness on the part of the majority of people in the government to shoot down civilians peacefully protesting.

We in the independent peace movement had a commitment over the previous nine years to non-violent resistance. But I have to confess that our movement attached to the Church was a rather small one; I would guess that the number of people involved in it didn't exceed 3,000-4,000 people. So the moment the masses took to the streets by the millions, we were only a small percentage of the protesters. Still the people from the peace movement were on the streets and they had developed an approach over a number of years and were able to talk to, and influence others to keep to this peaceful way.

The peace movement provided a kind of paradigm from which others learned. The mood among everybody was to act peacefully. It wouldn't have been like that if say very aggressive, violent groups had been at the forefront of the campaign. The situation could then very easily have become ugly. There was, in fact, no aggressive mood of this kind – or at least if it existed it was overshadowed by the peaceable mood of the majority of people. During the demonstrations, people would discuss how to do things, and how to avoid any kind of violence. I have the feeling that the successful non-violent revolution will provide a paradigm for other countries. There have been several historical examples of non-violent resistance which succeeded; now we have one more.

MR: Within the peace movement, did people look to the example of Gandhi? Were his campaigns a conscious reference point for them?

Knud Wollenberger: I think the film *Gandhi* was on East German television at some point, though I'm not sure when that was. But probably for most participants in the demonstrations there was no consciousness of the Gandhian tradition. For some of us in the peace movement, there was that consciousness. Some of us had read Gandhi, especially his own autobiography which was translated and published in East Germany, and books about him. The non-violent approach was mainly developed over many years within the peace movement as a genuinely Christian idea, though probably some people had an eye on Gandhi too.

MR: On a somewhat related point, what moved people to overcome their fear and take to the streets, despite the obvious dangers involved?

Knud Wollenberger: It was mainly due, I think, to the conviction among people that things could not go on any longer as they had done. The mass exodus through Hungary and Czechoslovakia demonstrated for all to see that this was the case.

Back in November 1987 when the Stasi had raided the Environmental Library, six young people were arrested and taken to prison. Four were released the followed day, but the other two were detained. We then developed the Vigil as a form of non-violent protest. We could only do so on Church property, and we stood in the entrance of the Zion Church. This attracted a lot of attention, including attention from the media. It was something very new for the East German government, and they were faced with a dilemma. On the one hand they didn't want to intervene again on Church premises; on the other hand they did not want the continued embarrassment of the demonstration which was attracting unwelcome attention. After about ten days, they released the two other young people, and we had the feeling that this was an important victory for a non-violent form of demonstration.

By that time the meetings were well attended, and even the big Churches were rather full. In January and February 1988, after the arrests at the Liebnecht-Luxemburg demonstrations, the largest Church in East-Berlin, the Gethsemene Church, was filled with 3,500 people. At that time people could still just about squeeze in and find a seat or somewhere to stand. But just under a year and a half later in Leipzig, the Churches simply weren't big enough to contain all the people wanting to attend the meetings. That was the point at which people gathered in the street. Finally there were so many people in front of the Church, that they started to march around Leipzig. It was a step by step process – it didn't happen overnight.

MR: What role did the media play in this development?

Knud Wollenberger: The media, especially the Western media, accelerated the whole process. If you look at Romania, the people there had no access to Western media. They could only hope that developments in Romania were being picked up and reported in the Western media. But in East Germany, most of the population could tune in to West German television and learn from it what was happening in different parts of the country.

MR: You and Vera were involved since 1980. Did either of you experience any personal difficulties – were you ever arrested or attacked by the police?

Knud Wollenberger: We were never beaten up, but Vera was arrested three times. On one occasion, in January 1988, she was sentenced to six months imprisonment. That was a hard time. But a big campaign developed round her case and that of the other people sent to prison with her, and finally the government retreated. Those imprisoned were given the option of leaving the country while being allowed to retain their East German passports. Previously, everyone who left the country in such circumstances lost their citizenship. Again it showed that the old methods of the regime couldn't be adhered to any more. The regime had two choices: either to retreat, or to use force on a much larger scale. Neither in respect of internal public opinion, nor of the inevitable international reaction, could they go back to bloody, Stalinistic repression. Slowly, bit by bit, they therefore stepped back.

MR: Do you see a role in present-day Germany for the kind of non-violent resistance that overthrew the old order? Or is it now no longer relevant in the context of a more democratic political system?

Knud Wollenberger: I see a very important, continuing role for non-violent action. The social problems in East Germany will become more and more acute within the next few years, and people need to have a means of protesting against the way of life they have been thrown into. However, I'm not only referring to resistance as such, but to a non-violent approach which includes learning how to build a democratic culture. It was not only the dramatic street protests that were significant in the East European revolutions, but also the fact that, at least within the framework of the peace movement, people learned to deal with each other despite holding different ideas. It was learning to accept that opposing views could be expressed in the same room without one side or the other being forced to back down. It took years for us to learn that. And I guess it will take years for the majority of the population, or of the politically interested population, to learn, even emotionally, how to live in a pluralist society.

MR: Turning now to the realm of defence and security, was there at all the idea, even within the peace movement, that the kind of resistance that was helping to overthrow an unpopular regime could be used as the basis of defence for a future democratic society?

Knud Wollenberger: Personally, I was always conscious of that dimension – and, in general, that the non-violent resistance would be a paradigm relevant for many other situations. But I'm not sure that many other people looked at it in this light, even within the peace movement. My feeling is that, just as the 1968 revolutions in the West provided a paradigm for many things that occurred in Western Europe, including the whole change in the culture there since then, so the East European experience of non-violence will prove a crucial paradigm for Eastern Europe for many years to come – and maybe not for Eastern Europe alone.

MR: We now have a new situation in Europe where the old bloc system has broken down, at least on the Eastern side. Is there any discussion of this paradigm of non-violent resistance being relevant to national security.

Knud Wollenberger: I can say that the idea of non-violent resistance to defend the country was discussed in the East German peace movement. There was a widespread feeling that it doesn't make sense to defend the country with nuclear weapons, or even with the immensely destructive weapons of modern warfare; even without atom bombs the country would be destroyed. Therefore if someone was occupying the country, it would make sense to use different means – and that could only imply peaceful means. However, with the breakdown of the Eastern European bloc, security issues are not currently being given much attention.

MR: Is there any longer a clear sense of who the enemy might be – or of the existence of any external threat to the new united Germany?

Knud Wollenberger: I can't answer that for sure. My impression is that most East Germans do not feel there is any external threat for which a military system might be necessary – though perhaps they might want to see some kind of force to control the borders. I don't think, generally speaking, that East Germans have given the question much thought. There are so many other more immediate problems to be tackled that defence issues in general do not really figure in the political debates taking place. People are very preoccupied with their own individual situation and with adjusting to a new way of life. That takes up the energy of most people. The election result also shows that people are not analysing what is happening, but responding rather to their feelings.

MR: Are you optimistic about the future in Germany, and in Europe generally in the light of developments over the past year?

Knud Wollenberger: I think that at the moment we have somehow the feeling that things are rolling over our heads – that for a time we were the subjects of history and that now again we have become its objects. However I think that in the long run the gaining of much more freedom than we enjoyed before is a very positive thing. Now, also, because we don't have the East-West division of Europe any more, the North-South division could become much more important. You can see this already beginning. In my view the problems are accumulating very fast. In the realm of ecology, we are at the point where a big change of climate could occur. This could hit Europe very hard, and other regions even harder. So I cannot be too optimistic. But at least the situation is clearer now, and the means that we can use to resist such a catastrophe occurring are also more obvious.

MR: Do you see a role for non-violent action in preventing it?

Knud Wollenberger: I think it could play a crucial role. If you use violence, it is usually because you cannot get the majority of the population on your side. So if you do succeed, you have to suppress the majority and institute some form of dictatorial regime. However, for a sound ecological approach, you need the co-operation and active participation of the population which is really only possible in a democratic society. Thus the demise of dictatorial governments in Eastern Europe should make it easier to shift the countries of the North towards a more ecologically sound approach.

But we should not deceive ourselves about the extent of resistance there is likely to be to this. Overcoming the comsumerist culture will be the biggest problem, for it means persuading people to adopt a new style of life. This cannot be done by *diktat*; people have to make the decision themselves. And they have to do this before the catastrophe occurs.

Appendix I

Selected Chronology: Eastern Europe

Poland

June 1956	Demonstration by 100,000 in Poznan ends in riots.
Oct 1956	Gomulka becomes party leader. Soviet invasion narrowly avoided.
Mar 1968	Student demonstrations. 1,200 students arrested in Warsaw.
Dec 1970	Food riots in Gdansk and other cities. Gierek replaces Gomulka as Party leader.
June 1976	Strikes and demonstrations in protest against rises in food prices. Formation of the Committee for the Defence of Workers' Rights (KOR).
Sept 1976	KOR extends scope of its work and adds the title Committee for Social Defence (KSS-KOR).
Oct 1978	Cardinal Karol Wojtyla of Krakov becomes Pope John Paul II.
June 1979	Pope visits Poland. Over 1,000,000 people attend open-air mass in Warsaw.
Aug 1980	Strike at Lenin shipyard in Gdansk leads to formation of Solidarity.

Appendix I

Sept 1980	Kania replaces Gierek as Party leader.
Dec 1981	Martial Law: Solidarity outlawed.
Oct 1984	Murder of 'Solidarity priest' Father Jerzy Popieluszko.
June 1987	Pope's second triumphal visit to Poland. Solidarity demonstration in Gdansk.
Nov 1987	Proposed government reforms rejected in national referendum.
Apr-May 1988	Wave of strikes ends inconclusively.
Aug 1988	Renewed strikes. Curfew in Gdansk and other cities. Walesa calls for end of strikes after Interior Minister, General Czeslaw Kiszczak, agrees to meet him and a representative of the Catholic Church to discuss Round Table Talks.

1989

Feb-April	Round Table Talks between Government and Solidarity.
April	Agreement at Round Table Talks on political reforms and re-legalisation of Solidarity.
June 4-18	Solidarity wins landslide election victory in the seats it is permitted to contest.
July 19	Jaruzelski chosen by *Sejm* to occupy the new post of executive President for a six year term.
Aug 24	Tadeusz Mazowiecki of Solidarity chosen as Prime Minister by the *Sejm* after the Communist Party's junior allies, the United Peasants Party and the Democratic Party, desert it.
Sept 12	Formation of coalition government under Mazowiecki. Four key Ministries retained by communists.
Nov 23	*Sejm* abolishes 600,000 strong workers' militias.
Dec 29	New constitution abolishes guaranteed leading role of the

	communist party and changes country's name to the Polish Republic.

1990

Jan	Introduction of market-oriented reforms.
Jan 27	Dissolution of the Polish United Workers Party (Communist Party). Splits into two parties: Social Democracy of the Polish Republic and the Social Democratic Union.
Feb	IMF and World Bank make new credits available. Paris Club governments agree to reschedule Poland's debt.
April	Solidarity conference underlines growing divisions.
May 27	Local elections. Solidarity-backed citizens committees win 41 per cent of seats nationwide; independents, 38 per cent.
July	Mazowiecki reshuffles Cabinet in response to pressure from Walesa.
Sept	Decision to hold Presidential Election.
Nov 26	Mazowiecki resigns as Prime Minister after coming third behind Lech Walesa and Polish-Canadian businessman, Stanislaw Tyminski, in first round of Presidential elections.
Dec 9	Walesa elected President by massive majority.

East Germany

Oct 1949	Establishment of German Democratic Republic.
June 17 1953	Demonstrations in Berlin and other cities crushed by Soviet tanks.
May 1955	Creation of Warsaw Treaty Organisation with GDR as member.

Aug 12 1961	Building of Berlin Wall to halt exodus of East Germans to the West.
May 3 1971	Ulbricht replaced by Honecker as Party leader and dialogue opens with the West German Chancellor, Willi Brandt.
Dec 1972	Signing of Basic Treaty between East and West Germany.
Sept 1986	Opening of the Environmental Library at the Zion Church, East Berlin.
Nov-Dec 1987	Raid by Stasi and members of the State Prosecutor's office on the Environmental Library, Zion Church. Seven arrested. Daily protest vigil widely reported and finally secures release of those detained.
Jan 1988	100 independent demonstrators arrested at official rally to commemorate Rosa Luxemburg and Karl Liebknecht. Two members of the Initiative for Peace and Human Rights charged with treason. Tens of thousands attend twice weekly 'intervention services'.
Feb 1988	Release of those detained.

1989

May 7	Protests at the rigging of local elections.
Aug-Sept	Mass exodus of East Germans via Hungary and Czechoslovakia.
Sept 19	Formation of New Forum.
Oct 7	GDR 40th Anniversary Celebrations attended by Gorbachev amid growing unrest.
Oct 9	70,000 demonstrate in Leipzig – no interference by police.
Oct 18	Daily mass demonstrations force resignation of Honecker as

	Party leader and Head of State. Replaced by Krenz.
Nov 8	New Forum legalised.
Nov 9	Opening of Berlin Wall. Huge street party. Travel restrictions lifted.
Nov 17	Reform communist Hans Modrow becomes premier in coalition government.
Nov 28	Chancellor Helmut Kohl of West Germany proposes German Federation.
Dec 1	*Volkskammer* ends guaranteed leading role of the SED (Communist Party).
Dec 6	Krenz and Politburo resign.
Dec 8	Round Table talks begin.
1990	
Jan 15	Demonstrators ransack Stasi Headquarters in Berlin.
Jan 28	Agreement to form government of national responsibility, taking office on February 5 under Modrow's premiership.
Feb 13	Four wartime Allies and two Germanies agree to hold talks on security implications of unification.
Mar 18	Christian Democrats and allied parties win landslide victory in general election.
Apr 12	Lothar de Maiziere of Christian Democrats heads grand coalition government.
May 5	First round of two-plus-four talks in Bonn.
May 18	Two Germanies sign state treaty on economic, monetary and social union.
June 21	Both German parliaments recognise the inviolability of Oder-Neisse border with Poland.

June 22	Second round of two-plus-four talks in Berlin.
July 1	Economic and monetary union introduced.
July 15-16	Gorbachev and Kohl meet in Stavropol and reach agreement that a united Germany is free to join whichever bloc it wishes.
July 16	Two-plus-four talks – also attended by Polish Foreign Minister – reach agreement on external aspects of unification.
Aug 31	Signing of Unification Treaty.
Sept 12	Treaty on the Final Settlement regarding Germany signed in Moscow at final two-plus-four meeting.
Sept 13	Twenty year German-Soviet co-operation treaty signed.
Oct 3	Unification.
Dec 2	Kohl and his Christian Democrat Party (CDU) win sweeping victory in all-German elections. Coalition partners, Christian Democrats, Christian Social Union (CSU) and Free Democrats (FDP), win 55 per cent of overall votes. The Social Democrats (SPD) win 33.5 per cent, the reformed communist party, the Party of Democratic Socialism (PDS), win 2.2 per cent overall, but 10 per cent in east Germany. Greens eclipsed in west Germany but fare better in east Germany.
Dec 17	Former East-German Prime Minister, Lothar de Maiziere, resigns all government and party posts over allegations that he had collaborated with the secret police, the Stasi, during the communist period.

Hungary

Oct-Nov 1956	Hungarian revolution crushed by Soviet invasion. Janos Kadar installed as party leader in place of Imre Nagy.

June 1958	Execution of Nagy.
1968-70	Government introduces 'New Economic Model'.
June 25 1987	Caroly Grosz becomes prime minister with brief to tackle economic problems
Sept 1987	100 intellectuals write to all MPs calling in effect for 'no taxation without representation'.
	Formation of Hungarian Democratic Forum after meeting between reform communist, Imre Pozsgay, and critical intellectuals.

1988

Jan 1988	600 attend first public meeting of Hungarian Democratic Forum.
March	5,000 join march called by opposition to celebrate Hungary's Republic Day, 15 March. Formation of the Association of Young Democrats – FIDESZ.
May	Formation of Network of Free Initiatives, and of independent trade union, the Democratic Union of Scientific Workers.
May 20-23	Grosz replaces Kadar as Party leader. Purge of old Politburo. Reformers Imre Pozsgay and Rezso Nyers join Politburo.
Nov 24	Miklos Nemeth takes over premiership from Grosz. Grosz remains Party leader.

1989

Jan	Hungarian Parliament passes Law on Associations, legalising independent parties.
Mar 15	80,000 people from thirty-one independent groups join Republic Day march.
May 2	Dismantling of border fence with Austria begins.

June 16	Re-burial of Imre Nagy and other leaders of 1956 revolution. Ceremony attended by 250,000.
July 6	Death of Kadar. Supreme court rules Nagy innocent.
July 22	First opposition MP, Gabor Roszik, elected to the Hungarian Parliament since last multi-party elections in 1947. Sponsored jointly by Hungarian Democratic Forum, Alliance of Free Democrats and Federation of Young Democrats.
Sept 11	Border with Austria opened to permit exodus of thousands of East Germans.
Oct 18	Hungarian Socialist Workers Party reconstituted as a social democratic party, renaming itself the Hungarian Socialist Party (HSP). Resignation of Grosz as party leader.
Oct 23	Multi-party system approved. New Hungarian Republic declared.
Nov 26	Victory for opposition parties in national referendum in which voters opt for postponement of presidential election until after general election.
Nov	Series of legislative measures passed to create a 'state of law', covering establishment of political parties, electoral law, reform of penal code etc.

1990

Mar-April	Centre-right Hungarian Democratic Forum (HDF) wins majority of seats in general elections and forms coalition government under premiership of Jozsef Antall. Alliance of Free Democrats form principal opposition party.
May 3	Writer Arpad Goencz, a Free Democratic MP, elected Speaker and interim President by parliament.

Cechoslovakia

Jan 1968 — Alexander Dubcek becomes Secretary of the Communist Party of Czechoslovakia (CPCz)and introduces far-reaching economic and political reforms – the 'Prague Spring'.

Aug 1968 — Soviet and Warsaw Pact forces invade Czechoslovakia. Dubcek, Premier Cernick and other leaders taken to Moscow. Unprecedented civil resistance by population. Dubcek and Cernik released and reinstated – but with strings attached.

Jan 1969 — Czech student, Jan Palach, immolates himself in Wenceslas Square in protest against Soviet occupation.

Aug 1969 — 100,000 people demonstrate in Wenceslas Square on the first anniversary of the Soviet-led invasion.

April 1969 — Dubcek forced out of office. Replaced by Gustav Husak.

Jan 1977 — Formation of human rights organisation, Charter 77. Though small in numbers it exerts profound influence on Czechoslovak politics in late 1970s and 1980s. Playwright Vaclav Havel one of its leading spokespersons.

April 1988 — Independent Peace association formed: calls for freedom of Information and right of conscientious objection.

1989

Jan 15 — Demonstration by 1,000 people in Prague to mark anniversary of death of Jan Palach attacked by hundreds of riot police.

Aug 21 — 10,000 demonstrate in Wenceslas Square on anniversary of Soviet-led invasion.

Nov 17 — Student-led demonstration of 30,000 attacked by police. The repression, and the rumour that one student has been killed, sparks series of mass demonstrations in Prague and other cities.

Nov 19 — Formation of Civic Forum – encompassing twelve opposition groups, including Charter 77.

Nov 21	Prime Minister Adamec opens talks with opposition.
Nov 22	Dubcek addresses demonstrators in his home town of Bratislava.
Nov 23	People's Militia refuses orders to disperse another mass demonstration in Prague.
Nov 24	Czech television broadcasts film of police attack on Nov 17 demonstration. Dubcek and Havel address crowd of 250-300,000 in Wenceslas Square. Jakes and the Politburo resign.
Nov 26	Havel, Dubcek, and Prime Minister Adamec address crowd of 500,000 on outskirts of Prague.
Nov 27	General Strike for democracy gains overwhelming support.
Nov 29	Abolition of the leading role of the communist party.
Dec 3	Swearing in by President Husak of a new communist-dominated Federal government provokes widespread anger. Move denounced by Civic Forum and People Against Violence who demand formation of a genuine coalition government and the resignation of Husak.
Dec 4	Further mass rally of 200,000 in Wenceslas Square and in cities across Czechoslovakia.
Dec 7	Resignation of Adamec.
Dec 8	Resignation of Husak.
Dec 10	Formation of coalition government led by reform communist, Marian Calfa.
Dec 29-31	Dubcek appointed Speaker of Federal Parliament; Havel becomes President.

1990

June 8-9	Civic Forum and its Slovak ally, People Against Violence,

	win largest share of vote in elections for Federal Parliament and Czech and Slovak National Councils. Marian Calfa heads coalition government.
July 5	Havel re-elected President by the Federal Assembly for a transitional two-year period.
Oct 19-21	Helsinki Citizens Assembly in Prague – opened by President Havel.
Feb 1991	Civic Forum divides into two political parties – a Centre Right party, the Civil Democratic Party, led by Finance Minister Vaclav Klaus, and a Liberal Club led by Foreign Minister, Jiri Dienstbier and Deputy Prime Minister Pavel Rychetsky.

Romania

Mar 1965	Nicolae Ceausescu becomes First Secretary of the Communist Party following death of Georghe Gheorghiu-Dej.
Aug 1977	Strikes and protests by coalminers in the Jiu Valley.
Nov 1987	Force used to suppress protests by thousands of workers in Brasov.

1989

March 12-13	Six former senior government and party officials send open letter to Ceausescu denouncing his policies.
Dec 16-17	In Timisoara, parishioners form cordon round home of Hungarian priest, Father Laszlo Tokes, to prevent his expulsion. Police, army and Securitate open fire on protest marches. Many killed and injured.
Dec 21	Ceausescu booed and jeered as he addresses crowd in front of Presidential Palace. More killings during overnight protests.
Dec 22	Crowd storms Presidential Palace, as army refuses to open

	fire. Ceausescus flee by helicopter. Pitched street battles for four days between army and Securitate.
Dec 23	National Salvation Front declares itself in charge.
Dec 25	Summary execution of Nicolae and Elena Ceausescu.

1990

Jan	President Ion Iliescu announces abolition of the death penalty in New Year's Day broadcast. Demonstrations and counter demonstrations by pro- and anti-NSF supporters.
Feb 1	Creation of Council of National Unity to act as 'a transitional mini-parliament'.
Feb 18-19	Protesters storm NSF Headquarters. Miners from Jiu Valley brought in to crush the protest.
March 20	Violence against ethnic Hungarians in the Transylvanian town of Tirgu Mures. At least three people killed and 300 injured.
	Protest demonstration by 70,000 ethnic Hungarians in Bucharest.
April 22	Demonstrators, many of them students, occupy University Square in Central Bucharest, demanding resignation of all former high-ranking communists from the NSF government.
May 20	National Salvation Front wins decisive victory. Iliescu elected President, gaining 86 per cent of popular vote; NSF also win landslide victory in parliamentary elections. Opposition parties complain of manipulation and unfair practice in lead-up to election.
June 13	Riots after police move in to try to end occupation of University Square.
June 14	Miners from Jiu Valley again bussed in to Bucharest and attack protesters and suspected opponents of NSF with clubs and iron bars. Four people reported dead and

	hundreds injured. Western governments condemn brutality and threaten to suspend economic aid.
June 20	Iliescu sworn in as President. Petre Roman re-nominated as Prime Minister.
Nov	Widespread protests against devaluation and cuts in subsidies.
Nov 15	Newly formed Civic Alliance co-ordinates protest march of 100,000 in Bucharest.

Bulgaria

1989

May	Sixty Ethnic Turks killed demonstrating against enforced assimilation.
June	Exodus of 350,000 Turks.
Oct 16	Eco-glasnost mounts demonstrations to coincide with a conference on the environment in Sofia under CSCE auspices.
Oct 26	Government forced to apologise after forty demonstrators beaten and arrested in front of conference delegates.
Nov 3	5,000 environmentalists allowed to march unmolested through Sofia.
Nov 10	After thirty-five years in power, Todor Zhivkov replaced by Petar Mladenov.
Nov 18	50,000 demonstrators in Sofia call for democracy.
Dec 11	Communist Party agrees to establishment of a multi-party system.
Dec 14	Another 50,000-strong pro-democracy demonstration in Sofia.

Appendix I 211

1990

June 10, 17 — Election in two stages gives Bulgarian Socialist Party (formerly the Bulgarian Communist Party) victory with 47.15 per cent of vote. The main opposition grouping, the Union of Democratic Forces, gains 37.84 per cent.

June 11 — 100,000 students and others demonstrate in Sofia calling for fresh elections and investigation into video evidence that on 14 December President Petar Mladenov had suggested tanks should be used to crush anti-government demonstrations.

July 6 — Mladenov forced to resign over video. Replaced by Zhelyu Zhelev.

July — Strikes, sit-ins and other protests continue.

Nov 29 — Socialist government of Andrei Lukanov forced to resign in face of a general strike, student sit-ins and other demonstrations, and an opposition boycott of parliament. Fresh elections set for March 1991.

Yugoslavia

1944-45 — Victory of communist partisans led by Tito, and establishment of communists government.

1948-49 — Breach with Moscow.

1980 — Death of Tito.

1980-90 — Period marked on the one hand by pressure from below for greater democracy, leading to changes in the Federal constitution and that of individual republics, and on the other by increasing tensions between certain ethnic groups and republics. The list of events noted below is necessarily selective and incomplete:

Mar-May 1981 — Civil unrest amongst Albanians in Kosovo.

Oct-Nov 1987	Emergency security measures in Kosovo province of Serbia, a province mainly inhabited by ethnic Albanians. Trials of Albanian separatists.
Dec 1987	Split in Serbian leadership over handling of Kosovo crisis.
May-Nov 1988	Slovene military secrets trial over publication in the official youth magazine *Mladima* of an open letter alleging plans for a military clampdown in Slovenia – an allegation based on a leaked military document. Defendants, three journalists and a Slovene warrant officer, convicted and imprisoned. Trial galvanises opposition movement in Slovenia, and leads to the formation in January 1989 of the Democratic Alliance.
July 6 1988	Federal Assembly building occupied by striking workers from Croatian footwear factory.
Oct 1988	Resignation of presidium in Serbian province of Vojvodia following mass demonstrations.
Nov 18 1988	100,000 ethnic Albanians demonstrate in Pristina, capital of Kosovo.
Nov 25 1988	Federal Assembly approves new Constitution designed to facilitate introduction of market economy.

1989

Jan 11	Formation of opposition Democratic Alliance Party in Slovenia. Resignation of state presidency of Montenegro following demonstrations in capital Titograd involving up to 120,000 people.
Jan 19	Ante Markovic appointed Federal Prime Minister.
Feb 1	League of Communists of Yugoslavia dismisses from its ranks ethnic Albanian leader, Azem Vlasi. Protest demonstrations and general strike by ethnic Albanians in Kosovo.
Feb 2	First meeting of the Initiative for a Democratic Yugoslavia in Zagreb, capital of Croatia.

Feb 28	700,000 Serbians demonstrate outside Federal Assembly to protest against 'chauvinism and separatism' of Albanians in Kosovo.
Sept 27	Slovenian Parliament amends the republic's constitution, giving itself the right to secede and ending communist party's guaranteed leading role.
Oct 31	Start of trial of ethnic Albanian leader, Azem Vlasi, and fourteen others over the unrest in Kosovo. 62 miners stage sit-in strike in Trepca zinc mine. Mass rallies in Croatia and Slovenia to demand their release.
Nov 10-12	First round of Serbian local, parliamentary and presidential elections. Confirms as President the communist and strongly nationalist Slobodan Milosovic.
Nov 29	Slovenia bans demonstration by Serbs in Ljubljana.
Dec	Serbia imposes economic blockade on Slovenia.
	Official communist party newspaper, *Borba*, publishes plans for introduction of multi-party system in Yugoslavia.

1990

Jan	Communist Party Secretary, Stefan Korosec, tells editors that opposition parties are to be allowed.
	Extraordinary Congress of the League of Communists of Yugoslavia ends in disarray: Slovenian delegation walks out in protest against the rejection of its demand for republic-based communist parties.
	Yugoslav Prime Minister, Ante Markovic, announces plans to change constitution so as to create a multi-party system.
Jan 24, 30	Further demonstrations in Kosovo demanding sacking of local communist party leaders, free elections, and the release of political prisoners. Demonstrations broken up by security forces using batons and tear-gas. Twenty people reported killed.

Feb	Army sent in to quell unrest in Kosovo. Demonstrations by ethnic Albanians; counter-demonstrations by Serbs. Imposition of curfew in provincial capital, Pristina. Further deaths.
Feb 4	Communist Party in Slovenia breaks away from the League of Communists of Yugoslavia.
March	Unrest in Kosovo continues. Many ethnic Albanian activists arrested.
March 8	Slovene Parliament drops title 'Socialist' from the official name of the republic.
April 8, 22	The six party coalition, Demos, wins the direct elections to the Slovene Assembly Socio-Political Chamber and Chamber of Municipalities. But Milan Kucan of the Party of Democratic Renewal (former Slovene League of Communists) voted President in direct elections.
April 12	Head of government and leading ministers resign in Kosovo province in protest at Serbian crackdown.
April 22, May 6-7	In elections in Croatia, overwhelming victory for nationalistic Croatian Democratic Union (HDZ) led by Franje Tudjman.
May 25	Yugoslav Prime Minister, Ante Markovic, announces plans to set up new party.
May 26	Resumed Communist Party Congress agrees to re-launch Party at special congress in September.
June 26	Serbian authorities declare dissolution of Kosovo Provincial Assembly.
July 2	New Constitution for Serbia approved in referendum. Constitution to introduce multi-party system but end special status of Kosovo. Kosovo Assembly declares province independent of Serbia.

July 5	Serbian Assembly votes to dissolve Kosovo Assembly permanently. Imposition of direct Serbian rule.
July 18	Launching of new Socialist Party by Slobodan Milosevic, President of Serbia, to succeed the Communist Party.
July 24	Yugoslav President Borislav Jovic announces that individual republics will be allowed to secede.
July 26	Serbian minority in Croatia declare their sovereignty and autonomy. 50,000 Serbs demonstrate in Srb to protest against proposed changes in Croatian constitution.
Sept 7	Kosovo Provincial Assembly re-constituted unilaterally by 111 of its Albanian, Turkish and Moslem deputies. Several subsequently arrested.
Sept 28	Serbia adopts a new constitution, abolishing the semi-independence formerly enjoyed by Kosovo and Vojvodina.
Oct 4	Yugoslav Federal army intervenes in the Slovene capital, Ljubljana, to take command of the republic's territorial defence. Move countered with passive resistance including cutting off electricity supplies and telephones to building.
Dec 23	Massive vote for independence in Slovenia's plebiscite.

1991

Jan	Republics of Croatia and Slovenia co-ordinate plans to resist any military intervention by the Federal army.
Jan 25	President Franjo Tudjman of Croatia and President Slobodan Milosevic meet and reach temporary accommodation.
Feb 20	Slovenia's parliament declares all Federal Yugoslav laws invalid and prepares to quit Federation.
March	Huge pro-democracy demonstrations in the Serbian and Federal capital, Belrade.
	Resignation of the Yugoslav President, Borisav Jovic (16

March). Serbia's President, Slobodan Milosovic, pulls Serbia out of the collective federal presidency.

Albania

1944-5	Establishment of communist government under Enver Hoxha following partisan war against Italian and German occupation.
1961	Breach with Moscow.
1978	Rejection of the teachings of Mao Tse-tung finalises breach with China.
1985	Death of Enver Hoxha. Succeeded by Ramiz Alia.

1990

April	Alia announces that Albania will seek to re-establish relations with the US and USSR.
May	Reports of unrest in various cities.
May 10	Package of reforms approved by Parliament, including giving all citizens right to have a passport.
July	Thousands of Albanians emigrate after taking refuge in Italian, West German, French and Greek embassies in Tirana. Further pro-democracy demonstrations.
Dec	Students spearhead renewed wave of protests.
Dec 12	After three consecutive days of student protests, the Albania Party of Labour (communist party) authorises the establishment of opposition political parties. Five senior members of the Politburo sacked.
Dec 13	Formation of opposition Democratic Party.
Dec 14	Troops clash with demonstrators in northern town of Shkoder.

Dec 15	Tanks used to suppress riots in the main industrial city of Elbasan. Unrest in other cities.

1991

Jan-Feb	Protests by students and others continue.
Feb 20	Thousands of protesting students in Tirana topple the statue of Enver Hoxha in city centre.
Feb 22	Alia takes direct control of government. Threat of civil war as some army units pledge to uphold system created by Enver Hoxha.
Mar 31	Despite opposition successes in the towns, the communist Party of Labour wins major victory in a general election.

Appendix II

Selection of significant dates marking changes in the Soviet Union

Mar 1985	Gorbachev becomes Secretary of the Community Party, (CPSU).
Apr 1985	Plenum of the Central Committee approves *perestroika*.
	Geneva summit meeting between Gorbachev and Reagen.
Apr 1986	Disaster at Chernobyl nuclear power station.
Oct 1986	Rykjavik summit fails to reach accord on Euromissiles.
1987	
July	Crimean Tartars demonstrate in Red Square.
Aug	Demonstrations in the Baltic State of Estonia.
Nov	Boris Yeltsin dismissed from post as Head of the Moscow Party organisation.
Dec	Signing of the INF Treaty with the US at summit meeting in Washington.
1988	
Feb	Mass demonstrations in Armenia call for return of Nagorno-Karabakh.

June	Moscow summit meeting between Gorbachev and Reagan consolidate US-Soviet dentent.
Jun-Jul	19th Party Conference of CPSU approves moves to market economy and democratisation of party and government Powers of Elected Soviets (parliaments) increased at expense of the Party. Legal system to be reformed. But leading role of Party to be retained.
Aug	60,000 demonstrate in Lavian capital, Riga, calling for independence and greater democracy.
	80,000 Russians in protest strike in Moldavia against adoption of Moldavian as official language.
Sept 12	300,000 people – a third of Estonia's population – demonstrate in Tallinn for independence.
Sept 22	Estimated 500,000 people confront Soviet troops in Armenian capital, Yerevan.
Sept 30	Gorbachev ousts Gromyko and other members of old guard from Politburo and Central Committee.
Sept-Oct	Inter-ethnic violence between Azeris and Armenians over status of Nagorno-Karabakh.
Oct 8-9	Establishment of Popular Front in Latvia, outside the Communist Party.
Oct	Unrest in Tbilisi, Georgia.
Oct 26	Moscow declares intention to free all political dissidents.
Nov 3	10,000 demonstrate for *perestroika* in Byelorussian capital, Minsk.
Nov 16	Estonian Parliament claims power to veto USSR legislation.
Nov 21	Supreme Soviet acknowledges right of Estonia to secede.
Dec 7	Gorbachev addresses the UN and calls for a new world politics, 'universal human values', and end to the Cold War.

	Announces cut of half a million in Soviet forces.
	Armenian earthquake.
Dec 26	Crackdown on nationalists in Azerbaijan.
1989	
Jan	Moscow announces major cutbacks in its forces in Europe.
Feb	Demonstrations in Moldavia, and Georgia.
Feb 15	Soviet withdrawal from Afghanistan completed.
Mar 26	Freest election since the Revolution to choose the Congress of People's Deputies. Many radicals and nationalists elected; old guard fares badly. Andrei Sakarov among the new Deputies.
Apr	New law on rights of Republics to secede.
	Twenty killed and many injured as Soviet troops attack demonstrators in Tbilisi.
	Gorbachev visits Britain.
May 15	Gorbachev visits China.
May 25	Opening session of new Congress marked by free debate.
Sept 8	800,000 demonstrate in Baku.
Sept 10	Founding of Ukrainian Popular Front.
Oct	Strikes by miners in Ukraine and Siberia.
Oct 3	Strikes banned in key industries.
Oct 8	Pro-democracy demonstrators in Moscow form human chain.
Oct 25	Soviet Foreign Minister, Eduard Shevardnadze, proclaims 'Sinatra Doctrine' at meeting in Warsaw.

Dec	Gorbachev meets Pope on way to Malta summit.
Dec 2-3	Malta summit between Presidents Bush and Gorbachev.
Dec 4	Soviet Union condemns the 1968 invasion of Czechoslavakia.
	Communist Party of Lithuania declares itself independent of the CPSU.

1990

Jan	Gorbachev visits Lithuania amid growing nationalist unrest.
	Latvian Supreme Soviet votes to end communist monopoly of power.
	Anti-Armenian pogroms in Azerbaijan. Popular Front in Azerbaijan poised to seize power but crushed by Soviet forces. Many killed in Baku as Soviet troops open fire. 750,000 attend mass funerals.
Feb 5-7	Communist Party plenum backs Gorbachev's proposal to end Party's monopoly of power. 150,000 demonstrate in Moscow on eve of meeting to support the measure – the largest demonstration in the city since just after the revolution of 1917.
Feb	Unrest in Central Asia, Transcaucasia, and Moldavia.
	Estonian Supreme Soviet abolishes Article 6 guaranteeing the leading role of the Communist Party.
	Soviet Union agress to withdraw all troops from Czechoslovakia by mid-1991.
Feb-Mar	Sajudis, the pro-independence movement, sweeps to power in multi-party elections in Lithuania. Lithuanian Supreme Soviet declares Lithuania independent.
	Further gains by nationalists, and by communist parties supporting nationalist demands, in republican and local elections. In Moscow, reformist coalition, Democratic

	Russia, wins fifty-five of the city's sixty-five Supreme Soviet seats.
Mar 12-13	Congress of People's Deputies establishes post of President of the USSR and elects Gorbachev.
	Soviet Union agrees to withdraw all troops from Hungary by July 1991.
	Lithuanian Supreme Council declares restoration of independence from the Soviet Union.
	Gorbachev sends in Soviet troops to Lithuania.
Apr 18	Moscow applies oil sanctions against Lithuania in start of blockade.
May 1	40,000 supporters of opposition groups demonstrate in Red Square.
May 12	Presidents of the three Baltic Republics meet in Tallinn to re-establish a 'Baltic Council'.
May 29	Boris Yeltsin elected as Chairman of the Russian Supreme Soviet.
June 1-3	Gorbachev and Bush declare end of Cold War at Washington summit.
June 4	Ethnic violence in Kirghizia between Kirghiz and Uzbeks. Reports of 193 killed and 1,275 injured.
June 12	USSR Supreme Soviet passes law guaranteeing press freedom.
	Russian Parliament declares independence of Russian Federation but delays putting it into effect.
June 15	Lithuanian Council declares moratorium on its independence declaration to allow talks with Moscow to begin.
July 2-13	28th Congress of the Communist Party of the Soviet Union. Gorbachev re-elected General Secretary. Resignation of

Appendix II 223

Boris Yeltsin from Party.

July 11 Political strike by tens of thousands of coalminers.

July 16 Ukraine proclaims its sovereignty: laws of the republic to take precedence over Soviet law.

Sept 21 USSR Supreme Soviet grants Gorbachev emergency powers.

Oct 1 USSR passes law on freedom of conscience and religious organisations.

Oct 9 Law on public associations legalises establishment of political parties and independent trade unions.

Oct 15 Gorbachev wins Nobel Peace Prize.

Sept 30,
Oct 14 Communist Party wins majority in Azerbaijan elections, marking reversal of fortunes for Popular Front.

Oct 17 Resignation of Ukrainian Prime Minister, Vitaly Mazol, following student hunger strikes, and demonstrations by 100,000 in Kiev.

Oct 24 Russian Federation Parliament declares USSR laws will apply in its territory only after it has ratified them.

Oct 25,30 Kazakhstan and Kirghizia respectively issue independence declarations.

Oct 23-27 All Union Central Council of Trade Unions reconstitutes itself as General Confederation of USSR Trade Unions and declares its independence of government bodies and political and public structures.

Oct 26 Miners hold founding congress of independent trade union in Donetsk, Ukraine.

Oct 28 Nationalist Coalition bloc, Round Table-Free Georgia, wins majority of seats in Georgian Parliament.

Nov 7	Shots in Red Square during parade to mark 1917 October Revolution possibly intended to assassinate Gorbachev.
Nov 11	Discussions between Gorbachev and Yeltsin.
Nov 14	Emergency debate in the USSR Supreme Soviet on the political and economic crisis.
Dec 18	Gorbachev proposes referendum in all Soviet republics on a new Union Treaty. Moldavian delegation walks out of Congress of People's Deputies.
Dec 20	Shevardnadze resigns as Foreign Minister and warns of menace of dictatorship.
Dec 26	Soviet Parliament grants Gorbachev power to issue decrees and impose state of emergency or direct presidential rule.

1991

Jan	Soviet troops move in to Latvia and Lithuania, seizing the TV station and other public buildings in Vilnius. Parliament buildings in Riga and Vilnius besieged.
Feb 10	Lithuanians vote massively for independence in referendum.
Mar 3	Latvia and Estonia also vote massively for independence in referenda.
Mar 17	Referendum on Gorbachev's proposed new Union Treaty has ambiguous outcome. Majority approve the Treaty, but six republics – the Baltic States, Armenia, Georgia, and Moldavia – refuse to participate. Majority in Russian Federation support demand for a directly elected Russian President.

Recognition of Reality
Reflections & Prose Poems
Adam Curle

Those of us living in the modern Western world (or 'North') have daily access to visual and factual images which travel with unprecedented rapidity from their place of origin to our newspaper page or television screen. Seemingly these aim to 'inform' us about contemporary war, famine, poverty, summit meetings, human suffering, or other newsworthy events. How much of this we actually digest or comprehend is another matter. For many it is often enough to grapple with understanding our individual positions here and now, at this time, during this event or in this moment. And yet we are part of a wider world.

Adam Curle's mediation work over the past twenty-two years has taken him to international and personal situations of great tension, despair, hope, pain and change. Previous to and during this period he has been involved in problems of Third World development and has held professorships in psychology, education, development and peace studies at Exeter, Ghana, Harvard and Bradford Universities.

In **Recognition of Reality** he chooses not to lecture. This is a book of reflections; glimpses of inner and outer worlds caught in poetic form and always based on true experience. At times gentle, at times painful, these pieces combine to offer our Age a compassionate interpretation of reality, and vision for the future. **Recognition of Reality** seeks to convey the essential truth and spiritual essence so often distorted or unseen amid human suffering and despair. Only by coming to terms with our fundamental being will we succeed in transforming and renewing this earth.

Social Ecology Series
HAWTHORN PRESS
ISBN 1 869 890 12 4

TOOLS FOR TRANSFORMATION
A Personal Study
Adam Curle

Three main areas are considered in depth: Mediation, Development and Education. Mediation and peacemaking are described in both large scale, violent conflict situations. Development is concerned with the character and structure of human society (for the good of the people) rather than with purely 'economic growth' considerations.

Education is viewed in the social context of communities as well as in the essence of learning/teaching relationships. Each area draws on wide practical experience and examples. Here to, are the rich influences of contemporary depth psychology, modern physics, Buddhism and Quaker practices.

Specific topics include: mediation, approaches to violence, negotiation, the nature of democracy, consensus management, community development, non-violence and learning for life. Case studies are drawn from the Nigerian Civil War, Bangladesh and Pakistan, Northern Ireland, Zimbabwe, the Afghan Powindahs, the Chakmas of Bangladesh, Chitral in Hundu Kush, the Arusha Declaration, and contemporary Britain.

Wary of the potential gap between ideas and implementation, between theory and practice, Adam Curle makes his views and suggestions accessible to any reader – on varied levels for personal choice. He reminds us of our participation and potential in a wider wholeness ... our interconnectedness with the fabric of life.

This is a book about transforming ourselves, and the world we live in.

... readers enter this book at their own risk. The risk is that you too will be called upon to re-examine your own illusions, to seek the reality behind the illusions, and to find a hitherto unsuspected part of yourself in the long slow work of transformation for humanity.

Elise Boulding

210 x 135mm; 224pp; sewn paperback;
ISBN 1 869 890 21 3.

MANAGING CONFLICT
Fritz Glasl

This comprehensive book on managing conflict is being translated for a 1992/3 publication. The author, based in Austria, works with conflict questions in both Eastern and Western Europe.

LIFE PATTERNS
Responding to life's questions, crises and challenges
Jerry Schöttelndreier

This life is not a dress rehearsal – it is the real thing!
Nurses of dying people have observed sometimes that patients are very angry because of the things they did not do, at their postponed lives. However, responding with awareness to life's questions, crises, turning points and challenges is not easy. The more freedom you have, the more choices there are.

Life Patterns offers a helping hand. It enables people to take stock, understand their roots, gain practical, human and spiritual insights into their present life situation and consider the next steps to take. This guide offers a process, a method, which can be used at any time in life.

There are, however, 'no easy answers'. Often living with 'the questions life asks' can lead the way. *Life Patterns* enables you to take your life more in hand – as opposed to letting life happen to you.

The author runs biography workshops and offers individual biographical counselling. He works for the N.P.I. Institute for Organisational Development founded in Holland by Bernard Lievegoed.

Biography and Self Development Series
Hawthorn Press
ISBN 1 869 890 27 2

CONFLICT AND PEACEMAKING SERIES

The CONFLICT AND PEACEMAKING SERIES aims to further the understanding and analysis of social conflicts and their resolution. Beginning with the publication of *TOOLS FOR TRANSFORMATION* by Adam Curle in 1990, it promotes the accessibility of information and ideas for individuals and groups who are concerned with aspects of peace-making; on inter-personal, collective or international levels. We live in a complex and specialized age which reaps a harvest of split families and communities, ethnic violence, wars and questions of peace and justice. Hawthorn Press hopes to look at the seeds of these dilemmas, the situations (through case studies such as Michael Randle's *People Power*), practices and ideas for change. It also hopes to promote dialogue and new thought in these areas.

Judith Large

Orders

If you have difficulty ordering from a bookshop, you can order direct from Hawthorn Press, Bankfield House, 13 Wallbridge, Stroud, Glos GL5 3JA, UK.
Telephone: (0453) 757040
Fax: (0453) 753295